S0-BKO-587

WITHDRAWN

*Detroit
Reprints
in
Music*

**Frederick Freedman, General Editor
Case Western Reserve University**

Above and below: Scenes from Gessner and Balk's *Faust Counter Faust.* See page **XXIV**.
Photos by McKay.

THE FAUST LEGEND IN MUSIC

BY
JAMES WILLIAM KELLY

WITHDRAWN

ML
63
.K4
1976

Detroit Reprints in Music
INFORMATION COORDINATORS
1976

Except for the addition of pages I-XXVII by the author,
this is a reprint, with minor changes, of a dissertation
originally presented in 1960 at Northwestern University, Chicago.

Copyright 1976 by Information Coordinators, Inc.
Library of Congress Catalog Card Number 74-75893
International Standard Book Number 911772-81-2

Designed by Vincent Kibildis
Printed and bound in the United States of America
Published by
Information Coordinators, Inc.
1435-37 Randolph Street
Detroit, Michigan 48226

CONTENTS

INTRODUCTION

WHEN MY FRIEND FREDERICK FREEDMAN†, Music Librarian of Case Western
Reserve University and General Editor of *Detroit Reprints in Music*, asked me to
update my 1960 dissertation, *The Faust Legend in Music*, my ingrained laziness
at first caused me to refuse. Once I got to the task of updating the bibliography,
however, I was surprised at the results of peering under a number of scholarly
rocks such as *The Catalogue of the British Museum*, *The Library of Congress
Catalogue of Music and Phonograph Records*, *The New York Public Library
Dictionary of Music*, *Music Index* and *RILM*: 132 new books, 13 new editions
or translations of books listed in my 1960 bibliography, 24 journal articles, 1 play,
and 17 musical compositions. And this figure does not include reviews and articles
relating to the several productions and recordings of Gounod's *Faust*. Some of
these items predate 1960, as I missed them the first time around. But most
publications date from 1960 onward, including four editions in several languages
of the old history of Dr. John Faustus published in the last eight years.

I think the aforementioned list indicates without doubt the viability of the
Faust legend. Perhaps the title of Herman E. Hinderks' 1957 lecture is symptomatic
of this: *Goethe's Faust and the Crisis of Modern Man*. Candoni and Nascimbene's
opera, *Faust in Manhattan* (1963), the Minnesota Opera's production of *Faust
Counter Faust* in 1971 and the Los Angeles ProVisional Theatre's production of
Dominus Marlowe/A Play on Doctor Faustus, first performed in July, 1973 and
which toured during February-March, 1974—all are examples of this viability.

In my first Chapter I remarked: "The legend deals with religions and philosophical
problems that are vital to man—the role that good and evil play in his life, his desire
to pierce nature's secrets to the core, and the dichotomy between the sublimity and
mystery of human life." Is this not even more true today as we continue ever more
urgently to plumb the depths of the secrets of body, mind, spirit, universe. . . ?

I wish to thank Miss Betty Lou Hammargren and Miss Betty Engebretson of
the staff of the Minneapolis Public Library for their generous assistance.

JAMES W. KELLY

Minnetonka, Minnesota
January 1974

BIBLIOGRAPHY/ADDITIONAL LITERATURE

ADEL, Kurt. *Die Faust-Dichtung in Österreich.* Vienna: Bergland Verlag, 1971.

ADOLF ALTENBERG, Gertrude. *La storica figura del Doktor Faust ed il motivo faustiano nella letteratura europea.* Milan: C. Marzorati, 1960.

ANDREWS, William Page. *Goethe's Key to Faust; a Scientific Basis for Religion and Morality and for a Solution of the Enigma of Evil.* Port Washington, NY: Kennikat Press, 1968. Reprint of the (Boston/NY: Houghton Mifflin, 1913) ed.

ANKARA. Devlet Konservatuvari. *Goethe: Faust; tragedya 3 perde* (Faust: insan, efsane, dram). Ankara: Millî Eğitim, Basimevi, 1946.

ANTONUCCI, Emil. *Faust*, written and illustrated with linoleum cuts by the author. NY: [Hand Press], 1963.
Printed in an edition of fifty copies.

AVANZI, Giannetto. *Bibliografia Italiana su Goethe.* Florence: L. S. Olschki, 1972.

BACH, Rudolf. *Leben mit Goethe; gesammelte Essays. Fausttagebuch,* hrsg. von Thea. Bach. Munich: C. Hanser, 1960.

BAHR, Ehrhard. *Die Ironie im Spätwerk Goethes; ". . . diese sehr ernsten Scherze . . ." Studien zum West-östlichen Divan, zu den Wanderjahren und zu Faust II.* Berlin: E. Schmidt, 1972.

BALDENSPERGER, Fernand. *Bibliographie Critique de Goethe en France.* NY: Burt Franklin, 1972. Reprint of the (Paris: Hachette, 1907) ed.

BATES, Paul A. *Faust: Sources, Works, Criticism.* NY: Harcourt, Brace & World, 1969.

BAUMBERGER, Otto. *28 Kompositionen zu Goethes Faust 1. und 2. Teil.* Weiningen-Zürich: J. & R. C. Baumberger, 1966.

BENTZON, Niels Viggo. "En Faust-opera," *Dansk Musiktidsskrift* XXXVIII/5
      (1963), 182-87.

BIELSCHOWSKY, Albert. *The Life of Goethe*, authorized translation by William
      A. Cooper. NY: AMS Press, 1970. 3 vols. Reprint of the (NY/London:
      G. P. Putnam's, 1905-1908) ed.   See: p. 155.

BIERMANN, Berthold, ed. *Goethe's World as Seen in Letters and Memoirs*.
      Freeport, NY: Books for Libraries Press, 1971. Reprint of the (NY: New
      Directions, 1949) ed.

BINDER, Alwin. *Das Vorspiel auf dem Theater; poetologische und geschicht-
      philosophische Aspekte in Goethes Faust-Vorspeil*. Bonn: H. Bouvier, 1969.

BIRVEN, Henry Clemens. *Der historische Doktor Faust: Maske und Antlitz*.
      Gelnhausen: H. Schwab, 1963.

BLAUKOPF, Kurt. "Berlioz, Goethe, Faust," *Hifi-Stereophonie* IX/1 (Jan 1970), 3-4.
      Settings by Berlioz as a reflection of French romanticism.

BLÜHER, Karl Alfred. *Strategie des Geistes: Paul Valerys Faust*. Frankfurt am Main:
      V. Klostermann, 1960.

BRANDT, Heinrich. *Goethes Faust auf der Kgl. Sächsischen Hofbühne zu Dresden,
      ein Beitrag zur Theaterwissenschaft*. Nendeln/Liechtenstein: Kraus Reprint,
      1967. Reprint of the (Berlin: E. Ebering, 1921) ed.

BRESSEM, Margarethe. *Der metrische Aufbau des Faust II und seine innere
      Notwendigkeit*. Nendeln/Liechtenstein: Kraus Reprint, 1967. Reprint of
      the (Berlin: E. Ebering, 1929) ed.

BROWN, Peter Hume. *Life of Goethe*. NY: Haskell House, 1971. Reprint of the
      (NY: Henry Holt, 1920) ed.

BROWN, Peter Hume. *The Youth of Goethe*. NY: Haskell House, 1970. Reprint of
      the (London: J. Murray, 1913) ed.

BRUYR, Jose. "De Jean Fust (1500-1545) aux 'Faust'," *Journal Musical Français*
      Nos. 161-62 (Sep-Oct 1967), 29-33.

BRUYR, Jose. "La Premiere (et douteuse) Incarnation de Faust," *Musica* [Chaix]
    No. 72 (Mar 1960), 6-10.

BURCKHARDT, Sigurd. *The Drama of Language: Essays on Goethe and Kleist.*
    Baltimore: Johns Hopkins Press, 1970.

BUTLER, Eliza Marian. *Ritual Magic.* NY: Noonday Press, 1959. See: p. 158.

CALGREN, Franz. *Faust am Goetheanum.* Dornach: Philosophisch anthroposo-
    phischer Verlag am Goetheanum, 1967.

CASTILLO, Guido. *Fausto*, 1 ed. [Montevideo] : Casa de Estudiante, 1960.

CASTILLO, Guido. *Fausto de Goethe.* Montevideo: Editorial Letras, 1969.

CITATI, Pietro. *Goethe.* Milan: A. Mondadori, 1970.

COTTI, Jürg. *Die Musik in Goethes "Faust."* Winterthur: P. G. Keller, 1957.

CROCE, Benedetto. *Goethe*, with introduction by Douglas Ainslie, translation by
    Emily Anderson. Port Washington, NY: Kennikat Press, 1970. Reprint of
    the (London: Methuen, 1923) ed.

DABEZIES, André. *Visages de Faust au XXe siècle, littérature, idéologie et mythe.*
    Paris: Presses universitaires de France, 1967.

DAVIDSON, Thomas. *The Philosophy of Goethe's Faust*, edited by Charles M.
    Bakewell. NY: Haskell House, 1969. Reprint of the (NY: Ginn, 1906) ed.

DIECKMANN, Liselotte. *Goethe's Faust: a Critical Reading.* Englewood Cliffs, NJ:
    Prentice-Hall, 1972.

DIENER, Gottfried. *Fausts Weg zu Helena, Urphänomen und Archetypus;
    Darstellung und Deutung einer symbolischen Szenenfolge aus Goethes Faust.*
    Stuttgart: E. Klett, 1961.

DUKAS, Paul. "Le Faust de Goethe et la musique," in his: *Les Écrits de Paul Dukas sur la musique*. Paris: Société d'éditions françaises et internationales, 1948.

EBERZ, Jakob. *Die Drei Dichtungen vom Schicksal des Abendlandes: Aeneis-Commedia-Faust [von] Otfried Eberz* [pseud. 1. Aufl.]. Munich-Solln: Sophia-Verlag, 1959.

ELIAESON, Åke, & Percy GÖSTA. *Goethe in der Nordischen Musik*. Stockholm: Erling Winkel-Seelig, 1959.

EMRICH, Wilhelm. *Die Symbolik von Faust II: Sinn & Vorformen*. Bonn: Athenäum, 1964.

ENGEL, Karl. *Bibliotheca Faustiana: Zusammenstellung der Faust-Schriften vom 16. Jahrhundert bis mitte 1884*. Hildesheim/NY: G. Olms, 1970. Reprint of the (Oldenburg: A. Schwartz, 1885) ed. See: p. 159.

ESTEVE BARBA, Francisco. *Fausto, célebre poema de Goethe*, adaptado para la juventud por Francisco Esteve; con ilustraciones de J. Segrelles. Barcelona: Araluce, 1933.

Paraphrases, tales, etc.

FÄHNRICH, Hermann. "Dreimal Helena; die Helena-Tragödie von Euripides, Goethe und Richard Strauss," *Neue Zeitschrift für Musik* CXX/1 (Jan 1959), 9-12.

FAUST - Recently published materials on the historical Doctor Johann Fausten:

Historia von Doctor Johann Fausten, dem weitbeschreyten Zauberer und Schwarzkünstler, mit einem Nachwort hrsg. von Richard Edmund Benz. Stuttgart: P. Reclam, 1964.

Die Faustdichtung vor, neben und nach Goethe. Darmstadt: Wissenschaftliche Buchgesellschaft, 1969. 4 vols. Reprint of the (Berlin: Morawe & Scheffelt, 1913) ed.

The Historie of the Damnable Life and Deserved Death of Doctor J. Faustus, translated by F. E. Gent. NY: Da Capo Press, 1969. Reprint of the (London: 1952) ed.

Das aelteste Faustbuch; Wortgetreuer Abdruck der editio princeps des Speis'schen Faustbuches vom Jahre 1587, mit Einleitung und Ammerkungen. Amsterdam: Radopi, 1970.

L'histoire du docteur Faust (1587), traduction, introduction, notes, et glossaire par Joël Lefebvre. Lyon: 1970. (*Bibliothèque de la Faculté des lettres de Lyon*, 17.)

FERCHAULT, Guy. *Faust: une légende et ses musiciens*. Paris: Larousse, 1948.

FESTER, Richard. *Eros in Goethes Faust*. Munich: Verlag der Bayerische Akademie der Wissenschaften, 1933. (*Sitzungsberichte der Bayerische Akademie der Wissenschaften, Philosophisch-historische abteilung*, 8.)

FLÖSSNER, Franz. *Reichardt, der hallische komponist der Goethezeit*. Halle-Saale: Gebauer-Schwetschke, 1929.

FRANZ, Erich. *Mensch und Dämon: Goethes Faust als menschliche Tragödie, ironische Weltschau und religiöses Mysterienspiel*. Tübingen: M. Niemeyer, 1953.

FRIEDRICH, Theodor, & L. J. SCHEITHAUER. *Kommentar zu Goethes Faust, mit einem Faust-Wörterbuch und einer Faust-Bibliographie*. [Neubearbeitung] Stuttgart: P. Reclam, 1960.

FRYKENSTEDT, Holger. *Goethes Faust; Verket och forskningen*. Stockholm: Norstedt, 1969.

GEERDTS, Hans Jürgen. *Johann Wolfgang Goethe*. Leipzig: P. Reclam, 1972.

GEHRING, Jacob. "Goethes Musikerlebnis," *Schweizerische Musikzeitung* CVII/4 (July-Aug 1967), 199-202; CVII/5 (Sep-Oct 1967), 264-67.
    Deals with periods 1770-1776 & 1788-1823.

GERSTEL, Judith. "'Faust Counter Faust'; Has the Center Opera Company Gone Too Far?" *High Fidelity/Musical America* XXI/5 (May 1971), MA 26-27.

GIAMATTI, A. Bartlett. "Marlowe: The Arts of Illusion," *The Yale Review* LXI/4 (June 1972), 530-43.
About the Faust story.

GIELEN, Josef G. W. "Goethe en de Muziek," *Mens en Melodie* XV/1 (Jan 1960), 11-14.

GOERNE, Dieter. *Faust auf der Bühne unserer Zeit.* Weimar: Nationale Forschungs- und Gedenkstätten der klassischen deutschen Literatur, 1970.

GOETHE, Wolfgang von. *Faust*, translated by Barker Fairley. Toronto: University of Toronto Press, 1970.
Illustrated by Randy Jones.

GOETHE, Wolfgang von. *Faust;* texte français de Gérard de Nerval. *Le Second Faust;* texte français de Aléxandre Arnoux et R. Biemel. Paris: Mazenod, 1963.

GOETHE, Wolfgang von. *Faust*, the Bayard Taylor translation revised & edited by Stuart Atkins. NY: Collier Books, 1963.
Bilingual ed, German & English.

GOETHE, Wolfgang von. *Faust, Part II*, a prose translation by Bayard Quincy Morgan. Indianapolis: Bobbs-Merrill, 1964.

GOETHE, Wolfgang von. *Faust*, with an introduction & appreciation by Louis Liebrich; illustrations by Eugene Delacroix. London: Heron Books, 1970.

GOETHE, Wolfgang von. *Faust, First Part; Faust, erster Teil;* edited by Peter Salm, the original German text translated, with introduction & notes by the editor. NY: Bantam Books, 1962.

GOETHE, Wolfgang von. *Faust: der Tragödie erster Teil;* edited by Walter Horace Bruford. London: Macmillan; NY: St. Martin's Press, 1968.

GOETHE, Wolfgang von. *Fausto*, traducción [por] Teodoro Llorente, illustración [por] Chico Prats. Barcelona: Editorial Maucci, 1961.

GOETHE, Wolfgang von. *Goethe über den Faust*, hrsg. von Alfred Dieck, mit einem Nachwort von Kurt Schreinert. Göttingen: Vanderhoeck & Ruprecht, 1958.

GOETHE, Wolfgang von. *Goethe's Faust;* the original German with new translation & introduction by Walter Kaufmann; part one and sections from part two. NY: Doubleday, 1961.

GOETHE, Wolfgang von. *Goethes Faust; Der Tragödie erster und zweiter Teil*, Urfaust, Kommentiert von Erich Trunz. Hamburg: C. Wegner, 1963.

GOETHE, Wolfgang von. *Goethe's Faust*, translated by John Shawcross, with a foreword by Dr. G. P. Gooch. London: Allan Wingate, 1959.

GOETHE, Wolfgang von. *"Urfaust," Faust in its Original Version*, edited by R. H. Samuel. London: Macmillan, 1958.

GOLLWITZER, Gerhard. *Die Geisterwelt ist nicht verschlossen: Swenderborgs Schau in Goethes Faust*. Stuttgart: Faust-Verlag, 1968.

GOTTHOLD, Friedrich August. *Ueber des Fürsten Anton Radziwill Kompositionen zu Göthe's Faust; Nebst Göthe's Späteren Einschaltungen und Aenderungen*. Königsberg: Gräfe & Unzer, 1839. [Copy in the New York Public Library.]

GRIMM, Herman Friederich. *The Life and Times of Goethe*, translated by Sarah Holland Adams. Freeport, NY: Books for Libraries Press, 1971. Reprint of the (Boston: Little, Brown, 1880) ed.

GRÜNDGENS, Gustaf. *Meine Begegnung mit Faust*. Frankfurt am Main: Suhrkamp, 1959.

GUNDOLF, Friedrich. *Goethe*. NY: AMS Press, 1971. Reprint of the (Berlin: G. Biondi, 1925) ed.

HAMMER, Carl. *Longfellow's "Golden Legend" and Goethe's "Faust."* Baton Rouge, La: Louisiana State University Press, 1952. (*L.S.U. Humanities Studies*, Series No. 2.)

HELLER, Otto. *Faust and Faustus; a Study of Goethe's Relation to Marlow.*
NY: Cooper Square, 1972. Reprint of the (St. Louis: Washington University
Studies, 1931) ed. See: p. 164.

HENDEL, Gerhard. *Von der deutschen Volkssage zu Goethes Faust.* Weimar:
Nationale Forschungs- und Gedenkstätten der klassischen deutschen Literatur;
Vertrieb. Berlin/Weimar: Aufbau-Verlag, 1967.

HENNING, Hans. *Faust-Bibliographie.* Berlin/Weimar: Aufbau-Verlag, 1966.

HENNING, Hans. *Faust in fünf Jahrhunderten; ein Überblick zur Geschichte
des Faust-Stoffes vom 16. Jahrhundert bis zur Gegenwart,* [1. Aufl.].
Halle/Saale: Verlag Sprache und Literatur, 1963.

HINDERKS, Hermann E. *Goethe's Faust and the Crisis of Modern Man; an
Inaugural Lecture Delivered before Queen's University of Belfast.*
Belfast: Marjory Boyd, 1957. (*Q.U.B. Lectures,* New Series, No. 5.)

HÖFLER, Otto. *Homunculus, eine Satire auf A. W. Schlegel; Goethe und die
Romantik* [Bibliographie Übersicht von Helmut Birkhan]. Vienna/Cologne/
Graz: Böhlau, 1972.

HOLZHAUER, Helmut. *Faust, Signatur des Jahrhunderts; Eine Analyse die
Welt und Menschenansicht Goethes in sein Hauptwerk.* Weimar:
Nationale Forschungs- und Gedenkstätten der klassischen deutschen
Literatur, 1970.

IGO, John N. *A Chamber Faust: A Lyric Suite* [1st ed]. Coral Gables, Fla:
Wake-Brook House, 1964.

JACOB, P. Walter. "Faust in der Oper," *Das Musikleben* VI/6-8 (July-Aug 1953),
256-60.

JANTZ, Harold Stein. *The Mothers in Faust; the Myth of Time and Creativity.*
Baltimore: Johns Hopkins Press, 1969.

JARRAS, Felix. *La Foi, les Oeuvres et le Salut dans le "Faust" de Goethe.* Paris: Lettres modernes, 1969.

KÁNSKI, Józef. *"Faust* w Lodze," *Ruch Muzyczny* XIV/2 (1970), 13.

KIPP, Heinrich. *Goethes "Faust," Einführung auf Grund theosophischer Forschung.* Calw/Württ: Schatzkammerverlag H. Fändrich, 1967.

KOCH, Rudolf. *Goethe-Faust; 12 originale Exlibrisradierungen,* mit einer Einleitung von Klaus Rödel. Copenhagen: Exlibristen, 1969.

KOMMERELL, Max. *Geist und Buchstabe der Dichtung, Goethe, Schiller, Kleist, Hölderlin,* [4. Aufl.]. Frankfurt am Main: Verlag Klostermann, 1956. Studies *Faust,* part 2.

KRAKER, Lojze. *Goethe in Slovenien; Die Rezeption seines Werkes bis zu ersten Übers. von Faust I.* Munich: Trofenik, 1970.

KROGMANN, Willy. *Goethes "Urfaust."* Nendeln/Liechtenstein: Kraus Reprint, 1967. Reprint of the (Berlin: E. Ebering, 1933) ed.

KUBE, Karl Heinz. *Goethes Faust in französischer Auffassung und Bühnendarstellung.* Nendeln/Liechtenstein: Kraus Reprint, 1967. Reprint of the (Berlin: E. Ebering, 1932) ed. See: p. 167.

LAWRENCE, Les. "Magic, Myth, Illusion," *Opera Canada* XI/3 (1970), 36-37.

LUKÁCS, György. *Goethe and His Age,* translated by Robert Anchor. London: Merlin Press, 1968; NY: Grosset & Dunlap, 1969.

LUN, Luigi. *Genesi del Faust goethiano.* Rome: Arte della stampa, 1969.

MAMPELL, Klaus. *Die Geschichte des berüchtigten Zauberers Doktor Faust; aufgezeichnet von seinem Famulus Christoph Wagner, sowie des Doktors nachgelassene Schriften nebst einem Dokument von des Teufels eigener Hand.* Frankfurt am Main: Nest Verlag, 1962.

MASON, Eudo Colecestra. *Goethe's Faust: Its Genesis and Purport*. Berkeley, Calif: University of California Press, 1967.

MELCHINGER, Siegfried. *Faust für uns;* Bilder der Hamburger Aufführung. Frankfurt am Main: 1961.

MENDELSSOHN-BARTHOLDY, Karl. *Goethe und Felix Mendelssohn-Bartholdy*, translated with additions from the German by M. E. von Glehn, with portraits and facsimile, and letters by Mendelssohn of a later date. NY: Haskell House, 1970. Reprint of the (London: Macmillan, 1872) ed. See: p. 170.

MEYER, Herman. *Diese sehr ernsten Scherze; Eine Studie zu Faust 2*. Heidelberg: Stiehm, 1970.

MILLER, Ronald Duncan. *Understanding Goethe's Faust I: a Scene by Scene Interpretation*. Harrogate (Yorkshire): Duchy Press, 1970.

MINTZ, Donald. "Schumann as an Interpreter of Goethe's *Faust*," *Journal of the American Musicological Society* XIV/2 (Summer 1961), 235-56.

MOMMSEN, Katharina. *Natur- und Fabelreich in Faust II*. Berlin: de Gruyter, 1968.

MONTGOMERY, Paul. *Review Notes and Study Guide to Goethe's Faust*. NY: [Distributed by] Monarch Press, 1964.

MÜLLER, Joachim. *Die Figur Homunculus in Goethes "Faust."* Berlin: Akademie-Verlag, 1963.

MÜLLER, Joachim. *Prolog und Epilog zu Goethes Faustdichtung*. Berlin: Akademie-Verlag. 1964.

MÜLLER, Joachim. *Zur Motivstruktur von Goethes Faust*. Berlin: Akademie-Verlag, 1972.

MÜLLER-BLATTAU, Joseph. *Goethe und die Meister der Musik*. Stuttgart: Klett, 1969.

MÜLLER-BLATTAU, Joseph. "Goethes Weg zu Bach," in: Heinz BECKER & Reinhard GERLACH, eds, *Speculum Musicae Artis. Festgabe für Heinrich Husmann zum 60. Geburtstag am 16. Dezember 1968* (Munich: W. Fink, 1970), 245-52. RILM[70] 3172.

NAUMANN, Hans-Peter. *Goethes "Faust" in schwedischer Übersetzung.* Stockholm: Almquist & Wiksell, 1970.

NEVINSON, Henry Wood. *Goethe: Man and Poet, Written for the Centenary of Goethe's Death on March 22, 1832.* Freeport, NY: Books for Libraries Press, 1971. Reprint of the (NY: Harcourt, Brace, 1932) ed.

NEWMAN, Ernest. *Musical Studies.* NY: Haskell House, 1969. Reprint of the (London/NY: John Lane, 1914) ed. See: p. 173.

PALMER, Philip Mason, & Robert Pattison MORE. *The Sources of the Faust Tradition, from Simon Magus to Lessing.* NY: Haskell House, 1965; also NY: Octagon Books, 1966. Reprints of the (NY: Oxford University Press, 1936) ed. See: p. 173.

PANOFSKY, Walter. "Faust auf der Opernbühne," *Musik und Szene* VI/9 (1961-1962), 105-7.

PETSCH, Robert. *Faustsage und Faustdichtung.* Dortmund: Ruhfus, 1966.

POHL, Wilma. *Russische Faust-Übersetzungen.* Meisenheim am Glan: A. Hain, 1962.

PRIEST, George Madison. *Faust*, revised edition. NY: A. A. Knopf, 1963. See: p. 175.

RAPHAEL, Alice Pearl. *Faust, a Tragedy, Part One*, translated by Alice Raphael; introduction and notes by Jacques Barzun; illustrations with eighteen lithographs by Eugene Delacroix. NY: Heritage Press, 1959; NY: Holt, Rinehart and Winston, 1961. See: p. 176.

REQUADT, Paul. *Goethes Faust I; Leitmotivik und Architektur.* Munich: W. Fink, 1972.

RESENHÖFFT, Wilhelm. *Existenzerhellung des Hexentums in Goethes "Faust"* [Mephistos Masken, Walpurgis] ; *Grundlinien axiomatisch-psychologischer Deutung.* Bern: Herbert Lang, 1970.

RESENHÖFFT, Wilhelm. *Goethes Rätseldichtungen im Faust* (mit Hexenküche und Hexen-Einmal-Eins) in soziologischer Deutung. Bern: Herbert Lang, 1972.

RESKE, Hermann. *Faust, eine einfuhrüng.* Stuttgart: Kohlhammer, 1971.

RICHARDS, Ivor Armstrong. *Tomorrow Morning, Faustus! An Infernal Comedy.* NY: Harcourt, Brace & World, 1962.

ROBERTSON, John George. *The Life and Work of Goethe, 1749-1832.* Freeport, NY: Books for Libraries Press, 1971. Reprint of the (NY: Dutton; London: Routledge, 1932) ed.

RUSSO, Wilhelm. *Goethes Faust auf den Berliner bühnen.* Nendeln/Liechtenstein: Kraus Reprint, 1967. Reprint of the (Berlin: E. Ebering, 1924) ed. See: p. 177.

SALM, Peter. *The Poem as Plant; a Biological View of Goethe's Faust.* Cleveland: Press of Case Western Reserve University, 1971.

SAMS, Eric. "Schumann and Faust," *The Musical Times* CXIII (June 1972), 543-46.

SANTAYANA, George. *Three Philosophical Poets: Lucretius, Dante and Goethe.* NY: Cooper Square, 1970. Reprint of the (Cambridge: Harvard University Press, 1910) ed.

SCHADEWALDT, Wolfgang. "Faust und Helena; zu Goethes Auffassung vom Schoenen und der Realität des Realen im zweiten Teil des Faust," *Deutsche Vierteljahrsschrift für Literatur und Geist* XXX/1 (1956), 1-40.

SCHEFFEL, Helmut. "Eine Faust-Oper zum Mitspielen," *Melos* XXXI/3 (Mar 1964), 77-8+.

SCHNEIDER, Frank. "Faust bei H. Berlioz," *Musik und Gesellschaft* XIX/3 (Mar 1969), 164-69.

SCHRÖDER, Rolf. *Gorkis Erneuerung der Fausttradition; Faustmodelle im russischen geschichtsphilosophischen Roman.* Berlin: Ruetten & Lowning, 1971.

SCHÜPBACH, Werner. *Die Menschwerdung als zentrales Phänomen der Evolution in Goethes Darstellung der klassischen Walpurgisnacht.* Freiburg: Verlag Die Kommenden, 1967.

SCOTT, Michael R. "Why 'Faust?'" *Music and Musicians* XVIII/12 (Dec 1969), 28-29.

STAWELL, Florence Melian, & G. Lowes DICKINSON. *Goethe and Faust*, an 1971. Reprint of the (London: Seeley, 1894) ed.

SIME, James. *Life of Johann Wolfgang Goethe.* Port Washington, NY: Kennikat Press, 1972. Reprint of the (London: W. Scott; NY: T. Whittaker, 1888) ed.

STAHL, Ernest Leopold. *Creativity; A Theme from Faust and the Divino Elegies. An Inaugural Lecture, Delivered before the University of Oxford on 2 March 1961.* Oxford: Clarendon Press, 1961.

STAWELL, Florence Melian, & G. Lowes DICKINSON. *Goethe and Faust*, an interpretation with passages newly translated into English verse. NY: Haskell House, 1972. Reprint of the (NY: L. MacVeagh, The Dial Press, 1928). See: p. 180.

STEFFEN, Albert. *Goethes Geistgestalt*, 2. Aufl. Dornach: Verlag für Schoene Wissenschaften, 1970. First edition, 1932.

STEINER, Jacob. *Erläuterungen zu Goethes Faust I.* Stockholm: Natur och Kultur, 1959.

STEINER, Rudolf. *Die Rätsel in Goethes Faust, exoterisch und esoterisch: zwei vorträge gehalten am 11. und 12. märz 1909 in Berlin.* Dornach: Verlag der Rudolf-Steiner-Nachlassverwaltung, 1970.

STERNFELD, Frederick W. "Goethe and Music," *Dissertation Abstracts* XXXI/12 (June 1971), 6654-A. See: p. 180.

STERNFELD, Frederick W. "Renaissance Music in Goethe," *Germanic Review* XX/4 (1945), 241-60.

STRICH, Fritz. *Goethe and World Literature*, translated by C. A. M. Sym. Westport, Conn: Greenwood Press, 1971. Reprint of the (NY: Hafner, 1949) ed.

STRICH, Fritz. *Goethes Faust* [Aus dem Nachlass, hrsg. von Gertrud Strich-Sattler]. Bern/Munich: Francke, 1964.

STUMME, Gerhard. *Faust als Pantomime und Ballett*. Leipzig: Druck der Offizin Poeschel & Trepte, 1942.

STUMME, Gerhard. *Meine Faustsammlung*, bearb. von Hans Henning. Weimar: Jahresgabe der Nationalen Forschungs- und Gedenkstätten der Klassischen Deutschen Literatur, 1957.

SZABOLCSI, Bence. "Mozart's Faustische Dramaturgie," *Österreichische Musikzeitschrift* XXIII/8 (Aug 1968), 393-97.

TAK, Willem G. van der. *Spinozistische gedachten in Goethe's Faust*. Leiden: E. J. Brill, 1950. (*Mededeelingen van wege het Spinozahuis*, 9.)

TILLE, Alexander. *Die deutschen Volkslieder vom Doktor Faust*. Wiesbaden: M. Sändig, 1969. Reprint of the (Halle: M. Niemeyer, 1890) ed.

TREVELYAN, Humphry. *The Popular Background to Goethe's Hellenism*. London/ NY: Longmans, Green, 1934.

UNGER, Max. *Ein Faustopernplan Beethovens und Goethes, ein Doppelbildnis in neuer Betrachtung, mit zwei Sepiazeichnungen des Verfassers*. Regensburg: G. Bosse, 1952.

VALENTIN, Erich. *Goethes Musikanshauung*. Olten: Vereinigung Oltner Bücher-freunde, 1960.

VAN ABBÉ, Derek Maurice. *Goethe: New Perspectives on a Writer and His Time.* London: Allen & Unwin, 1972.

VICKERY, John B., & J'nan SELLERY, eds. *Goethe's Faust, Part One; Essays in Criticism.* Belmont, Calif: Wadsworth, 1969.

VICTOR, Walther. *Carl Friedrich Zelter und seine Freundschaft mit Goethe.* Berlin: Aufbau-Verlag, 1970.

VISCHER, Friedrich Theodor von. *Faust, der Tragödie dritter Teil; Treu im Geiste des zweiten Teils des Goetheschen Faust gedichtet von Deutobold Symbolizetti Allegoriowitsch Mystifizinsky.* Berlin: Haude & Spener, 1969.

VISCHER, Friedrich Theodor von. *Göthe's Faust: neue Beiträge für Kritik des Gedichts.* Osnabrueck: Biblio Verlag, 1969. Reprint of the (Stuttgart: A. Benz, 1875) ed.

VON HOFE, Harold H. *Faust: Leben, Legende und Literatur.* NY: Holt, Rinehart & Winston, 1965.

WADEPUHL, Walter. *Goethe's Interest in the New World.* NY: Haskell House, 1973. Reprint of the (Jena: Frommann [W. Biedermann], 1934) ed.

WEGNER, Wolfgang. *Die Faustdarstellung vom 16. Jahrhundert bis zur Gegenwart.* Amsterdam: Verlag der Erasmus Buchhandlung, 1962.
With special reference to illustrations for Goethe's *Faust;* reproductions.

WENZLITSCHKE, Kurt. *Faust, neu interpretiert.* Frankfurt am Main: Biebergasse 2, Selbstverlag, 1967.

"Wessen 'Faust'?" *Musik und Gesellschaft* XIX/5 (May 1969), 325.

Yale University Library. *The William A. Speck Collection of Goethiana: Goethe's Works; a Catalogue Compiled by Members of the Yale Library Staff,* edited & arranged with notes & a biographical sketch of William A. Speck by Carl F. Schreiber. New Haven: Yale University Press, 1940. See: p. 178.

BIBLIOGRAPHY/MUSICAL COMPOSITIONS

BECKER, John Joseph. *Faust Triptych:* a Television Opera in 3 Monodramas.
[NYPL: Holograph, pencil.]

BENTZON, Niels Viggo. *Faust III.* Copenhagen: S. A. Roewade, 1964. Performed
in Kiel, North Germany, 1964.

CANDONI, Luigi, & Mario NASCIMBENE. *Faust a Manhattan, opera in un tempo,*
1963. (libretto in Italian) [Piano score in the Library of Congress.]

CASSIMIR, Heinrich. *Hymnus aus "Faust" für Männerchor und Blasorchester
oder Orge- oder Klavierbegleitung.* Karlsruhe: F. Müller, Süddeutscher
Musickverlag, c.1931. [Score in NYPL.]

DESSAU, Paul. *7 Lieder zu Goethes Faust, für mittlere Stimme und Klavier.*
Weimar: Thüringer Volksverlag, 1949. [Score in NYPL.]

DVORÁK, Antonin, & Adolf WENIG. *Cert a Káca* [The Devil and Kate], *Opera
o 3 jednánich . . ., Op. 112.* Prague: Hudebni matice umědecké besedy, 1926.
[Score in NYPL.]

EISLER, Hans. *Doktor Johann Faust.*

Puppet schema with Marxist propaganda. Eisler published the libretto in Berlin in 1952
but became discouraged by official criticism and died in 1962 without completing the music.

GESSNER, John & H. Wesley BALK. *Faust Counter Faust.*

This two-act music-theatre collage incorporates music by John Gessner, dialogue by
H. Wesley Balk, and music and words from the following works: Berlioz, *The Damnation
of Faust;* Boito, *Mefistofele;* Goethe, *Faust;* Gounod, *Faust;* Kipphardt, *In the Case of
J. Robert Oppenheimer;* Marlowe, *The Tragical History of Doctor Faustus;* Marowitz,
Prologue to Doctor Faustus. Premiere January 30, 1971 in Minneapolis. Philip Brunelle,
Music Director; H. Wesley Balk, Stage Director. Also performed in New York, Chicago,
Philadelphia, and San Francisco. The work consists of an opera-within-an-opera whose
setting is an insane asylum, where the latest Faust, John, who believes himself to be
a reincarnation of the original, is incarcerated along with all the past characters from
previous "Fausts." Materials are available from the Minnesota Opera Company, formerly
the Center Opera Company, 1812 South Sixth Street, Minneapolis, Minnesota, 55404.

Phone: 612-339-6726. The reception of this work has been mixed. After referring
to the fact that the single Chicago performance "went off like clockwork" Bernard
Jacobson of the Chicago *Daily News* goes on to say: "The result is as stimulating an
evening in the theater as you are likely to find."

HEIDEN, Bernhard. *Euphorion: scene for orchestra*, 1949. NY: Associated Music
Publishers, 1962. [Score in NYPL.]

MOSZKOWSKI, Moritz. *Anton Notenquetscher am Klavier.* Parodistischer Scherz
von Alexander Moszkowski. Parodie der Schülerscene aus Goethes "Faust."
Berlin: H. Steinitz, 1896. [Score in NYPL.]

MUELLER, Charles P. [Special Music for Pathé frères colored film, *d'art Faust.*]
NY: Pathé frères, 192-?. [Score in NYPL. Music adapted from Gounod's
opera, *Faust.*]

PANIZZA, Giacomo. *Faust Selection*, arranged for piano. Milan: G. Ricordi, 1848.
[Score in NYPL.]

RAPHAEL, Günther. *Gesang der Erzengel, Prolog im Himmel aus Goethes "Faust,"
Op. 79, für 3 Solostimmen und 16 Bläser (Klavier a uszug).* Wiesbaden:
Breitkopf & Härtel, 1954. [Piano score in NYPL.]

REIN, Walter. *Türmerlied, Intrada nach Worten des Türmers aus Goethes, "Faust,"*
für Männerchor und Bläser. Mainz: B. Schott's Söhne, 1932. [Score in NYPL.]

RUBINSTEIN, Anton. *"Faust": Ein musikalisches Characterbild für grosses Orchester,
Op. 68.* Leipzig: C. F. W. Siegel, 1864. [Score in NYPL.]

SEIBER, Mátyás. *Faust; suite per coro misto e orchestra su testo di Johann
Wolfgang von Goethe.* Testo inglese di Louis MacNeice. Milan: Edizioni
Suvini Zerboni, 1965.

SEIBER, Mátyás. *Two Songs from Goethe's Faust: Es war ein König in Thule,
Meine Ruh ist hin.* London: Augener, 1951. [Score in NYPL.]

SONNEBORN, Daniel. *Incidental music for "Dominus Marlowe/A Play on Doctor
Faustus"*—a play in progress in two acts by Michael Monroe first presented
by the ProVisional Theatre on July 11, 1973 in Los Angeles, California.
For details, see: Michael Monroe, under PLAY.

PLAY

MONROE, Michael. *Dominus Marlowe / A Play on Doctor Faustus.*

A play in progress in two acts with musical compositions by Daniel Sonneborn. It was first presented by the ProVisional Theatre on July 11, 1973 in Los Angeles, California. In a letter dated November 20, 1973, Michael Dowdy, one of the members of the cast says, "We still consider the piece a work-in-progress, so there is not yet a final version of the script available." In a review in *The Orange County Evening News*, Larry Taylor gives a synopsis of the play: "Starting out with the events surrounding the death of Elizabethan poet Christopher Marlowe, it soon becomes a surrealistic examination of his life and art. As we enter his unconscious state while he slips into death, we see Marlowe standing back, his life flashing before him, his revolutionary ideas up for examination. 'A trial!' he shouts. Paralleling his life's trial, often merging with it in simultaneous action, is an enactment of Marlowe's masterpiece, 'Dr. Faustus.' Faustus' temptation and his pull between heaven and hell are finally the death issues for Marlowe himself." Further information may be obtained from the ProVisional Theatre Foundation, 857 N. Virgil Ave. (Office E), Los Angeles, California, 90029. Phone: 213-664-2450.

Below and opposite: Scenes from *Dominus Marlowe / A Play on Doctor Faustus.*
Photos by Claire Henze.

XXVII

THE FAUST LEGEND IN MUSIC

Overleaf: Witches' orgy scene. Yale University Theater, 1949.

NORTHWESTERN UNIVERSITY

THE FAUST LEGEND IN MUSIC

A DISSERTATION

SUBMITTED TO THE GRADUATE SCHOOL

IN PARTIAL FULFILLMENT OF THE REQUIREMENTS

for the degree

DOCTOR OF PHILOSOPHY

Field of Music History

By

James William Kelly

Evanston, Illinois

August, 1960

TABLE OF CONTENTS

PREFACE

I wish to express my appreciation and gratitude to the following:

Dr. John F. Ohl, Chairman of the Department of Music History and Literature, Northwestern University, for his advice and encouragement.

Rev. Roland Behrendt, O.S.B., of the Modern Language Department, St. John's University, Collegeville, Minnesota, for his practical assistance and advice.

Dr. Meno Spann, German Department, Northwestern University, for his interest and advice.

Professor Kurt von Faber du Faur, Curator of the William A. Speck Collection of Goethiana at Yale University, and the Supervisor, Mrs. Hedwig J. Dejon, for their many kindnesses and invaluable assistance.

Mr. James T. Babb, Librarian of Yale University, for permission to photograph the Wagner manuscript.

Miss Mary Grahm, Librarian, and Mr. Lamont Moor of the Yale Drama Department.

Miss Alberta Kneeland, Curator of the Allen A. Brown Collection, Boston Public Library.

Donald Krummel of the staff of the Music Division, Library of Congress.

Mr. Frederick Freedman of the staff of The New York Public Library.

Mrs. Rita Benton, Music Librarian of the State University of Iowa.

ILLUSTRATIONS

CHAPTER I

HOW OLD IS FAUST?

Contemporary man, like his Renaissance counterpart, is restless and thus Faustian. He makes frenzied efforts to reach far beyond his puny sphere into boundless space and is determined to attain power over life and death by penetrating the very heart of matter. Daily, perhaps hourly, the barriers of ignorance are thrust back another arm's length by scientific discoveries. It is man's penetration into the makeup of the atom that will make his dreams of exploring the universe come true. Man is reaching for power, for fulfillment.

This search is, in a way, a search for God, his creator. Man is made in God's image. It is but natural for him to seek God, to seek to become God-like. Man simultaneously seeks and flees God. St. Augustine declares in his Confessions, "...for Thou hast made us for Thee and our heart is unquiet till it finds its rest in Thee."[1] Francis Thompson expresses it thus in "The Hound of Heaven":

> I fled Him, down the nights and down the days;
> I fled Him, down the arches of the years;
> I fled Him, down the labyrinthine ways
> of my own mind; and in the mist of tears
> I hid from Him, and under running laughter.[2]

The story of Faust is as old as homo sapiens, but the Faust of

---

[1] St. Augustine Confessions, trans. Vernon J. Bourke (New York: Fathers of the Church, Inc., 1953), p. 4.

[2] Selected Poems of Francis Thompson (London: Jonathan Cape, 1908), p. 49.

the literary artists is not really a person. He may have had a counterpart in the Johannes Faust of the Spiess Faustbuch as well as in earlier figures, as we shall see, but he is only a symbol of the dichotomy, the two opposing forces, in man. The one draws him upward toward higher things; the other draws him down to base acts and unrestrained pleasures.

This curse of instability, of vacillation, was brought upon the first man by his failing the test God put him to, whether there was a tree and an apple or not. "And the serpent said to her, What is this talk of death? God knows well that as soon as you eat this fruit your eyes will be opened, and you yourselves will be like gods, knowing good and evil."[1] Eve ate of the "apple" and so did Adam. Thus man's state of original justice, that is, man's state of original friendship with God which provided him with special helps to overcome his inordinate impulses, was forfeited. Man since that fateful day has been subject to concupiscence which gets in the way of his striving for higher things, for the fulfillment, the perfecting of himself.

When Adam and Eve were driven out of paradise, man's long onslaught on nature and her secrets began. Man had to learn to fend for himself; he was on his own. God had made him in His own image and likeness and had given him the task of ruling over and subduing all the rest of God's handiwork. Like God, who rules the universe, he was to exercise dominion over the world. In the Garden of Eden are found prototypes of the three principal characters in Part One of Goethe's Faust, a man, a woman, and the spirit of evil.

---

[1]Gen., 3:4-6.

Père Teilhard de Chardin, the distinguished palaeontologist, makes the following comments regarding man as the terminus of biological evolution:

> A certain sort of common sense tells us that with man biological evolution has reached its ceiling: in reflecting upon itself, life has become stationary. But should we not rather say that it leaps forward? Look at the way in which, as mankind technically patterns its multitudes, the psychic tension within it increases, pari passu with the consciousness of time and space and the taste for, and power of discovery. This great event we accept without surprise. Yet how can one fail to recognise this revealing association of technical mastery over environment and inward spiritual concentration as the work of the same great force (though in proportions and with a depth hitherto never attained), the very force which brought us into being? How can we fail to see that after rolling us on individually--all of us, you and me--upon our own axes, it is still the same cyclone (only now on the social scale) which is still blowing over our heads, driving us together into a contact which tends to perfect each one of us by linking him organically to each and all of his neighbours?[1]

In his essay "Remarks on the Modes of Divine Action in the Universe," written about 1920, Père Teilhard de Chardin has the following to say about the origin of evil:

> We often represent God to ourselves as being able to draw a world out of nothingness without pain, defects, risks, without 'breakage.' This is conceptual fantasy which makes the problem of evil unsolvable. No, it is necessary instead to say that God, despite His power cannot obtain a creature united to Him without necessarily entering into struggle with some evil because evil appears inevitably with the first atom of being which creation 'unleashes' into existence. Creation and impeccableness (absolute or general) are terms which are as much repugnant (physically or metaphysically, matters little here) to divine power and wisdom as the coupling of the terms 'creature' and 'uniqueness'...[2]

The "taste for, and power of discovery" that Père de Chardin refers

---

[1]Pierre Teilhard de Chardin, S.J., The Phenomenon of Man, trans. Bernard Wall (New York: Harper & Brothers, 1959), p. 304.

[2]Quoted in: Claude Tresmontant, Pierre Teilhard de Chardin, His Thought, trans. Salvator Attanasio (Baltimore: Helicon Press, 1959), p. 96.

to in the first excerpt from his writings is certainly Faustian. The
second quotation implies that the spirit of evil, so essential to the
Faust legend, is inevitable. Therefore, the implications of the Faust
legend are as old as man himself. The legend deals with religious and
philosophical problems that are vital to man---the role that good and
evil play in his life, his desire to pierce nature's secrets to the
core, and the dichotomy between the sublimity and mystery of human life.

In the next chapter the manifestations of the Faust legend in
antiquity will be traced. An important element in the Faust legend is
the pact made between man and devil. We will see how the wise men of
old were called magicians and were thought to be in league with Satan.

CHAPTER II

THE FAUST LEGEND IN ANTIQUITY

In its irregular development the history of the Faust legend
resembles that of many other epic themes. Gilgamesh, the hero of
the Babylonian epic of the seventh century B.C., resembles Faust
in his desire to be young again. He is informed that there is a
weed that will restore his youth, but just as he obtains possession
of it, it is snatched from him. Prometheus, the Titan who stole
fire from heaven, has been likened to Faust in his role of inventor
and teacher of the arts of life.

Eliza M. Butler describes the origin of the legendary magician
thus:

> "...the facts would seem to show that the legendary magician de-
> rives from that dim and distant hero, who, as king, god or priest,
> died to be reborn in kingship or seasonal rites; and that, al-
> though he gradually became a creature sealed and set apart in the
> magic circle, he was originally one of the countless dying gods
> whose distribution is world-wide."[1]

She goes on to list ten "stock features" of the magus-legend: (1)
supernatural or mysterious origin of the hero, (2) portents at birth,
(3) perils menacing his infancy, (4) some kind of initiation, (5)
far distant wanderings, (6) a magical contest, (7) a trial of perse-
cution, (8) a last scene, (9) a violent or mysterious death, (10) a
resurrection and/or ascension.[2]

---

[1] Eliza M. Butler, The Myth of the Magus (Cambridge: University
Press, 1948), p. 2.

[2] Ibid., pp. 2-3.

Solomon has a high place among these magi, who may be considered the forerunners of Faust, "He is one of the most brilliant of the fixed stars in the magical firmament. As long as the word magic lasts, his name will endure; and as long as the practice of magic persists, his authority will be invoked in all civilised lands."[1] Legend attributes to Solomon a magic ring with four stones which gave him power over the forces of nature as well as over animals, men, and spirits.

Even the Book of Job has something in common with the story of Faust in the opening conversation between God and "the Enemy" in which Job's constancy is discussed.

> The idea of a compact with the devil for the purpose of obtaining superhuman power or knowledge is of Jewish origin, dating from the centuries immediately before and after the Christian era which produced the Talmud, the Kabbalah and such magical books as that of Enoch. In the mystical rites that accompanied the incantations with which the Jewish magicians evoked the Satanim we have the prototypes and originals of all the ceremonies which occupy the books of magic down to the various versions of the Hoellenzwang ascribed to Faust. The other principle underlying the Faust legend, the belief in the essentially evil character of purely human learning, has existed ever since the triumph of Christianity set divine revelation above human science.[2]

Stories about men in league with the Evil One have been current since early Christian time and before. Down through the centuries learned men and especially those who tried to unlock nature's secrets were given the appellation of magician or wizard and were generally regarded with suspicion. There is quite a list of them, and the

---

[1] Ibid., p. 37.

[2] Walter Alison Phillips, "Faust," Encyclopaedia Britannica, 11th ed., IX (1957), 121.

durability of some of the more sensational episodes in their lives
is shown by the fact that they show up in the Faustbuch. It must
be remembered that even during their lifetime many of these men were
legendary figures. As a consequence it is very difficult to separate
fact from fiction as far as they are concerned.

Zoroaster lived in the sixth century B.C. and founded the
ancient Persian religion named after him. Virgil (70-19 B.C.), the
great Latin poet, emerges as a magician around the beginning of the
eleventh century. He is supposed to have invented marvelous automata
which anticipated the robots of the future. Appolonius of Tyana
probably lived about the first century A.D. in Greece. He was a
great wanderer and is supposed to have had the power to transport
himself from place to place and to work miracles. Pope Sylvester
II, Gerbert, (999-1003) wrote a series of works on philosophical,
mathematical, and physical subjects.

> This great pope, who in the tenth century was already convinced
> that the earth was round and had designed a globe which showed
> the polar circle and the Tropic of Cancer! But the minds of his
> contemporaries, the science of his age could not follow his math-
> ematical calculations and discoveries. Some spread the rumor
> that the great prelate was experimenting with calling up the
> spirits of Parallelogram and Dodecahedron--magic, evil names
> which they had seen in the pope's notes with their own eyes.[1]

Robert the Devil, duke of Normany, who died in 1035, is said to have
been consecrated to Satan before his birth by his mother. He was a
demon of slaughter in his youth but later repented. Michael Scot
(1175?-1232) was a Scottish mathematician and astrologer who wrote

---

[1]Paul Tabori, The Natural Science of Stupidity (Philadelphia:
Chilton Co., 1959), p. 159. The first sentence is incomplete in
the source.

books dealing mainly with astrology, alchemy and the occult sciences.
In his notes to the poem "The Lay of the Last Minstrel" Sir Walter Scott
gives an interesting account of various exploits of the great magician:

> "He used to feast his friends with dishes brought by spirits from
> the royal kitchens of France and Spain and other lands. His em-
> bassy to France alone on the back of a coal-black demon steed is
> also celebrated, in which he brought the French monarch to his
> knees by the results of the stamping of his horse's hoofs."[1]

St. Albert the Great, Albertus Magnus (1193?-1280), was a German theo-
logian and philosopher. Roger Bacon (1214?-1292?), the English friar
and philosopher, was a remarkable man and was far ahead of his time.
He deprecated scholasticism when it was at its height and urged that
truth be sought by means of experimental science. Pope Paul II
(1464-1471) opposed pagan humanism. Agrippa von Nettesheim, Henry
Cornelius (1486-1535), was a German writer, soldier and physician,
who was a friend of Abbot Trithemius. Agrippa wrote his De occulta
philosophia in 1510. The learned abbot, who was decidedly not a
friend of Johannes Faust, may also be included in this list. Paracelsus, Philip Aureolus Theophrastus Bombastus von Hohenheim (1493-
1541), an alchemist and physician, was one of a group of alchemists
who attempted to create male and female homunculi in their labora-
tories from human seed and human blood. The mythical wizard Merlin
is found in the Vita Merlini written about 1148 and attributed to
Geoffrey of Monmouth. Merlin is said to derive from the Welsh bard
Myrrdhin Willt of the sixth century. He figures prominently in the
Arthurian legend. There remain a few others who will be considered

---

[1]Encyclopedia Britannica, 11th ed., XXIV, 411, n.n.

in more detail.

The Legend of Simon Magus[1]

Simon the magician is first mentioned in the Acts of the Apostles.[2] It is his distinction to have his name immortalized in the vice of simony. He was a Samaritan sorcerer who had been converted by the apostle Philip and was sternly rebuked by Peter for offering money to purchase the power of imparting the Holy Ghost. Since the second century there has been a gradual growth of legendary material about Simon. He is mentioned by the church fathers Justin Martyr, Tertullian, Irenaeus, Hippolytus and Arnobius. The most interesting account is found in the so-called "Clementines."[3] The story was well developed during the first four centuries and lasted until the close of the Middle Ages. The Kaiserchronik[4] narrates the legend at some length and there is some rearrangement of material. Later it was absorbed into the Legenda Aurea.[5]

---

[1]For much of the material on Simon and the other figures to be discussed in this chapter the writer is indebted to The Sources of the Faust Tradition by P. M. Palmer and R. P. More (New York: Oxford University Press, 1936).

[2]Acts 8:9-13, 18-24.

[3]They are also called the Clementine Homilies or the Clementine Recognitions. They are summaries of the sermons of St. Peter and have been falsely attributed to Pope St. Clement I. (Cf. An Outline of the Church by Centuries by Joseph McSorley (St. Louis: B. Herder Book Co. 1938) Vol. I, fn. p. 23.) The Recognitions were very popular in the Middle Ages. The strange history of Clement and his father Faustus, or Faustinianus is said to have originated the Faust legend.

[4]This document is thought to date from 1141 and is probably Bavarian in origin.

[5]A Collection of Saints' legends by Jacobus Voragine (d. 1298), Archbishop of Genoa. It became very popular and was translated into many other languages.

10

The following interesting details are taken from the Clementine Recognitions. Simon asserted "that his flesh is compacted of divinity, that it can endure to eternity." He fell in love with the woman called Luna. She is called Helena in the Homilies. He claims he can make himself invisible; he can "pass through rocks as if they were clay." In chapter nine he proclaims, "I shall be worshipped as God; I shall have divine honors publicly assigned to me, so that an image of me shall be set up and I shall be worshipped and adored as God." He wanted himself to be believed to be "an exalted power, which is above God the Creator and to be thought to be the Christ and to be called the Standing One."

In the light of the above claims Simon surely suffered from delusions. In chapter fourteen he tells Niceta that his mother Rachel conceived him while she was still a virgin and that he only pretended to be a man. In chapter fifteen he lays claim to the power of creating human life: "Once on a time, I, by my power, turning air into water, and water again into blood and solidifying it into flesh, formed a new human creature--a boy--and produced a much nobler work than God the Creator. For He created a man from the earth, but I from air."[1]

Further information regarding Simon is to be found in the apocryphal book Acts of the Holy Apostle Peter. Nero had commanded the magician to be brought before him. In the presence of the emperor, Simon changed his appearance to that of a child, an old man and a young man. "For he changed himself both in face and stature into

[1]Palmer and More, op. cit., p. 18.

different forms, and was in a frenzy, having the devil as his servant."
He claims he is God and denounces Peter and Paul and warns Nero that
his kingdom will be destroyed if he does not get rid of them.

Peter accuses Simon of falsely claiming to be Jesus Christ.
Peter challenges Simon to tell him what he is thinking about and what
he has done in secret. Simon is unable to do so and calls upon great
dogs to eat him up, but Peter has pieces of blessed bread up his
sleeves and shows these to the dogs which disappear. Later Simon
said he would fly to heaven from a high tower. Nero was convinced
of his reliability when he began to fly. Peter, at the urging of
Paul, looked steadily at Simon and prayed that by the power of God
and Jesus Christ the angels of Satan would drop him, and he perished
in the Via Sacra.

Additional material is to be found in the "Life of St. Peter
the Apostle" from the Legenda Aurea. Simon promised to make those
who believed in him live forever. He claimed to be able to do anything. He said to Peter, "I shall show to thee the power of my
dignity, that anon thou shalt adore me; I am first truth, and may
flee by the air; I can make new trees and turn stones into bread;
endure in the fire without hurting; and all that I will I may do."

Simon wished to prove to Nero that he was the very son of God
and asked him to order that his head be cut off, and he would rise
three days later. Simon cleverly substituted a ram by his magic art.

Simon went to the house of Peter's friend Marcellus and tied
a big dog before the door so that the dog might strangle Peter. But
Peter blessed the dog and the animal went after Simon. Later the

people drove Simon out of town and he could not return for a whole year. Many of these details resemble episodes in the _Faustbuch_.

The treatment of Simon Magus will be concluded by a quotation from Milman's _History of Christianity_:

> "Simon probably was one of that class of adventurers which abounded at this period, or like Apollonius of Tyana and others at a later time, with whom the opponents of Christianity attempted to confound Jesus and his apostles. His doctrine was Oriental in its language and in its pretensions. He was the first Aeon or Emanation, or rather perhaps the first manifestation, of the primal Deity. He assumed not merely the title of the Great Perfection, the Paraclete, the Almighty--the whole combined attributes of the Deity. He had a companion, Helena, according to the statement of his enemies, a beautiful prostitute, whom he found at Tyre who became in like manner the first conception (the Ennoea) of the Deity; but who, by her conjunction with matter, had been enslaved to its malignant influence, and, having fallen under the power of evil angels, had been in a constant state of transmigration, and, among other mortal bodies, had occupied that of the famous Helen of Troy."[1]

Cyprian of Antioch

The attempt has been made to find in St. Cyprian, whose feast, together with that of St. Justina, is celebrated according to the calendar of saints on September 26, a mystical prototype of the sixteenth century Faust. Yet my source says the story "...is probably pure invention although traces of older tales are to be found in it."[2] There are three Greek versions of the legend: The Conversion of St. Justina and St. Cyprian, The Confession of St. Cyprian, and The Martyrdom of St. Cyprian and St. Justina. That the legend was popular is attested by several subsequent versions and repeated references

---

[1] Henry Hart Milman, The History of Christianity (New York: Harper & Brothers, 1841), II, p. 51.

[2] Palmer and More, op. cit., p. 41.

to it in later centuries. Perhaps the most famous setting is that by the Spanish playwright Pedro Calderon de la Barca (1600-1681), El Magico Prodigioso, which was based on the version found in the Legenda Aurea.

After learning about the truths of Christianity from a deacon, Justina converted with her parents. A noble named Aglaidas (Acladius) became infatuated with her and tried to take her by force, but the maiden made the sign of the cross over him and subdued him. His pride wounded, he sought out the magician Cyprian for aid in the capture of the holy virgin.

According to the Golden Legend Cyprian was consecrated to the devil at the age of seven by his parents. As a young man he studied in Egypt and with the Chaldeans before coming to Antioch. He was a master of the elements as well as of demonology and prophecy. To aid him in the work of weakening Justina's resistance he summoned a devil, but she overcame his blandishments by ardent prayer. Then Cyprian sent a stronger demon who was routed in turn. He then made a third attempt by sending the father of all demons who went to her in the guise of a virgin seeking counsel. Justina recognized him and drove him out. The demon admitted to Cyprian that the crucified One "is greater than all."

Cyprian decides to become a Christian. He makes the sign of the cross over himself and is freed from bondage to the devil. He requests the bishop Anthimus to burn his books. Later on Cyprian is made a lector; then he becomes a subdeacon, deacon and finally a priest. He turned many away from the worship of idols and encouraged them to become Christians. He became the bishop's coadjutor and Anthimus, sensing that his days were drawing to an end, turned over his see to him. After he had set his affairs in order Cyprian appointed Justina to be superior in a convent.

The earl of the country heard of the fame of Cyprian and Justina and demanded that they sacrifice. They refused and were immersed in a caldron of boiling wax and grease, but they were unharmed. The priest of the idols came near and was consumed. Then Cyprian and Justina were taken out and beheaded 304 A.D.

Theophilus of Adana

The legend of Theophilus, a Cilician archdeacon of the sixth century, was one of the most popular down to the year 1500. The legend, originally written in Greek[1] between 650 and 850 A.D., became popular by means of Latin[2] translations which spread throughout Europe. The earliest poetic treatment of the Faust legend was that of Hroswitha, a celebrated nun-poetess who died about 1002. She set the legend of Theophilus in 455 verses. Another notable version is Rueteboeuf's dramatic mystery of the thirteenth century.

On the death of the reigning bishop of Adana the clergy and people wished Theophilus to take this high office. He protested his unworthiness and the metropolitan acceded to his wishes. After the

---

[1] Thirteen Greek versions are listed by Radermacher in his Griechische Quellen zur Faustsage. The Legenda Aurea gives 537 as the date.

[2] Of the twenty-five Latin versions the oldest is by Paulus Diaconus of Naples.

consecration of another man Theophilus was relieved of his stewardship. The devil filled his heart with envy and such wicked urgings that he called upon sorcerers for aid. He went to a Jew, who was a skilled practioner of the diabolical arts, to enlist his help against the bishop. The Jew introduced him to the Prince of Darkness who said, "Let him deny the son of Mary and Mary herself, for they are offensive to me." Theophilus writes a statement of denial and seals it with his ring.[1]

After some time had passed Theophilus thinks of the torments of hell and begins to repent. He regrets the pact he made with the devil and after fasting decides to approach the Virgin Mary, whom he had denied. After he had fasted for forty days and forty nights the Virgin appeared to him and inquired as to why he persisted in requiring her aid. Theophilus mentions the case of Cyprian who received remission of his sins and the grace of martyrdom. Our Lady calls upon him for a profession of faith. Weeping and with bowed head he professes his belief in Jesus Christ. Then the mother of God says she will speak to her Son on his behalf.

For three more days the steward gave himself over completely to prayer and weeping, beating his head against the floor and fasting. Our Lady returns and announces his forgiveness. Theophilus desires the return of the wicked compact he made with the devil. After three days the Virgin returned the pact to him with the waxen seal on it.

The next day he went to the church and, casting himself at the

---

[1]The version in the Legenda Aurea is very brief. It does not mention that the pact with the devil was signed with Theophilus' blood. Some versions have this detail.

feet of the bishop, told him the whole story. He turned over the compact to the bishop with the request that it be read to all present. The bishop welcomed him and asked him to burn the document. This was done. Three days later Theophilus died after distributing his possessions to the poor.

Echoes of some of the fantastic occurrences in the lives of these magicians will be found in the record of the life of Johannes Faust, who lived in Germany in the sixteenth century and died amid horrible torments as a result of his pact with the devil. The life of the historical Faust and details concerning the various written versions will form the subject matter for the next chapter.

CHAPTER III

THE HISTORICAL FAUST

Dr. Johannes (George) Faust (1480?-1540) was a wandering scholar, mountebank and charlatan. He is sometimes called Sabellicus. It may be that he Latinized his German name Zabel,[1] suggesting that he descended from the tribe of Sabellians in ancient Italy, who were thought to be experts in magic. His birthplace is uncertain. It is generally thought to be the Swabian city of Knittlingen,[2] where a monument has been erected to his memory in the city square and a Faust-Museum was opened in 1954. Some authorities derive his name from the Latin translation of Knittel, meaning stick, which is fustis in Latin. Then again he may have been boasting of his success in the black arts by adopting a Latin name for advertising purposes--that of Faustus, the fortunate one.

The documents dealing with the historical Faust are not of equal value.[3] A good bit of legendary material has got mixed up

---

[1]It became quite the thing for the German humanists of the sixteenth century to add an "us" to their names or to translate their guttural names into Greek or Latin.

[2]Other towns claiming to be Faust's birthplace are Anhalt, Brandenberg, and Rhodes.

[3]The number of references to Faust in the various European literatures are indicative of the interest in this character. Alexander Tille (1866-1912) made a collection of about 450 items in his Die Faustsplitter in der Literatur des Sechzehnten bis achtzehnten Jahrhunderts (Berlin: E. Felber, 1898-1901). Since the publication of his book about 90 additional items have come to light.

with the facts. Reliable information can be had from his contemporaries Abbot Trithemius, Conrad Mutianus Rufus, Philipp von Hutten, and Kilian Leib, as well as from the account book of the bishop of Bamberg, the Ingolstadt and Nuremberg records, and Luther's *Tischreden*. Other sources that could be mentioned like the Waldeck Chronicle seem to have been influenced by hearsay. However, the historical Faust never seems to materialize as more than a shadowy figure in the letters, diaries, and records of his contemporaries from 1507 to 1540 when all mention of him as a living figure ceases.

As was asserted in the previous chapter, Abbot Trithemius,[1] the great Benedictine abbot and scholar, was no friend of Dr. Faust. He wrote a book called *Antipalus Maleficiorum* in which he gives instructions how honest men can guard themselves against witches and their accursed arts. It is to him that we owe the first written account of the notorious necromancer. He comments sharply on the singular vanity of Faustus in a letter to his friend the mathematician, John Virdungo, dated Wuerzburg August 20, 1507.

> Observe the stupid thoughtlessness of the man! He is carried away with so great a madness that he presumptuously bestows upon himself the title of Source of Necromancy! A man so truly ignorant of all good literature ought to have called himself a fool rather than a teacher! But his wickedness does not escape me. When I returned from Brandenburg in March of last year, I found this very man in the town of Gelnhausen. More silly things which he had quite rashly declared in the town hospice were repeatedly related to me. As soon as he heard that I was present, he fled from the town hospice, and no one could persuade him to present himself to me. ...Certain priests in the

---

[1]John Trithemius, O.S.B. (1462-1516) became abbot of the monastery of Sponheim at the age of twenty-two. He numbered the learned men and the princes of the time among his friends. In twenty-three years he built up the abbey library to 2,000 volumes. He was abbot of St. Martin, Sponheim, 1483-1506 and St. James, Wuerzburg, 1506-1516.

town related to me that he had said in the presence of many: that
he had attained such a knowledge and memory of all wisdom that if
all the writings of Plato and Aristotle had perished from human
memory in their entirety together with their philosophical ideas,
he himself by his own ingenuity like another Ezras, the Hebrew,
would be able to restore the lot of them with greater elegance.
Afterwards,...he came to Wuerzburg; and driven by the same vanity,
is reported to have said in the presence of very many: that the
miracles of Christ the Saviour were no miracles at all, and that
he, too, could do all those things which Christ had done as often
as and whenever he would wish. ...He said that he was most perfect in the alchemy of all things that have ever existed, and
that he knew how and had the power to perform whatever men would
desire. In the meantime the schoolmaster's post in the afore-
said town was vacant. He had been taken on as an assistant to
this post because of the promotion of Francis Balivei, your
chief from Sickingen, who is very fond of mystics and mysticism.
He soon began the worst kind of character formation among the
students, namely, training them for base pleasure. When this
fact came to light, he fled at once unwilling to take the appropriate consequences of his activity. These are the things which
are most certainly known to me about that famous man whose arrival you are so eagerly awaiting. When he comes to you, you
will find him to be not a philosopher but a foolish man inflated
with an overdose of rashness.[1]

In a letter to his friend Heinrich Urbanus, Conrad Mutianus

Rufus[2] relates that he heard a soothsayer called George Faust brag-

ging at an inn in Erfurt and making idle claims. In writing to his

brother Philipp von Hutten, he seems to indicate that Faust made pre-

dictions concerning the fortunes of the expedition in Venezuela.[3]

An interesting item is found in the journal of Kilian Leib, prior

of Rebdorf in Bavaria, dated July, 1528:

"George Faust of Helmstet said in the fifth day of June that
when the sun and Jupiter are in the same constellation prophets

---

[1]Marquard Freher, Johannis Trithemii opera historica (2 vols.;
Frankfort: Typis Wechelianis apud Claudium Marnium, 1610), II, p. 559.

[2]Conrad Mutianus Rufus (1471-1526), humanist and philosopher,
was a canon of St. Mary's at Gotha.

[3]Philipp von Hutten (1511-1546) was one of the leaders of the
Welser troops in Venezuela, where he met his death.

Prologue in heaven. Yale University Theater, 1949.

are born (presumably such as he). He asserted that he was the commander or preceptor of the order of Knights of St. John at a place called Hallestein on the border of Carinthia."[1]

The account book of the Bishop of Bamberg records that 10 guilden was paid to Doctor Faust, who made a horoscope for the bishop. The records of the cities of Ingolstadt and Nuremberg attest to the unsavory character of Dr. Faust. This is the entry in the records of the city council at Ingolstadt: "On Wednesday after St. Vitus' Day, 1528, a certain man who called himself Dr. George Faust of Heidelberg was told to spend his penny elsewhere and he pledged himself not to take vengeance on or make fools of the authorities for this order."[2] The entry in the records of the city council of Nuremberg May 10, 1532 is more terse: "Safe conduct to Doctor Faust, the great sodomite and necromancer, at Fuerth, refused."[3] The next excerpt from the writings of Faust's contemporaries is taken from the Tischreden of Martin Luther.

Mention was made of magicians and the magic art, and how Satan blinded men. Much was said about Faust, who called the devil his brother-in-law: 'If I, Martin Luther, had given him even my hand, he would have destroyed me; but I would not have been afraid of him,--with God as my protector I would have given him my hand in the name of the Lord.'[4]

---

[1]From Karl Schottenloher, Der Rebdorfer Prior, Kilian Leib, und sein Wettertagebuch, translated in Palmer and More, op. cit., p. 89.

[2]Tille op. cit. item 4, translated in Palmer and More, op. cit., p. 90.

[3]Franz Neubert, Vom Doctor Faustus zu Goethes Faust (Leipzig: J. J. Weber, 1932), p. 16.

[4]This excerpt was recorded by Antonius Lauterbach in 1537 and first published by E. Kroker, "Luther's Tischreden," Der Mathesischen Sammlung (Leipzig: 1903), p. 422.

Our final quotation from the Christlich Bedencken by Augustin
Lercheimer[1] may be less reliable, but it has considerable interest.

> He (Faust) was born in a little place called Knittlingen, situ-
> ated in Wuertemberg near the border of the Palatinate. For a
> time he was schoolmaster in Kreuznach under Franz von Sickingen:
> he had to flee from there because he was guilty of sodomy. After
> that he travelled about the country with his devil; studied the
> black art at the university in Cracow; came to Wittenberg and
> was allowed to stay there for a time, until he carried things so
> far that they were on the point of arresting him, when he fled.
> He had neither house nor home in Wittenberg or elsewhere; in fact
> he had no permanent abode anywhere, but lived like a vagabond,
> was a parasite, drunkard, and gourmand, and supported himself by
> his quackery...He came at times to the house of Melanchton, who
> gave him a good lecture, rebuked and warned him that he should
> reform in time, lest he come to an evil end, as finally happened.
> ...He was choked to death by the devil in a village in Wuertemberg...[2]

The Faust Books

The last notable reference to Faust before the appearance of
the Faustbuch is the edition of De Praestigiis Daemonum by the learned physician Johannes Wierus in 1568. It is the opinion of Robert
Petsch that the stories which gradually encrusted the name of Faust
were the common property of university circles about 1550 and that
there was a collection of Faustian legends in Latin before 1570.[3]
The earliest tangible effort to gather these tales into a manuscript
was made by Christopher Rosshirt.

---

[1]Hermann Witekind Augustin Lercheimer von Steinfelden (1522-
1603) taught Greek at Heidelberg and Neustadt and later on taught
mathematics at Heidelberg. His real name was Hermann Witekind. In
the third edition of his work Christlich Bedencken und Erinnerung
von Zauberey (Speyer, 1597) he denounces the assertion by the unknown author of the Spiess Faustbuch that Faust had been brought up
in Wittenberg and had received degrees there.

[2]Translated in Palmer and More, op. cit., p. 121.

[3]Ibid., p. 129.

The Wolfenbuettel manuscript, probably written between 1572 and 1587, is of greater importance. It provides a rather pedestrian account of the life and doings of the notorious magician. It is crudely done and of no literary value. Its purpose was probably to warn good Protestants not to imitate Faust's ambition and his proclivity for trafficking with the Evil One. However, the public's interest was not so much in the awful fate of the necromancer as in the piquancy of some of the stories. It is typical of the sort of manuscript that formed the basis for the later printed works. Some of the first manuscripts to be circulated gave instructions as to how to perform some of the magic arts attributed to Faust. One of the most famous of these, a Hoellenzwang printed in 1607, lists the benefits to be obtained from its employment.

> Dr. Johann Faust's Juggler's Bag, concerning all kinds of un-
> heard-of, secret, merry feats, mysteries and inventions where-
> by a man may interpret dreams, tell fortunes, open locked doors,
> cure the gout, recognize adulterers and fornicators, inspire
> strange men, women and maids with love, increase his height by
> some ells, make himself invisible or invulnerable, change his
> shape, rouse the thunder and lightning, collect and disperse
> snakes, catch pigeons, fish or birds in his hands, overcome
> his enemies, and perform other innumerable, incredible and
> extravagant feats, both merry and advantageous, together with
> five other extravagant, excellent and authentic devices. Now
> for the first time from the original written with his own hand
> by Dr. Faust, published for the particular pleasure of all
> artists by Johann de Luna, Christoph Wagner's former disciple
> and well-experienced in the Magic Arts.[1]

The famous chapbook published by Johann Spiess in Frankfort on the Main in 1587 constitutes the first printed chronicle of Faust's life.

---

[1]Karl Engel, Zusammenstellung der Faust-Schriften vom 16. Jahrhundert bis Mitte 1884 (Oldenburg: A. Schwartz, 1885), pp. 150 and 158.

> Many features formerly attributed to other wizards were transfer-
> red to Faust including the Devil in the form of a black dog which
> always accompanied Cornelius Agrippa of Nettesheim, the enchanted
> garden conjured up by Albertus Magnus for the Emperor in the midst
> of winter and the exorcising of the spirit of Alexander the Great
> and other Greek heroes by the Abbot Trithemius.[1]

Although the author warns the reader in the course of the sixty-nine chapters about the fate of those who dabble in alchemistic inquiry, he is more attracted by the sensational elements of his story. The Lutheran point of view is adumbrated by the anti-papal sentiments expressed. The unknown author of the Spiess Faustbuch localizes the story at Wittenberg, the Saxon university town where the Refor- mation started. An important feature of this Volksbuch is the empha- sis on Faust's speculative ambition. This is not to be mistaken for the higher intellectual strivings which are characteristic of the eighteenth century Faust and especially of Goethe's Faust. The spec- ulation in the Volksbuch is directed toward finding ways of enjoying with impunity sinful acts resulting from the seven capital sins. To the author, Faust's fate is a striking example of what happens when man forgets God.

The text of the Spiess Faustbuch and that of the Wolfenbuettel manuscript are much the same indicating that they probably come from a common source. Spiess himself published several editions, and pirated editions began to appear by the end of the year 1587. In 1588 some students at the University of Tuebingen put out a rhymed edition, and Bulhorn published an edition in low German. In 1589 an enlarged account appeared including six new chapters based on the

---

[1]William Rose, Doctor John Faustus (London: George Routledge & Sons, 1930), p. 29.

Faust tradition around Erfurt. The Berlin edition of 1590 combines the Spiess account with the additions of 1589. The last Faustbuch of the Spiess type dates from 1598. After this the Spiess book fell into oblivion and was not rediscovered until the nineteenth century.

The popularity of the Faustbuch encouraged a Swabian, George Rudolff Widman, to produce a long-winded account published in Hamburg in 1599. Catering to a demand for the sensational, he blew up the demonic elements at the expense of the scientific.

During the seventeenth century interest in the Faustbuch lessened. This was due to three factors: the Thirty-Years' War, a more rational view of witchcraft, and the spread of the Faust drama. It was not until 1674 that the old tale was brought out in book form. This revision of Widman's book, written by Dr. Nicolaus Pfitzer of Nuremberg, restored the erotic elements and introduced the peasant girl who is Gretchen in embryo. His version underwent seven editions in fifty years.

The final German Faustbuch was the so-called Faustbuch des Christlich Meynenden. This was essentially a condensation of Widman. It underwent several editions the last of which was published in 1797 according to Goedeke. This version is important because from it were taken chapbooks which were sold at the fairs. Goethe very likely became acquainted with this booklet version in his youth. Details such as Faust's involvement with Gretchen and his infatuation for Helen of Troy seem to point to a familiarity with both Widman's and Pfitzer's versions. By the time Goethe read these versions he had already become familiar with the story through the puppet plays.

The Faustbuch was also popular in other countries. By the end of the sixteenth century the Spiess book or one of its versions had been translated into English, Dutch and French. The earliest mention of Faust in England can be found in the translation by R. H. of a book by Ludwig Lavater, Of Ghostes and Spirites, published in 1572:

> There are also conjurers founde even at this day, who bragge of themselves that they can so by inchauntments saddle an horse, that in a fewe houres they will dispatch a very long journey. God at the last will chasten these men with deserved punishment. What straunge things are reported of one Faustus a German, which he did in these our dayes by inchauntments?[1]

The English Faust book is a rendering into English of the Spiess edition of 1587 or possibly of a later one. The translation is signed merely P.F., and the identity of the translator has remained unsolved. He omitted some of the sermonizing material in Spiess, elaborated or condensed as suited him, and added material relating to Faust's travels. The earliest printed edition of the Faust book dates from 1592. This translation and reworking of Spiess is undoubtedly the source for Marlowe's great play.

A summary of the life of Faust according to the English Faust book, which is substantially the same as the Spiess Faustbuch, will now be given. He was born at Rhoda[2] and was raised by an uncle in Wittenberg, where he was a divinity student. He secretly studied necromancy and conjuration. Later he turned from theological matters

---

[1]Ibid., p. 42.

[2]The modern Roda, southeast of Weimar.

and became an astrologer, mathematician and quack. Desiring to know
the secrets of heaven and earth, Faust summons Mephistopheles.[1]
Faust demands that the spirit should serve him, bring whatever he
asks, and answer his questions without loss of his soul. The spirit
leaves and, when he returns, demands that Faust give over himself
body and soul to Lucifer and that he confirm this by signing the
pact with his blood. Faust agrees to turn himself over to the Prince
of the Orient after twenty-four years; falsely hoping that "the devil
was not so black as they use to paynt him nor hell so hot as the
people say,"[2] he signs. After the signing Faust calls the spirit and
asks that he always appear in the guise of a friar with a bell in
his hand.

The devil provides Faust and his servant Wagner with the best
food and fine apparel. Faust desires to marry and calls in the
spirit for consultation. The spirit advises against marriage, but
Faust insists and is almost killed by the devil. Faust questions
the spirit about the fall of Lucifer. Later he dreams about hell
and asks the spirit about hell. The devil replies that it is a con-
fused thing of no substance. Then he explains about the kingdoms

---

[1]The old spelling was Mephostophiles. He did not become
Mephistopheles until the eighteenth century. He was one of the
seven principal devils in medieval demonology. "It is a name remarkable both for its euphony, and for seeming to mean something,
although no one has yet discovered what, or even what language it
derives from, Persian, Hebrew, or Greek. A sinister ambiguity
haunts the syllables and seems to mock such conjectures as 'no
friend to light' (Mephotophiles), or 'no friend to Faust' (Mefausto-
philes), or 'destroyer-liar' (Mephiz-Tophel)." Eliza M. Butler,
The Myth of the Magus (Cambridge: University Press, 1948), p. 132.

[2]The English Faust book, quoted in Palmer and More, op. cit.,
p. 141.

of hell. After hearing this Faust laments his pact with the devil. He questions the spirit further about hell. The spirit tells him there is a very high ladder up which the damned struggle toward God. When they get to the highest point, they fall back again. He goes on to describe the horrible torments of hell. The spirit admits that Faust may hope to regain God's favor but says it is unlikely. Then Faust asks the devil what he would do if he were Faust to please both God and man. The spirit gives him good advice about humbling himself before the majesty of God and keeping His commandments. He reminds Faust that he has no one to blame but himself for the condition he is in and tells him it is too late to repent.

The second part of Faust's life begins with comments on his excellence as an astrologer and mathematician. Faust questions the spirit on matters of astronomy. The spirit urges Faust to learn how to do many wonderful things--how to fly as swift as thought, how to run through walls, doors and gates, and how to nourish himself on fire. Faust again falls into despondency over his condition. He asks the devil to explain how God made the world and why he made man after His own image. Faust is threatened with dire torments if he does not change his attitude. Faust desires to see hell and is taken there by a devil in the guise of a black bear with a chair of beaten gold on its back. After his visit to hell Faust goes on a trip through space in a wagon drawn by two dragons. After fifteen years of his allotted span were up Faust goes on a journey around the world with the devil, who had changed into a flying horse. This trip took twenty-five days (shades of Jules Verne!). In Rome, he

observes the pope at table and regrets that Mephistopheles had
not made a pope of him. On another trip Faust gets a glimpse of
paradise. It is about this time that the people question Faust
about comets, the stars and thunder. The Emperor Charles V summons
Faust for a demonstration of his arts. His specific request is to
see Alexander the Great and his paramour.

At this point in the second part of the Faust book an enumera-
tion of some of Faust's fantastic deeds and pranks is begun. Some
dukes visiting Wittenberg wish to be transported to a wedding in
Menchen. Faust grants their request. He borrows some money from
a Jew and gives his leg as a pawn. Faust eats a load of hay. After
raiding the wine cellar of the Bishop of Salzburg, Faust sets his
butler on top of a large tree. At various banquets for the students
he has the dishes as well as thirteen apes dancing and produces a
calf's head that cries out when a piece of it is cut off. At a
gathering of students he summons the shade of fair Helen of Troy
in a sumptuous gown of purple velvet. Faust has an encounter with
four jugglers who cut off one another's head as part of their act.
Faust is so jealous of their fame that he brought about the death
of one of them.

An old man mentions the account of Simon in the Acts of the
Apostles to Faust and urges him to repent. When Faust begins to
regret his pact, the devil attacks him and orders him to sign another with his blood. In his twenty-third year he makes Helena his
mistress. In due time a son is born to them called Iustus Faustus.[1]

---

[1]At this point the Spiess Faustbuch has an interesting notation
in the margin: "Quaestio, an Baptizatus Fuerit?"

Later on when the child dies both mother and child vanish. In his
will Faust names Wagner as his heir. Wagner desires to possess
Faust's cunning. He requests the help of a spirit in the form of
a bear named Akercocke. This is to be granted on condition that
after Faust's death Wagner write an account of his life.

With one month of his twenty-four year span remaining Faust
falls again to bewailing his lot. Mephistopheles consoles Faust
by telling him he will be in good company in hell with all the famous people there. Faust calls the students together for the last
time, tells them about his pact, and entreats them to let his sad
end be a warning to them "...that you have God always before your
eies, praying unto him that he would ever defend you from the temptation of the divel, and all his false deceipts..."[1]

The horrendous description of Faust's end is worth quoting
in full:

> It happened between twelve and one a clock at midnight, there
> blewe a mighty storme of winde against the house, as though it
> would have blowne the foundation thereof out of his place...
> The Students lay neere unto that hall wherin Doctor Faustus lay,
> and they heard a mighty noyse and hissing, as if the hall had
> been full of Snakes and Adders: with that the hall doore flew
> open wherin Doctor Faustus was, then he began to crie for helpe,
> saying: murther, murther, but it came foorth with halfe a voyce
> hallowly: shortly after they heard him no more. But when it
> was day, the Students that had taken no rest that night, arose
> and went into the hall in the which they left Doctor Faustus
> where notwithstanding they found no Faustus, but all the hall
> lay besprinckled with blood, his braines cleaving to the wall:
> for the Divel had beaten him from one wall against another, in
> one corner lay his eyes, in another his teeth, a pitiful and
> fearefull sight to beholde. Then began the Students to bewayle

---

[1] The English Faust book, quoted in Palmer and More, op. cit.,
p. 227.

and weepe for him, and sought for his body in many places: last-
ly they came into the yarde where they found his bodie lying on
horse dung, most monstrously torne, and fearfull to behold, for
his head and all his ioynts were dasht in peeces.[1]

The Spiess Faustbuch closes with the familiar words of St. Peter:

"Brethren, be sober and watch for the devil goes about like a roar-

ing lion seeking whom he may devour, whom resist ye strong in faith."[2]

Before leaving the historical Faust to take up a consideration

of literary works inspired by the legend it seems appropriate to con-

sider a fascinating series of twelve volumes edited by J. Scheible

called Das Kloster. Weltlich und geistlich. Meist aus der aeltern

deutschen Volks-, Wunder-, Curiositaeten-, und vorzugsweise komischen

Literatur. Zur Kultur- und Sittengeschichte in Wort und Bild.[3] The

second volume contains articles by various authors on Faust and his

forerunners, Widman's Faustbuch, Faust's Hoellenzwang, and a verbatim

reproduction of the first Faustbuch of 1587. The Hoellenzwang is

divided into several parts. The first part gives special directions

how to summon the evil spirits, especially Aziels, telling what time

of the day to do the conjuring, and so on. The second section has

a rather awesome title: Verus Jesuitarum Libellus seu fortissima

coactio et constrictio omnium malorum Spirituum cujuscunque generis,

conditionis, status vel officii sint. Et Conjuratio fortissima et

probatissima in Usielem Huic est annixa Cypriani Citatio Angelorum,

---

[1] The English Faust book, quoted in Palmer and More, op. cit.,
p. 229f.

[2] I Peter, 5:8.

[3] These volumes were published by Scheible in Stuttgart,
1845-1849.

qui thesaurum abscondit, una cum illorum Dimissione.[1] The conjuration formulas given therein are quite frightening. Part three of
the Hoellenzwang is Faust's wonder book, which contains many tanta-
lizing diagrams, cabalistic symbols, talismans, and demonic signa-
tures, as well as a list of the infernal hierarchy. The rather
complete title of this section is: Dr. Johann Faustens Miracul-
Kunst- und Wunder-Buch oder die schwarze Rabe auch der Dreifache
Hoellen Zwang genannt. Womit ich die Geister gezwungen, dass Sie
mir haben bringen muessen, was ich begehret habe. Es sey Gold oder
Silber, Schaetze gross oder klein, auch die Spring-Wurzel, und was
sonst mehr dergleichen auf Erden ist, das habe ich alles mit diesem
Buche zu Wege gebracht, auch die Geister wieder lossprechen koennen.

Pertinent materials in the third volume of Scheible's Kloster
are the life of Faust's servant Christopher Wagner and the life of
Abbot Trithemius. There are a number of very interesting inserts
in this volume. The fantastic one in the section on Trithemius is
reminiscent of the weird style of Hieronymus Bosch. In the center
of the picture three monks are being drawn by a strange animal in
what looks like an ornate circus wagon. They are Abbots Trithemius
and Dennis and Fr. Basilius Valentinus.

The Ulm puppet play may be found in the fifth volume. The
importance of the Faust puppet plays will be considered in the
next chapter along with the role of the legend in serious literature.

---

[1]The date at the bottom of the title page is Paris, 1508.

CHAPTER IV

FAUST IN LITERATURE

The great play by Christopher Marlowe (1564-1593) on the Faust theme has long been considered the first drama on this subject. The date of composition is thought to be between 1588 and 1593.

However, in an article titled "An Ur-Faustus" Barbara Cooper makes a fair claim that "a play of Faustus was extant in 1580 and that an earthquake during its performance caused considerable super-stitious fear--fear which continued to be expressed throughout the history of Marlowe's famous version."[1] She bases her claim on com-ments about an earthquake on stage in a report on Faustus perform-ances by Prynne and Stubs. In his Histrio-Mastix, The Players' Scourge, 1663, William Prynne describes the occurrences on which Miss Cooper bases her claim.

> Nor yet to recite the sudden fearful burning even to the ground, both of the Globe and Fortune Playhouses, no man perceiving how these fires came: together with the visible apparition of the Devil on the Stage at the Belsavage Playhouse, in Queen Elizabeth's day (to the great amazement both of the Actors and Spectators) whiles they were there profanely playing the history of Faustus, ...there being some distracted with that fearful sight.[2]

Soon after the publication of the Spiess Faustbuch in 1587 the

---

[1]Barbara Cooper, "An Ur-Faustus," Notes and Queries, (New Series), VI, No. 2, (February, 1959), pp. 66-68.

[2]Quoted in: William Rose (ed.), The History of the Damnable Life and Deserved Death of Doctor John Faustus (London: George Routledge & Sons, n.d.), p. 46.

legend became known in England. Marlowe's source for The Tragicall History of D. Faustus was the English version of the Faustbuch.

For Marlowe, Faust is a veritable superman who expected from science an insight into human life. His Faustus demands wider powers and is not content merely with tricking the peasantry but aims to have a hand in world politics. Marlowe's Faustus ranks with the great characters of Elizabethan drama. The play[1] follows the account of the Faust book fairly closely, but he molds his material into a compact dramatic composition.

There is a remarkable similarity between the structure of Marlowe's tragedy and what seems to have been Goethe's original plan. In Marlowe's version Faust is introduced by a long soliloquy in which he considers the four faculties of the medieval university and casts them aside in favor of magic. In both, the pact with the Devil is a sequel to two discussions. In Marlowe the reason for the second scene is the fact that Mephistopheles has to get the consent of Lucifer. In Goethe the reason for the scene is not so readily apparent. Marlowe's Faustus demands control over the wealth and power of this earth and is willing to forgo his eternal salvation.

In general there seems to be more than a merely accidental resemblance between the two dramas. It seems fairly certain, however, that Goethe was not cognizant of Marlowe's play at the time of the earliest conception of his own poem. He did get acquainted with

---

[1]In his edition of The Works of Christopher Marlowe (Oxford: Clarendon Press, 1929), p. 140, C. F. Tucker Brooke states that among the many versions he considers the text of 1604 "the most faithful representative extant of Marlowe's manuscript."

it in 1818 when it was translated into German. There may, however, have been a German Faust drama at the end of the sixteenth century that had the same source and structure as Marlowe's.

Marlowe's play employs prose as well as iambic pentameter. The comic elements found in the clown, the horse dealer and some of the comments of Faust himself foreshadow the treatment in the later puppet plays. The good and evil angels and the pageant of the seven deadly sins were not found in the Faust book. The play is not divided into scenes and acts. It begins with an announcement from the chorus that the good and bad fortunes of Faustus are about to be performed.

The conclusion of the play is worth noting. The clock strikes eleven, and Faust reminds himself that he has but an hour to live. He begs God to end his pain, to save him even after he has spent 100,000 years in hell. He curses his parents, himself and Lucifer. The clock strikes twelve. He wishes his body might be turned into air or into little drops of water so he will not be found. Mephistopheles and the devils come to get him. The chorus ends the play with a warning to the wise to refrain from unlawful things.

In the last two decades of the sixteenth century travelling troupes of English actors, the "English Comedians," began to visit the continent. During the following century it became common for these English companies to tour German cities or to appear before a sovereign. These groups had quite an influence on the German stage. The earliest productions were given in English with the exception of the role of the clown which was spoken in German. Gradually mutilated versions of the English plays, including Marlowe's, were given in German and eventually original German plays were staged. Gradually German players were added to these groups and finally German troupes were formed.

It seems the first recorded performance of a Faust play on the continent was given by an English company at Graz in 1608.

The play that the German public became familiar with was no longer Marlowe's History. Travelling companies did not regard the text as something sacred but rather approached it in the commedia dell'arte tradition, using the text as a springboard for their own inventions as determined by the changing taste of the public or the necessities of the company. The familiar essentials were, of course, retained. The Viennese actor Stranitzky played a prominent part in this phase.

One of the sources of changes in the drama was the local Faust tradition as found in Germany. There is no indication in the English Faust book or in Marlowe's play that the choice of a devil was based on his speed. Also the use of a prologue in hell is not found in Marlowe and is not part of the Faust tradition.

We do not have a single copy of the text of the play as it was given on the legitimate stage. The text was to be found in manuscript copies in the possession of the various troupes. Our knowledge regarding the play for the more than a century and a half that preceded Goethe's Faust stems from three sources: the diary of Georg Schroeder which describes the performance in Danzig in 1668, several theater programs which give an inkling of the changes as the play developed, and texts of the puppet plays.

Schroeder's account begins with Pluto's arrival from hell. He in turn summons one devil after another, the tobacco devil, the bawdy devil, the cunning devil, and sets them about their tasks of ensnaring men. Then Faust is introduced in his study. He conjures up the devils and is not easily satisfied but wants one who is as quick as the thoughts of men. The remainder of the story follows the familiar pattern. After his death Faust is portrayed being tormented in hell. These flaming words are seen as he is drawn up and down: *accusatus est, judicatus est, condemnatus est.*[1]

At first the comic element was brought in loosely. A character called Pickelhaering was introduced to amuse the audience with his crude humor. The Viennese influence tended to bring Harlekin or Hans Wurst[2] directly into the play, putting him in direct contrast with the principal characters.

"In fact, he became a sort of parody of Faust and second in importance only to the worthy Doctor himself, who in the end was dragged off to hell, while the clown had wit enough to cheat the devil."[3]

The public of the eighteenth century was less amenable to the mummery, superstition and vulgarity which had become such a large part of the play. Under the strong influence of Gottsched, a professor at Leipzig and literary arbiter in Germany during the third

---

[1] Palmer and More, op. cit., p. 245.

[2] I have often heard the word *Hanswurst* used in a deprecatory manner.

[3] Palmer and More, Ibid., p. 244.

decade of the century, their interest was turned toward French models.
This accounted for the transfer of the Faust play from the living
stage to that of the puppet theater. The German puppet play is first
mentioned in 1698. The last staged presentation seems to have oc-
curred in Hamburg in 1770. The puppet performances have continued
until the present time.[1]

The Ulm puppet play of 1698 is divided into two parts. Part one
is made up of a prelude and seven acts; part two also consists of seven
acts. Part one, apart from Pickelhaering's episodes, takes us up to the
point where Faust chooses Mephistopheles to be his servant because he is
as swift as men's thoughts. In part two Mephistopheles returns and says
after his period of service of twenty-four years Faust has to go to
hell. An angel pleads with Faust not to sign the compact. Faust wishes
to go to the court of Prague. The king asks Faust to produce Alexander
and his consort. Then Faust questions Mephistopheles about hell. The
devil tells him there is no redemption from hell. Faust asks about
heaven. Faust plans to reform his ways, but Mephistopheles brings him
Helena to dissuade him. The puppet play ends with the banquet with
the students during which Faust tells of his pact. As the hourglass
of his life runs out Faust warns all men not to be misled by the joys
of the world. Fireworks; hell opens, and the devils drag Faust off.

The puppet plays later became very farcical with the comic figures
of Wagner and Kasperle (or Hans Wurst) and the devils, Auerhahn, Asmodi,

---

[1] I witnessed a delightful one presented by Dr. Meno Spann, of
the German department, Northwestern University, Evanston, Illinois,
in the summer of 1959. Cf. the appendix.

Fitzliputzli, and so on. These appeared at the sound of the magic word "Perlicka" and vanished at the word "Perlacka." Faust gets cheated when instead of giving him the twenty-four years he had bargained for, the devils come after him at the end of the twelfth. When he tries to embrace beautiful Helen, she turns into the she-devil Teufelinne.

The puppet plays served to keep the figure of Faust before the public and undoubtedly planted the seed of later artistic ventures in the mind of authors like Goethe who were later to treat the story so impressively.

After Christopher Marlowe, the first literary man to do something in a concrete way about the Faust tradition was the great reformer of the German stage Gotthold Ephraim Lessing (1729-1781). He probably became familiar with the materials in his student days. It was a performance of the Schuch troupe in Berlin in 1754 that gave him the impetus to make his own setting of the drama. A letter from Moses Mendelssohn, dated November 19, 1755, is the first indication that Lessing was working on a Faust play. He worked on Faust for twenty years, but it is very doubtful that he ever completed a Faust drama. It seems he changed his mind from time to time and had several versions of the story in mind. All we have in Lessing's own hand is the scene published in the seventeenth Literaturbreif on February 16, 1759, and the Berlin scenario written at about the same time, which was a posthumous publication. These fragments plus reports of Captain von Blankenburg and J. J. Engel give a fairly good idea of what Lessing had in mind. It was von Blankenburg's opinion that Lessing completed a version of the Faust story. It seems a completed version of the story was in a box

The baroque Faust. (About 1680).

of papers that was lost in transit to Wolfenbuettel.

According to Engel the play begins with a meeting of the devils in a gothic church. Satan sits on the high altar; the rest of the devils on nearby altars. They are not seen. The devils are reporting on what they have done. Satan is not pleased with their reports. The fourth devil reports regarding a youth totally given over to wisdom. Satan decides to take on this one himself. At the end of the scene a heavenly voice is heard saying, "You will not be victorious."

The angel puts Faust into a deep slumber and constructs in his stead a phantom. Faust dreams all that happens to this phantom. At the end Faust thanks Providence for this warning. Engel says he does not remember the details of the devil's plan of seduction.[1]

If the plot reported by Engel is compared with the puppet plays or Marlowe's drama, definite progress toward a higher plane will be noted. There is a change in attitude toward wisdom. In Lessing's plot the desire for truth and striving for knowledge is regarded as among man's highest goals. In the Faust books, the puppet plays, and Marlowe's play intellectual curiosity is regarded as a sin. A second addition is the attempt to rationalize tradition by the use of the dream motive. The ennobling of Faust's character places the whole drama on a higher plane. Lessing's plan is unique in that his was to be the first treatment in which the old magician was not to be damned. By these changes he rescued the Faust tradition from the oblivion which threatened it and by his deepening of the implications of the story opened the way for Goethe.

[1]Robert Petsch, Lessing's Faustdichtung (Heidelberg: C. Winter, 1911), pp. 48-50.

Before taking up Goethe's <u>Faust</u> in particular it will be necessary to discuss the <u>Sturm und Drang</u> movement in Germany. This movement

> "burst forth as a sudden revolutionary convulsion, taking the German public unawares and threatening to demolish the still unfinished structure of literary tradition at which German writers had labored for half a century. The revolt miscarried, and the tradition survived. The brevity of 'Storm and Stress' neutralized its violences. It was left to another revolution--allied in doctrine, yet gentler in method and more gradual in onset--to the Romantic Movement, to achieve some twenty years later the reversal and rearrangement of values which had been the unsystematic but unmistakable aim of the men of 'Storm and Stress'."[1]

Social conditions in Germany afforded two factors which prepared the soil--total lack of large cities and the important role of universities. Communication was slow. Thus German talent instead of concentrating and sharpening itself in competition, was dispersed in the numerous provincial towns.

German literature remained provincial because the nobility from Frederick the Great down preferred French literature. The centers of German literature were found at the universities in Leipzig, Halle, Goettingen, Strassburg, Koenigsberg, and Jena. As a result of the pressures in the direction of age students instead of expressing themselves aped the dullness and pedantry of their professors. In the seventeen-seventies reverence for age came to a precipitous end in the universities.

Rousseau gave the impetus with his emphasis on the noble savage and youth untouched by the corrosion of civilization. This gave the immature a justification in their own right. However, the adolescent revolution needed a catalyst. This could come either through leadership of men young in their ideas or through repression.

---

[1]M. A. Garland, <u>Storm and Stress</u> (London: Harrap, 1952), p. 131.

"There were in German universities three separate outbursts, two strikingly different yet almost simultaneous in the early seventies, in Strassburg and in Goettingen, and a belated single-handed revolt in Stuttgart at the beginning of the eighties. The progenitors of the movement in Goettingen were of slight stature, and its character was moderate, even tame. Strassburg springs into the forefront of German literature through the fruitful meeting of two outstanding figures, Herder and Goethe...[1]

The destiny of German literature was to be shaped as a result of the meeting of Herder and Goethe in Strassburg in the autumn of 1770. The former was twenty-seven and the latter twenty-one.

"Herder's Journal of 1789 reveals the teeming wealth of fertile ideas which he was able to display before Goethe in their conversations. Much of what he had to say was derived from Rousseau, yet his mind transformed it into something which was new, profound and opportune...
Although Goethe soon left the University of Strassburg, and spent the remainder of his phase of 'Storm and Stress' at Frankfort, he is none the less an illustration of the students revolt, of the anger of unspoiled youth with a corrupt age, of untrammelled genius with pedantic authority. This theme, set moreover in a university environment, was the mainspring of his early work upon Faust."[2]

Goethe gathered around himself a group of young men and by force of his genius exercised considerable influence on them causing them to imitate his outlook, style and approach. It was Goethe's powerful personality which gave impetus to the revolution called Sturm und Drang. From him came the qualities of violence and excess, and without him the concept of "Storm and Stress" would probably never have arisen. The idea of genius as the untaught, instinctive human being, according to which the self-appointed geniuses of Sturm und Drang shaped their lives, stemmed from Rousseau. The utterance of passion was to be unrestrained and unimpeded.

---

[1] Ibid., p. 136.

[2] Ibid., p. 137.

There were a number of reasons for the failure of the movement. The volume level was _fortissimo_ and was bound to pall. The "geniuses" were of two strongly contrasting types--the one a man of violence and action, the other an introverted, sentimental dreamer. Goethe's poignant portrait of a misfit, _Werther_, one of his best works in this period, is a perfect portrait of the _Sturm und Drang_ genius. One of their favorite themes was that of the Marguerite episode in Faust, the seduced girl and the illicit love ending in infanticide. Their reverence for the sham folk prose of Macpherson-Ossian shows that they were unable to distinguish what was folk literature and what was not.

The effects of this violent romantic expansion can be found in Goethe and Schiller. After a few productive years they were silent, and comparatively sterile, between the ages of twenty-six and thirty-seven when they should have been most productive. None of the writers who went through the _Sturm und Drang_ period emerged unscathed. It was, indeed, a much easier task for the apostles of romanticism to replace the established order with their own in 1800 than it had been for their precursors in 1775. The collapse of the _Sturm und Drang_ movement was inevitable when Goethe, realizing the dangers inherent in it, withdrew from it by leaving for Weimar.

Johann Wolfgang von Goethe (1749-1832) spent a period spanning sixty years in giving the story of the inconsequential medieval magician its definitive setting. In _Faust_ he was to create the eternal type of man who seeks to grasp all, to encompass all, to understand all. Goethe became acquainted with the story in his student days, probably through one of the chapbooks. He saw the puppet plays; he came across

Faust in his studies of the Reformation; he viewed the paintings in the cellar of Auerbach's castle. In Book 10 of _Dichtung und Wahrheit_ he comments on the effect the puppet play had on him:

> Die bedeutende Puppenspielfabel (Faust) klang und summte gar vieltoenig in mir wider. Auch ich hatte mich in allem Wissen umhergetrieben und war frueh genug auf die Eitelkeit desselben hingewiesen worden. Ich hatte es auch im Leben auf allerlei Weise versucht und was immer unbefriedigter und gequaelter zurueckgekommen. Nun trug ich diese Dinge, sowie manche andre, mit mir herum und ergoetzte mich daran in einsamen Stunden, ohne jedoch etwas davon aufzuschreiben.[1]

He worked on _Faust_ sporadically, sometimes with eagerness, sometimes with repugnance, and had it not been for the prodding of his great friend Schiller, the great masterpiece might, very likely, never have been finished. There are several instances in his letters to his friend Zelter[2] which indicate the difficulties the seventy-eight-year-old genius experienced in attempting to bring his work to a satisfactory conclusion.

Weimar, May 24, 1827

...But now I mean to make a private confession to you, viz. that the encouraging sympathy of kind spirits has led me to take up _Faust_ again, exactly at that point, where, on descending from the cloud of antiquity, he again confronts his evil genius. Do not say anything about this to anyone; I will however confide to you, that it is my intention to proceed from that point, and to fill up the gap between

---

[1]Quoted in the introduction to _Goethe's Faust_, edited by R-M. S. Heffner, Helmet Rehder, W. F. Twaddell (Boston: D. C. Heath & Co., 1954), p. 18.

[2]Felix's father Abraham Mendelssohn called Carl F. Zelter (1758-1832) "the restorer of Bach to the Germans." Zelter was not an ordinary man. By trade he was a stonemason, by choice a musician. He was so successful that he became conductor of the Singakademie at Berlin. He also became Goethe's most intimate correspondent. Goethe, it seems, never swerved from his confidence in the opinions of Zelter. Zelter was always ready to lay down the law on any topic that Goethe might bring up. His pupil, Edward Devrient, dubbed him "excellent, but crusty." Felix Mendelssohn also studied with him.

it and the final conclusion, which was ready long ago...[1]

Weimar, November 21, 1827

...The Second Part of Faust is still shaping itself; the task here is the same as in the Helena,—so to formulate and arrange existing elements, that they may suit and accord with what is new; to accomplish this, much has to be thrown aside, and much to be remodelled. So it required resolution to begin the business; as I advance, the difficulties get less...[2]

Weimar, June 1, 1831

Do not fail, my good Friend, to continue sending me, from time to time, a few sheafs from the rich harvest of the outer world, to which you are sent, unlike myself who am confined wholly to the inner life of my garden-hermitage. In one word, let me tell you, that I submit to this, in order to finish the Second Part of my Faust. It is no trifle, in the eighty-second year of one's age, to represent objectively, that which was conceived at the age of twenty, and to furnish a living skeleton, like this, with sinews, flesh, and skin; probably also, I shall cast over it, when finished, some folds of drapery besides, so that the whole may be an open riddle, to delight mankind for ever and aye, and give them something to think of...[3]

Weimar, September 4, 1831

...You inquire about Faust; the Second Part is now complete in itself. I have for many years past known perfectly well what I wanted, but only worked out those particular passages which interested me at the moment. The consequence was that gaps became evident, and these had to be filled up. I firmly resolved to set all this to rights before my birthday. And so it was done; the whole work now lies before me, and I have only to correct a few trifles. So I shall put a seal on it, and then, it may add to the specific weight of the volumes that are to follow...[4]

It may have been Goethe's alchemistic investigations, 1768-1770,

that strengthened his interest in the Faust legend and stimulated his

---

[1] Goethe's Letters to Zelter, trans. A. D. Coleridge (London: George Bell & Sons, 1887), p. 288f.

[2] Ibid., p. 307.

[3] Ibid., p. 447.

[4] Ibid., p. 464.

first Faust sketches made in his early twenties. He wrote the Urfaust
1773-1775.[1] Barker Fairley in his A Study of Goethe makes the following
comment on the Urfaust: "The Frankfurt Faust, the Urfaust as we call it,
is without question the work in which he best succeeded in capturing...
the turbulent unrest that possessed him in early years...and the blind
worship of nature and of natural impulses on which it fed insatiably."[2]
The first Faust text made public was Faust: Ein Fragment, issued in 1790
in the seventh volume of an edition of Goethe's writings. In 1800 he
made the first draft of part of the Helena scene. The first part of
Faust as we now know it was published in 1808. Goethe felt that a number of matters were left unfinished in this Part I, and it was his intention of dealing with these in Part II. In 1816 he made a prose resume
of Acts I, III, and IV of Part II. He began work in earnest on the
Helena episode in 1825. At the same time he was engrossed in the study
of Greek history, geography, and mythology. These efforts resulted in
the publication of Helena: Klassisch-Romantische Phantasmagorie in 1827.
This text was later incorporated into Part II as Act III. Bit by bit
Acts I, II, and IV were drafted and polished. Parts of Act V, such as
Faust's death, had been completed thirty years earlier. The revision
of earlier sketches and the filling in of the gaps now became the poet's
main concern. By his eighty-second birthday, August 28, 1831, he had
completed, copied, and sealed Part II.

---

[1]A copy of Goethe's manuscript, or a large part of it, made by
Fraeulein Luise von Goechhausen of the Weimar Court, was discovered by
Erich Schmidt and published by him in 1887 as Goethes Faust in urspruen-
glicher Gestalt.

[2]Barker Fairley, A Study of Goethe (Oxford: Clarendon Press, 1947),
p. 178.

Goethe's _Faust_ owes much to the spiritual climate of the age, but it is not a direct outgrowth of those upheavals. Nor is it merely a dramatization of the poet's own personal experiences, nor merely the artistic treatment of a historical theme—the life and death of the arch magician Doctor Faustus. It is a colossal drama with humanity as its hero couched at times in cryptic language, portraying events, characters and problems of human life in terms of the cultural and intellectual history of modern times since the Renaissance. In it may be found echoes of the French Revolution (1789) and the War of Greek Liberation (1821-1829). However, any war or revolution can be recognized in the play since it spans a period of 3,000 years from the days of Helen of Troy to relatively recent events. A physicist or biologist will find references to problems in his field. A philosopher will find the wealth of abstract thought impressive.

Although many of the scenes are remote from modern life, none of the characters or presentation is "old fashioned." _Faust_ is timely for the present because it inquires into the purposes and values of human life. In _Faust_ may be found some of the desires and drives that account for the ups and downs of human existence. Faust symbolizes the scientific man who has hardly begun to exhaust the possibilities in the world around him. Since Faust is sometimes held back and sometimes driven forward by his own failings, he represents the upward course of the human race. In _Faust_ we find the colorful poetic portrayal of the two basic drives in man—to love and to know.

The procedure used in the composition of the drama is that of a dialogue between two characters. It is only in rare instances that more than two are engaged at any particular time. This practice manifests a basic feature of Goethe's art—his interest in the juxtaposition of opposites. In certain scenes like "<u>Auerbachs Keller</u>," "<u>Hexenkueche</u>," "<u>Walpurgisnacht</u>," and the court scenes the contrast between the principal characters is heightened by the colorful figures in the background. Even the soliloquies resemble dialogue since they portray the character in dramatic conflict with himself.

The character of Faust must be regarded from two viewpoints; he represents both a single individual and man in general. Even the Faust of Part I of Goethe's poem shows a dual character, that of the aged scholar attempting to reach beyond the limits of human knowledge and that of the gay blade setting out with Mephistopheles to run riot through the world. Goethe follows the lines of the old story but seasons it heavily with criticism and satire of university life.

When Margaret, the simple peasant girl, enters upon the scene a great change comes over the play. The play lingers at such length over this love-affair that the attention swings from Faust to Margaret, who holds the stage virtually alone in the final scenes of Part I. Thus Goethe with the introduction of Margaret changed the customary course of the legend. In Part II Margaret was to play an important role in Faust's salvation. Goethe overcame a great obstacle to the completion of the drama once he clearly visualized this later role of Margaret.

When Goethe resumed work on <u>Faust</u> in 1797 he changed his conception of the figure of Mephistopheles. Formerly he had been merely a spirit; now he became an urbane, crafty, witty "man of the world."

In Part II Faust is found at the court of the Emperor as is called for by the Renaissance legend, but this is not the court of Charles V of the _Volksbuch_. It now represents the world of politics with its disclosure of human ambitions and follies. In Part II Faust also conquers time by uniting himself with Helena in accord with the legend. In fact, more than half the Second Part is devoted to this adventure. However, this Helena is not the demonic ghost of the chapbooks and puppet plays. Goethe's Helena is the embodiment of beauty in actual form.

Part II also takes Faust through a number of colorful experiences which are not found in the tradition. The number of characters whom Faust meets and the number of involvements of Faust and Mephistopheles grow apace. In the figures of the Emperor and Helena and their entourages we recognize historical or mythological characters. But when we meet all the others, the Three Mighty Men, Dame Care, and so on, the symbolic complexity of the work impinges upon us.

In contradistinction to the Prologue God does not speak in the final scene when Margaret, in the role of one of the penitents, brings about Faust's salvation by her pleas to Mary, Queen of Heaven.

The Technical Structure of Goethe's Faust

Structurally speaking, _Faust_ may be considered a pageant or mystery play. Parts I and II can be placed under an arch, one side of which rests on the "Prologue in Heaven" and the other on the last scenes of Part II with the _Mater Gloriosa_. The whole dramatic action, as in a mystery play, consists of a series of temptations of Faust, permitted by the wager between God and Mephistopheles, and solved, insofar as there is a solution, by the intervention of the Madonna.

In strict symmetry of contents, though not in length of execution, each of the two Parts consists of three attempts of Mephistopheles (of three temptations) to make Faust pronounce the words:

> When thus I hail the moment flying:
> 'Ah, still delay - thou art so fair!'[1]

In both Parts the temptations rise, by comparison, in degree and gradation, in each Part the middle one receiving the greatest stress. Graphically expressed, the whole tragedy could be pictured as one large semi-circle, below which are two smaller semi-circles (Part I and Part II), each of which encompasses three arches of which the central one is the highest.

There are three temptations in Part I: the coarse sensualism of Auerbach's Cellar and the Witches' Kitchen; then the normal sensual love which is extended into the almost independent Gretchen tragedy; and finally the cunning perversions of the Walpurgis Night.

Part II exposes Faust to three temptations of a more intellectual kind. First, Faust as courtier and financier at the emperor's court (scientific theory of inflation); then, through Homunculus, the attractions of arts and sciences, including Greek mythology. Analogous to the Gretchen tragedy, these temptations climax in the vision of Helena as the symbol of consummate beauty. The last temptation shows Faust already "beyond good and evil": as the God-like dictator over human fate, master over the elements, engineer of a scope which lacks only the application of nuclear power (Philemon and Baucis).

---

[1] Faust, a Tragedy by Johann Wolfgang von Goethe, trans. Bayard Taylor (New York: Random House, 1950), I, p. 58, v. 1699f.

In chapter V the Christian elements in Goethe's _Faust_ will be examined in more detail. I should like to end the present discussion on Goethe's _Faust_ by quoting the conclusion of Stuart Atkins' fine commentary on _Faust_:

> The first great work of Western literature since Shakespearean tragedy to speak not, like French classical tragedy or the eighteenth century's bourgeois genres, for one social class; to speak not, like the morality play or its more sophisticated counterparts, the drame à thèse and "philosophical" tragedy, for one religious or philosophic system--Faust is a dramatic action set forth, despite the theatrical machinery for which its text gives full license, almost exclusively through the spoken word, so that with a few sound effects actors in any costume can, on a bare stage, project the many settings which it seems to demand. Long though it be as a drama, Faust is a remarkably close-knit text which, thanks to a structural economy made possible as much by the full exploitation of parallelistic variation as by the artistic shorthand of continuous use of standard literary conventions, communicates a highly complex poetic vision without ever giving the effect of skeletal bareness. As André Gide wrote of Faust in his journal under the date June 26, 1940, 'Everything in it is saturated with life. Thought is never presented in it in an abstract form, just as sentiment is never separated from thought, so that what is most individual is still heavy with meaning and, so to speak, exemplary.' With its symbols and motifs, its themes and its characters, its forms and its actions, all reciprocally strengthening their separate contributions to the total poetic statement, Faust must communicate to him, who temporarily suspends disbelief, that unique aesthetic experience which only the greatest works of the world's literature have the power to convey.[1]

There were many versions which made this theme very popular in Goethe's time. Some remained faithful to the tragical aspects as found in the chapbooks and popular plays. Others, more cynical, emphasized comical elements. On the stages of Catholic South Germany the anti-papal taunts of the _Volksbuch_ were removed and instances can be found where forgiveness was extended to a repentant Faust. Some plays were quite famous. Paul Weidmann's _Johann Faust_ (1775)[2] and Friedrich

---

[1]Stuart Atkins, _Goethe's Faust_ (Cambridge: Harvard University Press, 1958), p. 277.

[2]This was at one time thought to be Lessing's lost Faust play.

(Maler) Mueller's Situation aus Fausts Leben (1776) and Fausts Leben I
Teil (1778) are noteworthy products of the Sturm und Drang period.
Maximillian Klingsor's novel of 1791, Fausts Leben, Taten und Hoellenfahrt
has nothing in common with Goethe's Faust although they were associated
in the early days of "Storm and Stress." Klingsor's novel was a thinly
disguised inquiry into the origin of Evil and was a late product of
Rousseauism. Some other versions current while Goethe was working on
his were Doctor Faust by Julius Heinrich von Soden (1797), Johann Friedrich Schink's Johann Faust (1804) and Ernst Klingemann's Doctor Faust
(1814).

There are a few other German Faust settings that should be mentioned. Nikolaus Franz Niembsch von Strehlenau (1802-1850), better known
as simply Lenau, made a beautiful setting of the legend which was published in 1836. Heinrich Heine (1797-1856) paid a call on the aged Goethe,
October 1, 1824, and told him he, too, planned to write a Faust story. He
turns the story upside down with such details as heavenly teaparties and
Mephistopheles' love for the angels. His Doktor Faust: Ein Tanzpoem was
published in Hamburg in 1851. Thomas Mann (1875-1955) wrote a turgid
novel in 1947 entitled Doctor Faustus, which narrates the tortured life
of the composer Adrian Leverkuehn. It describes the struggle with de-
moniacal forces on the part of the creative man of the twentieth century.
The best known French work on this topic is Paul Valery's Mon Faust,
which appeared in 1946. The contemporary Spanish author Juan Valera,
whose favorite practice it is to treat an idea from different angles,
wrote two works on the Faust theme. In his El Doctor Faustino he por-
trays a weak, vacillating character whose life is a series of mistakes

that lead up to his tragic end; in _Morsamor_ he tells of an old monk who like Faust wants to relive his life and see the world. One of the purest tributes to Goethe's fame is the additional scene that Pushkin wrote for _Faust_ in 1828. Another Russian, Anatolli Lunacharski (1875-1933), had made impressive use of the Faust theme in his play for reading _Faust and the City_. Lunacharski was a great authority on music and the theater, and his text would seem to lend itself to musical treatment. A few American writers ought to be mentioned. Washington Irving's _The Devil and Tom Walker_ is usually called the comic New England Faust. Perhaps Nathaniel Hawthorne's _Peter Goldwaite's Treasure_ has more right to the title. As William Bysshe Stein remarks, "The controlling motivation of the Faust myth, the covenant by which man sells his soul to the devil, appears again and again in Hawthorne's fiction..."[1] The American poet, Hart Crane, has written (c. 1922) a strangely beautiful poem _For the Marriage of Faustus and Helen_. It must also be noted in conclusion that the Faust legend has not failed to make an impression on the "Beat Generation." Jack Kerouac has written a novel called _Doctor Sax_ (1959) which is subtitled Faust Part III. It tells the story of Jack Duluoz, like Kerouac himself a French-Canadian, growing up among the shadowy doorways and brown tenements of Lowell, Massachusetts, haunted by the ghost of Doctor Sax.

From a consideration of the literary Faust we turn in the next chapter to an examination of the Christian elements in Goethe's _Faust_.

---

[1]William B. Stein, _Hawthorne's Faust_ (Gainesville: University of Florida Press, 1953), p. 51.

CHAPTER V

THE IMPACT OF CHRISTIANITY IN GOETHE'S FAUST

The purpose of this chapter is not to discuss the question
whether or not Goethe was a believing Christian; nor does it attempt
to prove that he was a Christian poet or that Faust is Christian
poetry. The objective is restricted to the investigation of whether
any impact of Christianity can be found in Faust and, if so, to what
extent and with what consequences. The start will not be made from
theological or philosophical premises but from the work itself, considering solely its words and action. The inquiry will be restricted to two basic phenomena of Christian reality, the risen Christ and
His Church. The question may be stated thus: Do we find the resurrection of Christ and the Church in Goethe's Faust, and if so, to
what extent do they influence the outcome of the play?

At the end of the first scene of Part I the angels proclaim
the resurrection of Christ. However, not every proclamation of the
resurrection necessarily implies its Christian reality. One has
only to recall the nature of certain articles in newspapers and
magazines, supposedly treating of Easter, in order to realize the
extent to which the Christian Easter message can be made shallow and
profane. But in Faust, this is not the case. The angels' proclamation of the Lord's resurrection is in full accord with Catholic belief. No exhaustive dogmatic presentation should be expected in

Faust; that, in all fairness, cannot be expected of a work of poetry.
But it is of decisive consequence that with the announcement of the
risen Lord the angels point the way to a new and more perfect mode
of existence. For, from the dogmatical point of view, this is the
intrinsic implication of the Christian Easter message: the raising-
up of man to life eternal. Not only are Easter bells ringing, but,
in accord with theology, it is angels who announce the Easter message. If anyone at all witnessed the resurrection, it was angels
and not men. Angels represent the hierarchy of spirits as insti-
tuted by God to whom is quite rightly reserved the privilege of an-
nouncing the way to a new life. How far Goethe himself actually
believed in the risen Lord is inconsequential. The resurrection as
presented in Faust is in complete agreement with the Creed. Besides,
it is not meant to be merely a marginal note but will profoundly influence the actual progress of the tragedy. It is, of all things,
the announcement of the resurrection which causes Faust, desperate
as he was the moment before, to put down the poison and to embark
on the quest of his proper place in life. His development began in
the first scene in complete desperation, a desperation still aggra-
vated by his crushing encounter with the Earth Spirit and the subsequent meeting with his famulus Wagner who, to Faust, embodies the
disgusting mediocrity of mankind. The only escape from this unbear-
able situation, the only apparent means to reach "newer shores" was
offered by poison and suicide. Then in one all-important moment the
announcement of the resurrection shows the real road to "a new day
beckoning to newer shores." All this is clearly stated in this scene.

If ultimately Faust remains unaffected by the resurrection message, the fault does not lie with the message and its announcement. It lies rather with Faust, who, in spite of his initial step, is still too cowardly to disentangle himself sufficiently from his all too human pettiness to take up the challenge of belief. For the same reason his cowardice had prevented him from executing the sign of the Macrocosmos. In spite of his passionate yearning for the magic power of this symbol, he was satisfied with the Earth Spirit for the alleged but self-deceptive reason that this minor spirit was more akin to him. Likewise he now does not dare to strive for those spheres to which the message of Christ's resurrection bears witness and which it could have opened for him. He is deceiving himself by the subterfuge that this message is only for the young, a pretext utterly unjustified by the message itself as it is found and expressed in the play. Faust is consciously degrading the noble grandeur of the resurrection with its sublime vision of a new life. He reduces it to the level of sentimental youthful reminiscences. Still, his abstaining from suicide shows the impact of the resurrection on him. It must be remembered that the moment when Faust raises the cup to his lips constitutes the decisive turning-point of the drama, its very core. This moment decided between being or not being when Faust was pressed to the utmost fringe of life in this world. At this moment both Faust's life and drama would have come to an end had it not been for the unfathomable designs of a Higher Power which turn Faust back to life.

The energy of a magnetic field is immediate and most powerful in the center but still active, though to a lesser degree, at the periphery. Scene ii of Part I, "Before the City-Gate," still belongs to the mediate sphere of the impact of the resurrection. In the Easter landscape outside the city gate, too, the resurrection is being celebrated, although in a more or less external manner. The crowd in its Sunday's best and the country-side in all its spring finery still show a faint reflection of the glory of the resurrection, bestowed on all men and on the whole of creation.

The analogy of Christ's resurrection to the bestowal of new life on all creation must be admitted by all Christians. The renewal of life by the cycle of cosmic seasons is only a slight reflection of the work wrought by God. The objection may be raised against drawing the conclusion of an outright Christian impact in the scene "Before the City-Gate." Yet the progress of the action decidedly shows such an effect. After the walk, Faust has returned to his study. It is still the same old study which he had cursed in the first scene as being "a dungeon and drear, accursed masonry." These are still the same old books and shelves whose accumulated dust has robbed him of the pleasure of study and research. It is the same midnight hour as before. His surroundings have stayed as they were, but Faust himself has completely changed. Of necessity the question for the cause of this sudden transformation arises. How did it happen that Faust is now experiencing this very same old study in quite a different manner, that his better soul awakens to the light, the wild desires no longer win him, the deeds of passion cease to chain him, reason resumes her speech, hope again lends sweet assistance, the love of Man and love of God revive within him, and he again yearns to reach the rivers of existence, the very founts of Life? There is no other explanation for this change of mood and attitude in Faust than the announcement of the resurrection. Neither words nor the progressive action of the drama offer any other alternative, even if, in a way, the resurrection remains at the periphery. Already his own words, that the love of God is again reviving in him, furnish the proof that Christian reality is gaining impact. Still more decisive in this scene is his transcendence from the merely human order to the order of revelation, not a revelation forcibly obtained by magic from some spirit, but that indisputably Christian revelation for which we pine and thirst, "which nowhere worthier is and more nobly sent, than here in our New Testament."[1]

It is not faulty theology to conclude that Faust's positive turning to the concrete Christian revelation is based on the resurrection of Jesus Christ. The drama leads a desperate Faust by the power of the angelic message to the strictly Christian realities as they are revealed by the word of God in Holy Scripture.

Faust's colloquy with God begins with the words of the prologue of the Gospel according to St. John. The colloquy does not lead to a conclusion. Faust does not receive the revelation he so ardently desires because he insists on substituting his own words for the revealed word of God. His colloquy deteriorates into a monologue. Yet

---

[1] Taylor (trans.), op. cit., I, p. 42, v. 1218f.

the fault does not lie with the deficient impact of Christian reality;
it lies rather with Faust's hopeless egocentricity from which he is
unable to free himself. Nevertheless, it is striking that after his
conversation with God he does not continue talking merely to himself.
His monologue leads over into a dialogue with the devil. This is an
amazingly true picture of the situation in which man finds himself:
he cannot succeed by himself nor for himself. He lends his ear
either to the word of God or to the small-talk of the devil. Yet,
whichever way he turns, he still stands under the impact of the
resurrection. For the one who surrenders to the graces of faith,
there will be salvation and fulfilment; for him who refuses to surrender, there will be fatal judgment.

Moreover, it is theologically fitting that the poodle introduces himself in the midst of the Easter landscape and from this
very Easter landscape of the resurrection sets out for his evil purposes. For all Christian reality is exposed to seizure by demons
as long as it remains tied to the mode of this world. Hence, Satan
is an essential part of Christian reality. Whoever refuses to give
himself over to the risen Lord and His revealing word, surrenders
to Satan. This is not only part of Christian belief but it is also
unmistakably shown in the fate of Faust as the drama progresses.
At the moment when Faust, in his intellectual conceit, falsifies
Scripture, when he puts first the word and not the deed, Mephistopheles is already in his study; Faust's road under the guidance of
magic has already begun. When the Easter bells rang, salvation was
still possible. The second scene, "Outside the City-Gate," already

The pact. St. John's University Opera Workshop, 1957.

draws Faust into the magic power field of the poodle. When Faust
cannot refrain from calling him, another decisive word, a demonia-
cal one, is spoken. Only at the very end, through the mercy of God
and the intercession of penitent sinners, will Faust hear again the
chant of the angels, to which he now closes his ears when he calls
to Mephistopheles: "Come, follow us!"

The road on which Faust sets out with Mephistopheles need not
be followed in detail. It suffices to say that with the proclamation of Christ's resurrection the fate of Faust becomes inevitably
linked to the central forces of Christian reality and consequently
will be decisively influenced by their impact.

The Easter message was introduced rather strikingly by the
choir of the angels. There is no such cue for the second manifes-
tation of Christian reality, the Church. Nowhere is she proclaimed
in so many words; however, she is there. She is made visible in
Margaret. This may sound like a startling statement. But each and
every woman in Faust represents a distinct human or cosmic order.
This, obviously, is most true of Helena. She has always been recognized as representing Greek antiquity, and rightly so, since all
her words and actions are born of this particular age of history.
Likewise, the Mothers in Part II stand for a particular cosmic order,
the order of fruitfulness and fecundity. Margaret also represents
a distinct order in the hierarchy of human kind. Any a priori denial would make the Margaret part of the drama merely a love episode, differing only in the beauty of its poetic expression from
the every-day love affairs encountered in cheap literature: simple

girl falls in love with gentleman, or vice versa; seduction and child
murder; girl condemned and gentleman left unmolested. But the Margaret
of _Faust_ is not merely the simple girl adorned with blond braids. The
drama says nothing of the kind. Nor can she be taken merely as the
consummate incorporation of female sensuality by which she first wins
her man and then perishes. The drama reflects an entirely different
concept.

At the very beginning of the Margaret episode Mephistopheles
significantly admits that he has no power over her and that he is at
a loss to satisfy Faust's carnal desires. This admittance by Mephistopheles is of the utmost importance. To bring Faust together with
a woman, or with women, was precisely one of the points of Mephistopheles' premeditated program of temptation and seduction. In Scene
vi, "Witches' Kitchen," Mephistopheles made him behold the apparition
of an alluring temptress. Faust caught on then, but it is Margaret
who now becomes the first object of his passion. Mephistopheles is
very disturbed that it was, of all women, Margaret whom Faust met.
Obviously she does not correspond to the type of sensual woman con-
jured up in the "Witches' Kitchen." She stems from a completely
different realm over which Mephistopheles' powers fail. He himself
says so quite clearly, and he leaves no doubt why he has no power
over her: she comes from confession, from the sphere of influence
of the sacramental Church, of the Church founded upon and acting
through Christ's sacraments.

The question now arises whether Margaret's coming from confession remains an exterior and accidental circumstance which could

not legitimately be exploited in any Christian connotation, or whether
her subsequent words and actions remain within and are prompted by the
sacramental orbit of the Church, just as Helena's words and actions
are expressive of Greek antiquity. In this connection Margaret's inquiry into the religious belief of her lover assumes paramount importance. Her question is not caused by vain curiosity nor by the
desire of a simple girl to put on airs in the sight of the gentleman.
There can be no doubt of the essential seriousness of her question,
and it is imperative to probe into the relationship between this inquiry and her love. The mere fact that this question is being raised
suffices to show that Margaret is not just a victim of sensual passion, but that within her a spiritual component is active by which
she feels compelled to scrutinize, justify, and secure her love. By
her inquiry into the Faust's beliefs she confesses to her love in
the sight of God because this love of hers is embedded in the very
core of her existence and has its roots much deeper than in sensual
passion. This layer of her being is determined by her belief in the
sacramental Church. It is the voice of the Church which speaks
through her. If she were only a girl in love, there would be no
reason for this question weighing on her conscience. But in reality her love is subject to the order of the Church. This is shown
still more clearly when this uneducated girl, after Faust's very
poetical and very empty and utterly pantheistic profession of faith,
gains and maintains the upper hand. She has what theology terms the
discernment of spirits; and she asserts calmly and firmly that Faust
is no Christian.

Where the average girl in a similar situation would unreservedly yield to the deceptive speech of the man she loves, Margaret does not consent. Even in the face of Faust's lies she maintains her correct appraisal of Mephistopheles. The best indication of her real quality is that in the presence of Mephistopheles she is not only unable to pray but even feels her love for Faust wane. This last remark shows better than anything else that her love is in no way grounded on sensual impulses and desires but stems rather from that sphere of correlated body and spirit which has been sanctioned and sanctified by the existence and order of the Church. The fact that Margaret eventually falls into sin does not imply her separation from the Church of which even the sinner remains a part. It is again decisive for our judgment of the girl that her inner disposition compels her to carry her sin into the very arms of the Church. Just as she wanted to answer for her love in the face of God, so she will answer for her sin in the face of the Church. She does not yield to the promptings of the evil spirit who tries to drive her to desperation. Neither does she accept Faust's offer of rescue because it would depend on the help of Mephistopheles. Still to the very end, she is in love with Faust, yet she does not surrender herself to his safe-keeping. On the contrary, she severs her fate from his because she confidently believes in her submission to the judgment of God and in the certainty of salvation. In the touching prayer at the end of the Dungeon scene, which strongly alludes to the In Paradisum of the liturgy of the dead, she recommends herself to the mercy of God; she again manifests her profound insight

into the depth of Faust's depraved soul--at which she shudders.
Nevertheless, deep in her heart she remains united to him in love.
In her, as in the Church, the mysterium iniquitatis stands cheek
by jowl with love and charity. Everything without exception which
Margaret says and does points toward the moral order and power of
the Church, a Church which rules over her love and her sin, her
better insight and her final decision, her life and her death, a
Church which ultimately will lead her to repentance. To classify
Margaret simply with womanhood and humanity in general would mean
an arbitrary disregard of her own words and actions; it would mean,
without prejudice to her genuine naturalness and spontaneity, a
neglect of her total subordination to the Christian reality of the
Church.

Margaret's particular role in the drama becomes self-evident
in the closing scene of Part II. She is the only character in the
whole play who appears again. That alone would testify to her paramount importance. But she is presented not simply as "Margaret"
but as Una Poenitentium, a penitent formerly called Margaret. Together with three other penitent women she is united in the society
of the Mater Gloriosa, the Pater Seraphicus, and the Pater Marianus,
the representative members of the communion of saints in which the
Church militant achieves her final consummation.

What unmistakably makes this heaven a Christian heaven is the
fact that the decisive action is performed by penitents, to be exact,
by penitent women, and especially by Margaret. The penitents are in
themselves typically Christian in origin. What is even more remarkable,

these penitents are supported by the documentary evidence of Christian texts: Mary Magdalene by Luke 7, the Samaritan woman by John 4, and Mary of Egypt by the Acta Sanctorum of the Bollandists. The objection that these were but names without any real Christian meaning would imply a degradation of the dignity of Goethe's poetry and the incapacity of his poetic mind. Goethe was quite learned and well versed in Scripture.

Margaret, the deserted mother who has killed her child and who was an accomplice to the death of her own mother, though unknowingly, receives the commission from the Mother of God to lead Faust to higher spheres. The only words which the Mater Gloriosa speaks in the whole drama are addressed to Margaret:

> Rise, thou, to higher spheres!
> Conduct him who, feeling thee, shall follow there![1]

They are directed, and are directing Margaret, toward Faust's salvation. Faust was and remained God's servant, a latent vessel of grace. This is the presupposition of the whole tragedy, unsearchable as heaven itself, where this presupposition was announced. All of Faust's earthly experience involved guilt. It is only in the realm of the Mater Gloriosa, where Faust is raised by the power of love, that he will be re-created, redeemed.

In the very center of this Christian heaven Margaret appears as a penitent. There her work of love is consummated in Faust. By repentance she herself has been raised from her sin to the communion of saints in heaven, and all this has taken place within the sphere

---

[1] Ibid., II, p. 257, v. 12095f.

of the sacramental Church. Thus, in Margaret the sanctifying powers of the Church, and most essentially a charity which manifests itself in the transmission of salvation to others, attain their final efficacy. The first intimation of this power goes back to the early scenes of Part I when Margaret and her love seemed to exercise on Faust an influence which might have drawn him from his life of passion. When Faust entered her chamber for the first time, he almost surrendered to the purity of the surroundings, almost desisted from "the lust of instant pleasure." This was likewise the case in the scene "Forest and Cavern." There is only one kind of love, the love of God, of which every true love is but a reflection. And most certainly Margaret's love for Faust was just such a reflection, since her love could exercise a sanctifying influence on Faust. But what she then failed to achieve in the natural order of her love, she is now permitted to accomplish: she, a purified and sanctified penitent, is leading her lover to eternal bliss. In either case it is with the powers of the Church that Margaret intervenes in the formation of Faust's destiny. Neither the cosmic powers of the Mothers nor classical antiquity were able to save and transfigure the Faust of Goethe's tragedy. It is the penitent, called Margaret, who performs this transfiguration. And she it is over whom Mephistopheles holds no sway because in her the dispensation of graces within the Church of Christ is unfolded and displayed.

The fact that in this tragedy Faust could be saved at all proclaims the triumph of the love of God, whose handmaid Margaret became in order that, weak and strong at the same time, she too might be an instrument of God, just as the Church herself is God's tool. It makes little sense to object to the absence of repentance and penance in Faust, the erring man. The rehabilitated Faust is no longer the Faust of old. He enters into bliss in the company of penitents and thus shares in the atonement (at-one-ment) of the Church. This may not suffice for a theological treatise on justification but it does suffice for the creative work of a poet.

One should hesitate to claim that all this concerns only religious generalities. On the contrary the religious realities in Faust are very precisely Christian realities since they are proclaimed in New Testament revelation and in the order of the sacramental Church. Only an arbitrary interpretation of the text could escape such a conclusion. Goethe's tragedy in its own words and actions speaks a language that is quite unmistakable.

Since the Incarnation, the whole of the created universe is permeated with Christian reality. Its impact cannot be resisted by whoever wants to listen, and certainly not by those who are vates, seers, prophets, poets, and who have received the gift of scrutinizing perception. Goethe's personal Christian belief remains open to question. But the magnitude of his poetical genius can only be enhanced by the fact that in this drama, which embraces all of humanity and all its problems, he has made manifest Christian reality in its essence and impact, even though he personally, human and all too human, never was able to take the final step.

The treatment of the question of the Christian elements in Goethe's Faust will be terminated with some pertinent words by Stuart Atkins:

...As Faust is no paragon of virtue, so is Faust, however extraordinary it may be as a poetic achievement, the imperfect work of an imperfect man well aware of these facts. But for all his profound insight into human frailty, and because he understood men as only the greatest poets of all time have been able to understand them, Goethe still felt compelled to testify with Faust that he recognized in man's imperfect striving for natural truths a universally shared pattern of religious experience. And as long as it can be felt that the value attached to aspiration in Faust is rightly a positive one, so long also must Faust remain one of the greatest secular poetic statements of how man searches for the meaning of life and of God.[1]

From the treatment of the religious elements in Goethe's Faust we turn in the next chapter to a consideration of the Faustian man as portrayed by Oswald Spengler in his important work The Decline of the West.

---

[1]Atkins, op. cit., p. 276.

CHAPTER VI

THE FAUSTIAN MAN

In 1918 Oswald Spengler (1880-1936) published in Munich the
first volume of his The Decline of the West (Der Untergang der Abendlandes). Whatever the objective merits of Spengler's philosophy of
history may be, ever since its publication the Decline has exercised
a profound influence on European thinking. Many of Spengler's concepts and slogans, whether original or merely refurbished ideas of
bygone ages, have become common property. His influence has pene-
trated far and wide; it is present, sometimes perhaps only subcon-
sciously, wherever savants undertake to interpret history or to
mould the future. Whether his theories are accepted or not, they
are at issue, and a study of the development of the Faust legend
would be incomplete without reference to Spengler and his historical concepts since he made Faust, den faustischen Menschen, the
Faustic soul, the symbol and exponent of our own Western (European
and American) civilization.

> Thus, in Spengler's view, what the historian could learn from
> Goethe the natural scientist would eventually merge with the
> lessons of Goethe the philosopher. And behind the injunction
> to imaginative contemplation, there lay a further precept of
> philosophical apprehension. 'Alles Vergaengliche ist nur ein
> Gleichnis'--'everything transitory is only a metaphor': the
> final chorus of Goethe's Faust rang out again and again in the
> Decline as its most pervading leitmotif. All things human, all
> historical events, its author implied, were only passing reflec-
> tions of great hidden truths.[1]

---

[1]H. Stuart Hughes, Oswald Spengler--A Critical Estimate (New
York: Charles Scribner's Sons, 1952), p. 59f.

Spengler saw "in the contrast between the first and the second parts of _Faust_ an epitome of the things that separated the earlier era of creative thought from the 'purely practical, farseeing, outward-directed activity of the nineteenth and twentieth centuries'."[1]

In essence Spengler's way of regarding history consists in rejecting the traditional succession of ancient, medieval, and modern times and in substituting for it a study of comparative cultures, or in their later stages, civilizations. Every culture, like any living being, is born, grows, reaches its climax and then turns towards its decline until it dies—either simply disappears or is, at least in part, absorbed by a new, a younger culture. In brief, his is the cyclical theory of human development. What was traditionally defined as ancient history, Spengler redefined as the history of classical culture (Greek and Roman). The conventional medieval and modern periods form the history of the West, and we of the twentieth century are living through its late stage, i.e. its stage of civilization (in contrast to "culture") or decline. His method was to teach Western man that the society in which we live is no different in character from the societies that have preceded it, and that it, like its predecessors, is destined to pass away when its appointed time has been completed, when its cycle has reached its lowest point of productivity. The traditional view, Spengler argued, represented a distortion, a product of the pride and myopia of European man. The new method would put things in their correct focus.

---

[1] _Ibid._, p. 60.

Spengler called his method morphological. That is, it represented an application to history of the biological concept of living forms. Each culture, in this view, was an organism which like any other living thing went through a regular and predictable course of birth, growth, maturity, and decay. Or, in his more imaginative language, it experienced spring, summer, autumn, and winter. Within each culture, Spengler insisted, certain basic attitudes permeated all of life and thought. They exercised an equally pervasive influence in the realm of aesthetics as over the forms of economics, war, and politics, and even over so unlikely a field as mathematics. Taken together, these basic attitudes formed a characteristic cast of the human spirit working itself out in the history of every culture of which any record remains.

Every culture formed a distinct bloc of spiritual and physical reality, clearly set off from its predecessors, contemporaries, and successors. Yet each one went through the same morphological stages.

> I hope to show that without exception all great creations and forms in religion, art, politics, social life, economy and science appear, fulfil themselves and die down contemporaneously in all Cultures; that there is not a single phenomenon of deep physiognomic importance in the record of one for which we could not find a counterpart in the record of every other; and that this counterpart is to be found under a characteristic form and in a perfectly definite chronological position.[1]

First and most central perhaps to his style of thought was the concept of history as a universal symbolism. The record of man's existence ceased to be a casual succession of events or a mechanical chain of cause and effect and became the ordered, majestic unfolding

---

[1] Oswald Spengler, The Decline of the West, trans. Charles F. Atkinson (2 vols.; New York: A. A. Knopf, 1945), p. 112.

of the implications contained in a limited number of awe-inspiring symbols. This thinking in symbols broke sharply with the more usual notion of thought as a logical progression from one idea to another. In place of logic, he relied on feeling and intuition. Needless to say this conscious irrationality reflected a profound scepticism. The mainspring of human action was instinct rather than abstract ideals. Thus, progress in history is an illusion. In the field of morals and manners, it was impossible to establish what constituted "good and evil" for all time. If other men in other cultures had thought differently, their ideas were equally "true" for their time and their society. Man must be a relativist.

For the present purpose, the application of Spengler's theory will be restricted to Classical and Western Culture. In his scheme of things the soul of the Classical Culture, which chose the sensuously-present individual body as the ideal type of the extended, is designated by the name of the Apollonian, made familiar by Nietzsche. In opposition to it is the Faustian soul, whose prime-symbol is pure and limitless space, and whose "body" is the Western Culture that blossomed forth with the birth of the Romanesque style in the tenth century. The nude statue is Apollonian, the art of the fugue Faustian. Apollonian are: mechanical statics, the sensuous cult of the Olympian gods, the politically individual city-states of Greece, the doom of Oedipus. Faustian are: Galilean dynamics, the great dynasties of the Baroque with their cabinet diplomacy, the destiny of Lear, and the Madonna-ideal from Dante's Beatrice to the last line of Faust II. The painting that defines the individual body by contours is Apollonian, that which forms space by means of light and shade (Rembrandt!) is Faustian. The Apollonian existence is that of the Greek who describes his ego as soma (body) and who lacks all idea of an inner development and therefore all real history; the Faustian is an existence which is being led with a deep conscious-ness and introspection of the ego, and a resolutely personal culture evidenced in memoirs, reflections, retrospects and conscience.

For the Apollonian man the essence of existence expressed it-self as body and form. He confined his activities and speculations to the here and now; he abhorred the idea of size and distance. The free-standing nude statue with its harmonious contours and untroubled gaze symbolized in visible form the classical attitude of personal detachment and serene acceptance of an inscrutable destiny.

Faustian man, like his ideal prototype, the hero of Goethe, lived in eternal restlessness, and in longing for the unattainable. His is the art of endless vistas and limitless spaces. It began with the sky-ward striving of the medieval cathedrals, found a new outlet in the perspective color of the Renaissance and seventeenth century painting, and ended as music, which alone spoke a language sufficiently abstract to convey a sense of spiritual infinity. The world of Faustian man is the world of dynamic movement, where as the Apollonian contemplated it in static repose. In the will to con-quer distance Faustian man has created his most eloquent symbols: the Copernican view of the universe, the faith of the explorer and the mountaineer, and the machines that decade by decade have produced more and traveled faster than even their inventors had considered possible. Space is there to be conquered.

"Space," speaking now in the Faustian idiom, is a spiritual entity rigidly distinct from the momentary sense-presence of Apollonian man. In fact, Spengler claims that the Faustian space-concept could not be represented in an Apollonian language, whether Greek or Latin. But the created expression-space of the Apollonian arts is equally alien to ours. The tiny cella of the early Classical temple was a dark nothingness in contrast to the eternal vaults of Gothic naves. The closed ranks of the Greek columns were expressly meant to convey to the eye the fact that they surrounded a body confined to itself. The Doric column bores into the ground; in no other Culture is the firm footing, the socket so emphasized. In the Classical reliefs there is an interstice between the figures but no depth. A landscape of Claude Lorrain, on the contrary, is nothing but space; all bodies in it possess an atmosphere and perspective meaning purely as carriers of light and shade. The Faustian soul, in its springtime, arrived at an architectural problem which had its center of gravity in the spatial vaulting-over of vast cathedrals, dynamically deep from porch to choir. In Gothic (Faustian) architecture, the art of the vault and of the single column supporting a large arched room reached a perfection not attained again. And there is more to it than just being a device of functional art. The arch represents the most noble (most Faustian) possibility of stone architecture, and it embraces a mystery which, quite unjustifiedly, seems to be solved when some mathematical formula apparently discloses the value and forces of gravitation and

Goethe. Crayon drawing by Ferdinand Jagemann.

resistance and their mutual relation. But the forces themselves, gravity and inertia, remain original phenomena whose intrinsic nature is still unknown to man.

This art represents the overflow of the Middle Ages with the excitement of passionate deeds and spiritual traditional form and line into a fluid, bewildering succession of curves and structural deceptions, and the great painters of the seventeenth century push perspective and shadow to their farthest limits of metaphysical depth. H. Stuart Hughes aptly comments on the relation of the Faustian spirit to music: "Ultimately the Faustian spirit has no recourse but to take flight into the realm of music. From about 1670 on, music dominates the cultural life of the West."[1]

The eighteenth century is the autumn of the Faustian soul. It offers the last and most exquisite creations of fully-realized style and form: the perfection of diplomatic technique and aristocratic manners; the art of the Rococo; the music of Mozart; the philosophical writings of Kant and Goethe ("contemporaries" of Plato and Aristotle). In the rationalism of Enlightenment the city reveals its ultimate sterility. The century ends in a revolution (1789) in which the middle class assumes authority. In a futile attempt at self-preservation, the monarchy makes peace with its old enemies, the two traditional classes. Neither side can claim the final victory; this goes to Napoleon, the "romantic" tyrant and "contemporary" of Alexander the Great.

---

[1] Hughes, op. cit., p. 82.

With the opening of the nineteenth century the winter of the West, the "civilization" phase of the Faustian spirit is inaugurated. The end, Spengler's prediction of Caesarism, need not concern us here. In any case, there is undoubtedly much truth in what he says of the early stages of Western culture and for which he sees in Faust the very exponent: his unlimited striving, his unceasing yearning for unreachable heights, the two souls in his breast. His theories might be--and they are--open to dispute. But in any case, Faust remains the representative figure of much which holds true of our Western culture, independently of whether or not it will meet with the end which Spengler predicted for it.

The treatment of Spengler's idea of the Faustian man will be concluded with H. Stuart Hughes estimate of the importance of the Decline for twentieth-century man.

> Spengler's talent as an imaginative writer, however, and the accuracy of his major predictions do not exhaust, or even properly establish, his intellectual importance. It is somewhere between literature and prophecy that the Decline has made its most telling contribution. It is as symptom, as synthesis, as symbol of a whole age that Spengler's book remains one of the major works of our century...For when everything else has been said, the Decline bulks largest as the massive concretization of a state of mind--the state of mind of an old society anticipating its end...Hence, as imaginative literature, if not as history in the strict sense, The Decline of the West offers the nearest thing we have to a key to our times. It formulates more comprehensively than any other single book the modern malaise that so many feel and so few can express. It has become the classic summary of the now familiar pessimism of the twentieth-century West with regard to its own historical future.[1]

With the consideration of the Faustian man according to the

---

[1] Hughes, op. cit., p. 164.

ideas of Oswald Spengler the first part of the dissertation is brought to a close. Spengler claimed that the last of the Faustian arts died with Tristan.[1] However, we will see in part two how the Faustian spirit has truly flowered, even after Tristan, in a really amazing plethora of musical compositions of many types written in a great variety of forms.

---

[1] Spengler, op. cit., p. 291.

CHAPTER VII

FAUST IN OPERA

And now, behold a spirit-masterpiece!
Music is born from every wandering fleece.
The tones of air, I know not how they flow;
Where'er they move all things melodious grow.[1]

It is not surprising that music entered into alchemical conceptions
and practice; for besides flourishing among the Greeks and Arabs,
music provided an accompaniment from very early times to the rituals
and ceremonies of religion, magic and necromancy. Alchemical designs
often contain representations of musical instruments, sometimes borne
by mythological performers; and both Hermes and Minerva were recognized as patrons of the musical art. To a certain extent, therefore,
music was considered to exert a beneficial effect upon alchemical
operators.[2]

In letters to Eckermann dated January 29 and February 12, 1827,

Goethe expresses himself very plainly as to the manner in which he wished

the complete Faust drama to be performed:

It will make an unusual effect on the stage that a drama begins as
tragedy and concludes as opera. The first part requires a great
tragedian and later in the operatic portion, the roles must be filled
by the best singers. The role of Helena cannot be given by one
actress only. Two are required, because it is only rarely that a
singer is sufficiently great as a tragic actress. The composer
would have to be one who has lived long in Italy, so that he could
combine German nature and Italian ways. The music would have to be
in the character of Don Giovanni. Mozart would have been the ideal
composer for Faust.[3]

---

[1]Taylor (trans.), op. cit., II, p. 60, v. 6443-6446.

[2]John Read, Through Alchemy to Chemistry (London: George Bell &
Sons, 1957), p. 71.

[3]Frederick W. Sternfeld, "Goethe and Music" (unpublished doctoral
dissertation, Yale University, 1943).

On another occasion while conversing with Eckermann he ventured the opinion that Meyerbeer might have written a satisfactory _Faust_ score if he had not been so involved with Italian theaters.

It is perhaps surprising to discover upon a close examination of the text how frequently Goethe[1] calls for music. In Part I, Scene i, chiming of bells and choral song are required at the moment when Faust puts the goblet of poison to his lips. The Angels' Easter song is followed by the chorus of women and the chorus of disciples. Scene ii contains the beggar's song. Later on dance and song are called for under the heading "Peasants Under the Linden-Tree." In Scene iv there is the chorus of invisible spirits. It is not clear whether Goethe wanted this and many of the later choruses sung. The scene in Auerbach's cellar, Scene v, calls for singing several times, including Brander's "Song of the Rat" and Mephistopheles' "Song of the Flea." Scene vi, the witches' kitchen, requires the glasses to sing and the caldron to sound and make a musical accompaniment. In Scene viii Margaret sings the song of the King of Thule. Scene xix calls for a serenade to be sung by Mephistopheles.

---

[1] Speaking of the fact that poets are generally rather unmusical, Ernest Walker makes the following remarks in his article "Goethe and Some Composers," _The Musical Times_, No. 1072 (1932), p. 497.
"Goethe was the greatest of the few exceptions. For more than a quarter of a century he was an official producer of opera; his fine bass voice had been trained, and he played both the piano-forte and the violoncello (not very well, perhaps, but still...); he knew a good deal about Palestrina, Bach, Handel, and at any rate some of his contemporaries; he improvised tunes to all his own lyrics and composed some four-part vocal music ('in the style of Jommelli', he remarked); he conducted a choral society with a catholic taste for all music except the melancholy and the 'meteoric'; he developed a scientific theory of harmony, with individual speculations about the minor scale."

Scene xx, the cathedral, calls for organ and anthem. Scene xxi, Walpurgis Night, has Faust, Mephistopheles and Will-o'-the-wisp alternate
in song. Later on choruses of witches and wizards are called for.
Faust is dancing with a young witch. Scene xxii, Walpurgis Night's
Dream, calls for orchestra, _pianissimo_, before the final four lines.
In the final scene of Part I Faust hears Margaret singing when he comes
to open the door to her cell.

At the beginning of Part II Faust is revived by Ariel's song, which
is accompanied by Aeolian harps. This is followed by a chorus. Scene
ii, the emperor's castle, calls for trumpets at the beginning. Scene
iii contains a song by the garden-girls accompanied by mandolins.
Later the gardeners sing a song accompanied by theorbos. In Act II,
Scene iii, Goethe implies that the Sirens are to sing because he requires
that the Sphinxes mock them in the same melody. At the beginning of
Scene iv the stage directions indicate that the Sirens are reclining on
the surrounding cliffs while fluting and singing. In Act III there are
several choruses but again no indication whether they are to be sung or
not. Later in the same act the directions call for signals, explosions
from the towers, trumpets and cornets, martial music. After Euphorion's
death the chorus chants a dirge. At the end there is a note that there
is to be a complete pause and the music is to cease. Scene ii of Act IV
calls for drums and military music. Later a tremendous peal of trumpets
is required. The directions at the close of the scene indicate warlike
tumult in the orchestra, which is to change into lively martial strains.
Scene iv of Act V begins with Lynceus, the warder, singing in the watch
tower of the palace. Toward the end of Scene vi of Act V there are

several choruses of angels. The final scene opens with chorus and echo. Later there are choruses of blessed boys and women penitents, and at the close the Chorus Mysticus.

The importance of music in the play is shown by the fact that twice Faust is restored to life by the power of music, and in the end the poet requires the aid of music to communicate the salvation of Faust's soul.[1]

In his play Goethe makes telling use of several of the old church hymns. Faust himself confesses that he was saved by the strains of the old Easter hymn, Christ ist erstanden, which brought back pleasant memories of his youth. It was the custom in medieval times for the priest to intone this hymn; then the people would take it up while marching into the churchyard. Margaret's prayer to the Sorrowful Mother is a textual parody of the Stabat Mater. The strains of the old sequence from the Requiem Mass, the Dies Irae, is used with telling effect in the church scene.

I have been able to uncover the titles of forty-two operas on the Faust story. Of these the scores of only twelve were available to me. They vary greatly in length and in style from the simplicities of Kistler to the complexities of Busoni; from the terse one act versions of Boulanger and Delvincourt to the lengthy trilogy of Brueggemann. It is truly

---

[1]One should not overlook the fact that Goethe's lines are often very musical also, as in this example:

Rege dich, du Schilgefluester
Hauche leise, Rohrgeschwister,
Saeuselt, leichte Weidenstraeuche,
Lispelt, Papelzitterzweige,
            Faust II, v. 7249-7252.

a fascinating variety. Not all are based on Goethe. Some composers, as the case with Busoni and Reutter, prefer the old folk tale and puppet play.

The libretto for the first _Faust_ opera was written by the unknown playwright Heinrich Schmieder, who got the notion of preparing the Faust story for an opera while he was living in Mannheim. As the basis of his libretto he took the first part of Goethe's _Faust_ up to the episode of Marguerite's faintness in church. He also made use of other versions that were known to him from which he picked what suited him. His friend Ignaz Walter (1759-1822), who was a somewhat gifted imitator of Mozart, wrote the music. The opera was performed in Bremen in 1797 and in Hanover in 1798 by Walter's own troupe. It was not given elsewhere. The score has not been available to me but Hugo Holle gives some interesting information regarding Walter's setting of "The King of Thule."

> He gives two stanzas of the poem one musical setting. There is an introduction and a postlude. For the orchestral accompaniment he requires 3 flutes, 2 A-clarinets, 2 bassoons, string quintet and for the second part adds the bass viol. He demonstrates his technical resources in his clever use of the instruments, alternating woodwinds and strings. The harmony is simple and the melodic style is reminiscent of Mozart. Here and there in the prelude and postlude one can see traces of Papageno's figure. Walter does not succeed in capturing the inner spirit of the poem but gives it a spinning room setting that is half earnest, half joking.[1]

Ludwig Spohr (1784-1859) composed his opera _Faust_ in 1813. It was given its first performance in Prague in 1816. He refers in his autobiography to the fact that Theodor Koerner was to have provided him with a libretto but Koerner decided instead to join "Luetzow's light horse,

---

[1]Hugo Holle, _Goethes Lyrik in Weisen Deutscher Tonsetzer bis zur Gegenwart_ (Munich: Wunderhornverlag, 1941), p. 13.

and fight for the freedom of Germany."

I thus saw my hope of an Opera libretto from the pen of the youthful and gifted poet, destroyed, and was now obliged to look elsewhere for another. It was therefore very opportune that Herr Bernard had offered me his version of 'Faust' for composition, and we were soon agreed upon the terms....From the list of my Compositions, I find that I wrote that opera in less than four months, from the middle of May to the middle of September. I still remember with what enthusiasm and perseverance I worked upon it. As soon as I had completed some of the parts I hastened with them to Meyerbeer, who then resided in Vienna, and begged him to play them to me from the score, a thing in which he greatly excelled. I then undertook the Vocal parts and executed them in their different characters and voices with great enthusiasm. When my voice was not sufficiently flexible for the purpose, I helped myself by whistling, in which I was well practiced. Meyerbeer took great interest in this work, which appears to have kept its ground up to the present time, as he during his direction of the opera at Berlin put 'Faust' again upon the stage, and had it studied with the greatest care.[1]

Goethe's friend Zelter was very impressed with Spohr's opera as

he indicates in the following letter to Goethe.

November 15, 1829
"That fine word Faustus, Fauste, Faust, has been invested by you with such ominous importance, that by all laws, human and divine, you ought to be told of its further consequences. So listen! for the first time yesterday evening, I heard and saw, from beginning to end, Faust, the Grand Opera by J. C. Bernard and Spohr.
If I am not mistaken, the composer got together a Sanhedrin, or whatever they call it, in order that they might jointly sanction laws, which are to be universally current, alike for grand Opera and for light Opera, as is clear from the above stupendous work. In connection with this, he seemed especially to have reckoned on C. M. von Weber; whether an understanding was arrived at, I know not, nor have I asked.
Yesterday's performance of this full, highly wrought work, was worthy of the greatest praise, nor did the crowded house fail to applaud it. The Orchestra, the highest faculty of an Opera, was one man; the singers were as perfect as possible; machinery, decoration, witches, ghosts, and other monsters--all met with the fullest recognition and the best reception...Now, with regard to the work of the composer, who certainly merits more recognition as an artist in tones,

---

[1]Ludwig Spohr, Autobiography, trans. from the German (London: Longman, Green, 1865), p. 98.

than as a musician and melodist--everything--up to the smallest detail, is astoundingly worked out, with the greatest elaboration of art, so as to outwit, to outbid the most watchful ear. The finest Brabant lace is coarse work compared to it..."[1]

A year later Moritz Hauptmann describes the reception in Paris of Spohr's opera to his friend the singer Franz Hauser.

> Cassel, June 9, 1830
>
> ...Did you read of the reception given to Faust in Paris? I daresay it was a poor performance, but still I am surprised that Fetis and Castilblaze...should find absolutely nothing in it. Even supposing all the public criticism to be well founded, that is only the reverse side; the other side seems to have escaped their notice--or was it effaced by the performance? People have no right to pass a verdict under such circumstances.[2]

His comments to the same friend eight years later are not very flattering.

> Cassel, June 24, 1838
>
> ...Our last Opera was Spohr's Faust....Apart from poetry and music, what a mere puppet-show is Faust! The characters are so clumsy! How shapeless and awkward are those four comrades--too many as individuals, too few for a crowd! And much of it is now too long for me, that last finale, for instance....It is perfectly endless; five or six people come upon the stage, each singing a separate story, and how on earth are we to keep them all in our heads?[3]

Bernard's[4] libretto for Spohr's opera took hardly anything from Goethe. It was based on the old folk play as well as on Klinger's novel. The cast is as follows: Faust; Mephistopheles; Faust's four companions, Wohlhaupt Wagner, Kaylinger, and Moor; Roeschen; Franz; Kunegunde; Hugo;

---

[1]Coleridge (trans.), op. cit., p. 373.

[2]Moritz Hauptmann, The Letters of a Leipzig Cantor, trans. A. D. Coleridge (London: Novello, Ewer & Co., 1892), p. 102.

[3]Ibid., p. 132.

[4]J. R. B. Bernard (1780-1850) was editor of several journals in Vienna such as Thalia, a journal for dramatic art.

Gulf; and Sycorax. The role of Faust is to be sung by a bass. The opera is divided into two acts with nineteen musical numbers which were connected by spoken text. Number sixteen, the recitative and aria "Ich bin allein," was taken from his opera Der Zweikampf mit der Geliebten. A man by the name of Boerne made the observation after hearing a performance in Leipzig in 1860 that the story would hold together better without the dialogue. Spohr had prepared a version with composed recitatives instead of the dialogue in 1852. Mr. Gye, director of the Italian opera theater in London, had come to Spohr with a request from Queen Victoria for performances in London. Spohr was concerned that there be no discrepancy in the style between the set numbers and the recitatives.[1] The work took him four months. In its new form the opera now had three acts instead of the original two. The opera was presented in its new form in London, July 15, 1852, and was warmly received.

At the beginning of the opera, Faust is in love with Roeschen the daughter of a goldsmith from Strasbourg. Roeschen is in danger because the populace is aroused against her since they believe she did away with her mother. Faust is untrue to Roeschen and falls in love with Kunegunde. He snatches her from the hands of her abductor Gulf and restores her to Count Hugo to whom she is betrothed. In the Blocksberg he gets a potion from the witch Sycorax that will make him irresistible. On Kunegunde's wedding night he seduces her. Later overcome by remorse he would return

---

[1] In the Speck Collection at Yale I had the privilege of examining a manuscript fragment of the 1852 revision. He was working on the recitative in number nineteen. The manuscript shows quite a few emendations, and there are slight differences in the text and the music from the printed version of the score.

to Roeschen, but his time is up and he must go to hell.

Spohr's _Faust_ is considered a masterpiece of the German school.
The instrumentation and the choral passages are very fine. Spohr wrote
for his soloists in a rather violinistic manner; consequently the music
is quite difficult to sing. His music is notable for the freedom of its
key relationships and for the expressive suspensions and upward-resolv-
ing appogiaturas. He made considerable use of ornamentation. Carl
Maria von Weber comments as follows on the difficulties of the music.

> Die grossen Schwierigkeiten, die sich uebrigens in allen Arbeiten
> Herrn Spohr der Ausfuehrung in musikalish technischer Hinsicht
> entgegenstellen, moegen freilich die Auffuehrung dieses schoenen
> Werkes mancher Buehne erschweren.[1]

The overture is a fine piece. It begins _allegro vivace_ in the
key of C.

Overture, 1st theme, vocal score, p. 1

The middle section is made up of a short _largo_ in 8/8, after which the
opening _allegro_ resumes, this time in c minor. Unfortunately no indications of the instrumentation are given in the vocal score. The following examples from some of the vocal numbers show his rather florid
style of writing:

---

[1]Quoted in: Rudolf Wassermann, "_Ludwig Spohr als Opernkomponist_,"
Doctoral dissertation (Munich: University of Munich, 1909), p. 2.

No. 2. Faust, vocal score, p. 12

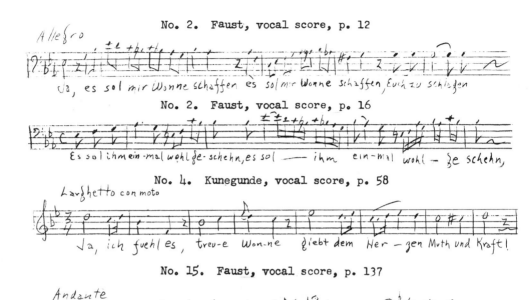

No. 2. Faust, vocal score, p. 16

No. 4. Kunegunde, vocal score, p. 58

No. 15. Faust, vocal score, p. 137

In number nineteen there is an interesting counterpoint between Kunegunde's vocal line and the accompanimental bass.

No. 19. Kunegunde, vocal score, p. 201

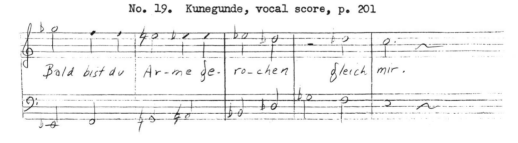

In defective translations Faust was becoming known to French paint-ers, poets, and composers. A melodrama <u>Faust</u> by Théaulon and Gondolier with music by Béancourt was presented in Paris, October 27, 1827. This version was a horrible distortion of Goethe's drama. According to accounts in the newspapers the text was laughable. The main characters were Mephistopheles, Frédéric, Marguerite and her father Konrad. The music was taken from various French operas. It is significant that the twenty-four year old music student Hector Berlioz was a member of the chorus in the theater where Béancourt's melodrama was given. It is Clement's opinion that Béancourt's music is powerful.

Fausto, a semi-serious opera, by Angelique Louise Bertin, was given its first performance in the Italian Theater in Paris, March 8, 1831. It was not a success, but Loewenberg says it is not unworthy of its great subject. The text was adapted from Goethe's Faust Part I, presumably by the composer. I was only able to examine a vocal score in the Brown collection. It is quite an impressive composition. The vocal score contained no indications of the instrumentation and no stage directions. The music consists of an overture and fourteen numbers.[1] There must have been spoken dialogue because the vocal parts do not make up a connected story.

Cast		Performers
Faust	tenor	Donzelli
Valentine	tenor	Bordogni
Mephistopheles	bass	Santini
Wagner	bass	Graziani
Marguerite	soprano	Meric-Lalande
La Maga	soprano	Corradi
Catherine	contralto	Rossi

The overture, marked andante maestoso, is quite short. After the opening there are several short sections that alternate slow and fast

---

[1] At the bottom of the page listing the musical numbers there is a note that indicates that numbers 1, 6, and 13 have been arranged for contralto and are to be found at the end of the score.

tempos. Several themes are employed.

Overture, 1st and 2nd themes, vocal score, pp. 1 & 3

Overture, 3rd and 4th themes, vocal score, p. 5

In the introduction the Easter chorus is treated in an interesting way. Faust sometimes sings with and sometimes alternates with the chorus. The trio that follows sung by Marguerite, Faust, and Wagner is quite florid. Mephistopheles' appearance and Faust's reaction in the next scene stem from comic opera.

No. 3. Duet. Mephistopheles and Faust, vocal score, p. 47

The sequence of keys used in the <u>finale</u> is rather striking: B flat, b, E flat, B flat, A. The composer provides an alternate for the high notes as Faust expresses his joy at having his youth restored.

No. 4. Act I, finale, vocal score, p. 79

Qual sarra ma-na pos — sa

In the canzonetta that opens Act II Margaret has a playful tune.

No. 5. Margaret, vocal score, p. 102

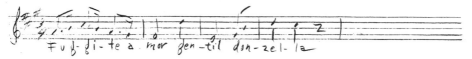

Fug-gi-te a mor gen-til don-zel-la

The duet that follows shows the Italianate character of the music as well as Bertin's method of composition by the repetition and extension of short phrases. The following example shows her breathless style.

No. 6. Faust, vocal score, p. 112

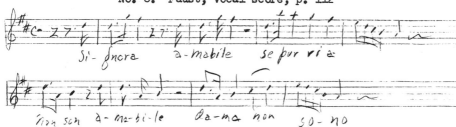

Si- gnora a-mabile se pur vi à

non son a-ma-bi-le da-ma non so - no

Number eight, the duet between Mephistopheles and Catherine, employs the stuttering device so common in opera buffa.

No. 8. Mephistopheles, vocal score, p. 122

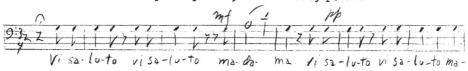

Vi sa-lu-to vi sa-lu-to ma-da ma vi sa-lu-to vi sa-lu-to ma-

da — ma si si si si si si vi sa-lu-to

94

In the church scene Margaret sings an impassioned melody against the chattering of the evil spirits.

No. 10. Margaret, vocal score, p. 167

In Valentine's aria, "ah mi batte il cor," no. 11, there is a ritornello played by trumpets and drums. In the **finale** of Act III Margaret protests her innocence in a coloratura passage.

No. 12. Margaret, vocal score, p. 190

There is a very interesting use of the chorus at the very end of the opera.

F. Lachner (1803-1890) probably wrote his opera on the Faust theme about 1850. At the Library of Congress I was able to examine a brief section "Wen ich meine? Kennst ihr fragen," which gave evidence of the Italianate style of vocal writing.

Gounod had started work on Faust in 1856. He and Jules Barbier and Michael Carré, the librettists, had called on M. Carvalho the director of the Theatre Lyrique. He encouraged the project at the time, but when Gounod had completed nearly half of his work, M. Carvalho informed him that there was to be an elaborate presentation of the drama Faust at another theater and he did not feel it wise to undertake the production of an opera on the same subject. For eight days Gounod was so upset he could not work. M. Carvalho had requested a comedy; so

Gounod wrote <u>Le Medecin Malgre Lui</u>, which was his first popular success in the theater. After the run of the Faust drama was concluded, M. Carvalho again took up the project of a <u>Faust</u> opera. Gounod rapidly completed it. <u>Faust</u> was put into rehearsal in September, 1858. <u>Faust</u> originally had the form of an opéra-comique. There was much spoken dialogue, and there was no ballet. The recitatives were added for a production at Strasbourg in April, 1860. The ballet music was added for a performance at the Opera in March, 1869.

Gounod's <u>Faust</u> has become so familiar that many individuals are inclined to look down their noses at the work.

> The Germans quite rightly insist on calling this work <u>Margarethe</u>, since it is concerned only with the love affair which is found in the first part of Goethe's drama. Gounod and his librettists did well to limit the subject in this way, for it is not imaginable that he could have risen to the heights necessary for an appropriate treatment of the second part. Berlioz, unusually for him, highly praised Gounod's music, singling out especially Faust's aria 'Salut, demeure chaste et pure' and the closing portion of the love duet (Act III); yet nearly every number of the score is famous.[1]

Some literary scholars have also expressed their sorrow that people should be introduced to Goethe's <u>Faust</u> via the Barbier-Carré libretto. The people of the time did not take to the work too well. Gounod was accused of being obscure and being a Wagnerite. The music is French, but at the same time it has Italianate qualities and quite often an air of solemnity. According to Loewenberg it became the most popular French opera ever written, receiving its two-thousandth Paris performance in 1934 and having been given in at least forty-five different countries

---

[1]Donald J. Grout, <u>A Short History of Opera</u> (New York: Columbia University Press, 1956), p. 335.

96

and twenty-four different languages.[1]

I consider it a splendid work. While preparing the score for three performances at St. John's University in 1957, I became intimately acquainted with the work. Despite the immediate appeal of many of the melodies, it is not the easiest thing in the world to make it come off. There are many subtleties that one might miss in a superficial examination of the score. From the first hesitant gropings in the overture to the tremendous prison scene with its apotheosis at the close, it is a masterwork of its kind.

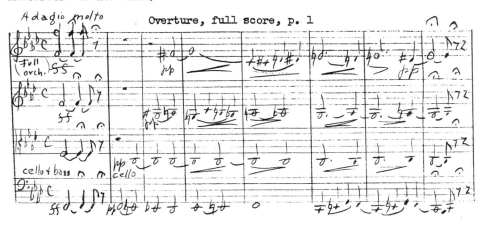

Overture, full score, p. 1

The opera Mefistofele, so-called to avoid confusion with Gounod's Faust, written by Arrigo Boito (1892-1918) perhaps comes closest to capturing the spirit of Goethe's poem. At the age of twenty-five, Boito conceived the idea of setting the whole of Goethe's Faust to music. He undertook the translation and remodelling of Goethe's text to fit the then current views on the forms for a music drama. His approach did

[1]Alfred Loewenberg, Annals of Opera (Geneva: Societas Bibliographica, 1955), pp. 481-482.

Berlioz, Huits Scènes de Faust, op. 1, no. 5, "Concert de Sylphes," p.49.

not meet with public approval; as a result the first performance at Milan in 1868, which took six hours was a complete failure. "For the young author had not only to fight against his obscurity, against tradition, and against anti-Wagnerism, but also the typical Faust opera by Charles Gounod which was well established even in those days."[1] His comprehensive plan had shrunk and only pictures and bits of Goethe's complete Faust remained. In 1875 the revised versions of Mefistofele had a triumphant reception in Bologna and from then on it met with great success.

Boito wrote two versions of the libretto. The first corresponds more exactly with Goethe's poem. The opera is made up of two parts plus a prologue and an epilogue. Part I consists of the first three acts and Part II of Act IV. The principals in Part I are Mefistofele, Faust, Margherita, Marta, and Wagner. In Part II they are Helen, Faust, Mefistofele, Pantalis, and Nereo. There are three ballet sequences: L'obertas, Act I, Scene i; Witches Sabbath, Act II, Scene ii; and Grecian Dance, Act IV, Scene ii. Boito calls for a large orchestra including two harps, organ, harmonium, fisarmonica, trumpets, horns, trombones, and bells. A number of instruments are required on the stage.

The prologue opens with a tremendous chord from the full orchestra. After this a powerful fanfare sounds played by the brass.

---

[1]Ferruccio Busoni, The Essence of Music and Other Papers, trans. Rosamond Ley (London: Rockliff, 1957), p. 169.

Prologue. Full score, p. 1

There follows a hushed salutation to the Lord of the heavens, the
voices, low in pitch, singing an open 5th. This later rises to a great
climax at the words "dei volanti cherubim d'or." The next section, a
scherzo stromentale, introduces Mephistopheles. After his measured
greeting, "Ave Signor," the jocular nature of Boito's devil is at once
indicated.

Mephistopheles, full score, p. 25

After Mephistopheles' long monologue in which he says the master
of the world is going to pieces so rapidly that he does not have the heart
to tempt him to evil, the mystic choir of basses asks the fateful question, "Is Faust known to you?" He makes a wager with God on his ability
to ensnare Faust. There are some charming passages for a children's
choir, representing the Cherubim. The prologue is concluded by a great
chorus of the Cherubim, the celestial host, and the penitents.

Act I, Scene i, is preceded by a quotation from Goethe, "If I
might once say to the fleeting moment: Stay thou art lovely...Then let
me die." The scene is that of a great gathering of people at Frankfurt
on Easter. It is introduced by the ringing of five bells. There ensues
dance music alternating 3/4 and 2/4 time. The obertas is danced. The
tune is very appealing.

Chorus. Full score, p. 113

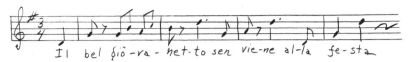

Il bel gio-va-net-to sen vie-ne al-la fe-sta

As the people drift off Faust notices a strange friar and speaks to Wagner about him. Wagner says it is only a pious friar muttering his rosary.

Act I, Scene ii, takes place in Faust's laboratory. An echo of the music of the first scene is heard, Faust intones a lovely hymn to love, a melody made up of short motives and phrases.

Faust, full score, p. 144

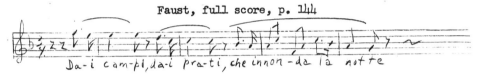

Da-i cam-pi, da-i pra-ti, che innon-da la notte

Faust prepares to read from the gospels when he hears a howling noise. The rushing figures in the clarinets, bassoons and lower strings are very effective here. It turns out to be the grey friar. Faust confronts him with the sign of Solomon and the friar is transformed into Mephistopheles, dressed as a gentleman. Faust asks him his name. There follows the brilliant whistling section in which Mephistopheles says, "Son lo spirito che nega sempre tutto." After Faust agrees to a reversal of roles down below, the contract is concluded by a handshake. Mephistopheles spreads his cloak and they prepare to leave.

Act II, Scene i, "The Garden," is preceded by the quotation from Goethe's Faust, "Who would dare affirm the saying: I believe in God?" Faust, under the alias Henry, is strolling up and down with Margaret. Margaret's entrance song is very simple. Boito asks that it be sung

quasi puerile. The flutes entering at the second phrase add to the
sweetness.

Margherita, full score, p. 260

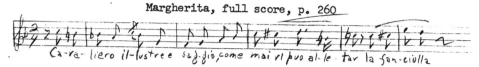

Later Faust gives her a phial with which to put her mother to
sleep so he can visit her undisturbed. There is a lengthy quartet sung
by Margaret, Faust, Martha and Mephistopheles. The scene closes as
Faust and Mephistopheles clasp Margaret and Martha tightly in their arms.

The second scene is that of the Witches Sabbath. The setting is
the Schirk Valley and the peaks of the Brocken. This section is introduced by a single note C played ppp by the bassoons, cellos and basses.
This is followed by an eerie, moaning, chromatic figure in the strings.
Mephistopheles is urging Faust to climb higher. A chorus of witches
appears and Mephistopheles demands homage as their king. They dance
around him and present him with symbols of authority and a globe. He
addresses it in a mocking song. Faust sees a vision of Marguerite in
fetters. This is the first time he mentions her name. The act is
brought to a conclusion by an infernal chorus celebrating the sabbath.

The quotation from Goethe for Act III is "She is condemned."
The death of Margherita takes place in this act. She is distraught.
After a strange, quiet orchestral introduction Margherita sings a lovely
aria with a strongly oriental flavor. Faust pleads with Mephistopheles
to save her. With the aid of a key provided by Mephistopheles Faust
slips into her cell. In a beautiful duet they sing of the happiness
they might have had. There is a powerful chordal close.

Faust and Margherita, full score, p. 357

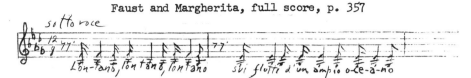

Act IV is again preceded by a quotation, "Tell me what I must do to speak that sweet language." Act IV transports the listener to the isles of Greece where the voice of Faust is heard offstage singing of his love for Helen. She welcomes him. Faust is entranced with the peaceful surroundings amid the nymphs and sirens. Mephistopheles, preferring the rougher pleasures of the Brocken, departs. A Grecian dance takes place. Faust re-enters and offers Helen his love. The act closes with an ecstatic love duet sung by Faust and Helen. This act is perhaps the weakest musically.

In the epilogue the scene is again Faust's laboratory. Mephistopheles is speculating as to why Faust has not yet spoken the decisive words, "Stay, thou art lovely." Faust sings of the approach of death. Mephistopheles seeks to carry him off but the heavenly voices of the prologue are again sounding in his ears. The brass fanfares of the prologue are heard again. Faust prays to be freed from Satan's temptations and pronounces the fatal words. A heavenly vision appears. Faust dies in the state of grace while Mephistopheles defeated sinks into the earth.

The return of the impressive music of the prologue acts as a unifying force. But it is not strong enough to weld the disparate elements together. The prologue is unquestionably the most powerful and satisfactory part of the score. Perhaps it is a pity that Boito did not wait

a few years more before undertaking the well-nigh impossible task of
condensing the two parts of Goethe's drama into the confines of a single
opera. The gaps between the acts can only be filled by a knowledge of
Goethe's poem.

Cyrill Kistler (1848-1907) composed his <u>Faust</u> opera in 1905. His
vocal line is generally quite simple and straightforward. The work
seems to be an effective setting of the Margaret story. The overture,
not so designated, however, employs mainly the keys of g and C. It is
marked <u>feierlich</u>. The instrumentation is for large orchestra including
a rather big percussion section, and harp. Two large bells are required
on stage. The introduction, or overture, suffers from too much sameness
of tempo. It begins in solemn march style. The harmony is quite chromatic. The third section of the overture has a rather arresting theme
in the bassoons, cellos, and basses.

Overture, full score, p. 10

At times his setting of the text is awkward as in the case of Faust's
first words.

Faust, full score, p. 173

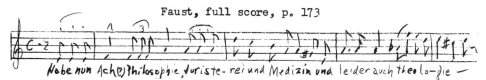

Nabe nun Ach(?) Philosophie, Juriste-rei und Medizin und leider auch Theolo-gie —

A continuous style of writing is used. The acts are not divided into
scenes or set numbers. The Easter chorus for SSAA is a fine one. The
first act ends as Faust gazes enraptured on the vision of Margaret. The

first theme quoted above is used here with telling effect.

Act II, which consists of the garden scene, begins with an agitated prelude. In Margaret's song, the "King of Thule," the movement of the spinning wheel is sometimes suggested in the orchestration. There is an unusual modulation in the middle section from b to e flat. The act ends as Faust and Margaret pledge their undying devotion to each other.

After the solemn prelude which begins Act III, Margaret sings her moving prayer before the <u>Mater Dolorosa</u>. During Mephistopheles' serenade the orchestra imitates the mandolin by the pizzicati in the strings. The act ends with the chorus praying for Valentine's eternal rest.

A very long and solemn prelude opens Act IV. The scene is the prison. When Margaret calls on God and His Angels there is a long, effective passage in the orchestra. An unseen chorus is heard from above.

Chorus, full score, p. 86

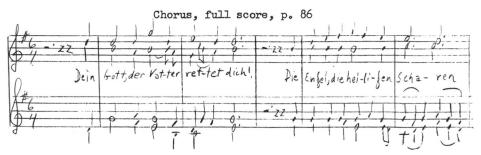

Later on the angels are seen descending the steps. They form a circle around Margaret. And thus the opera comes to a close.

It would probably not be a mistake to refer to the trilogy by Alfredo Brueggemann (1873-) as a monumental work. The first of the three full length operas is entitled <u>Doctor Faust</u>, the second <u>Margaret</u>, the third <u>Faust and Helena, Faust's Redemption</u>. The first opera was produced in 1907, the second around 1910, and the third was never

performed. The first is dedicated to Engelbert Humperdinck, who was his
teacher. The second is dedicated to Giacomo Puccini. In their general
appearance his scores resemble those of Puccini. There is similar continuous lyrical writing with frequent shifts of tempo and keys. Perhaps
this constitutes a reason that militated against the general acceptance
of these works. In his preface to the first opera he says:

> Pertanto io prego di voler accogliere con indulgenza le presenti
> 'Scene Faustiane' e conto ch'esse non vengano considerate sotto il
> falso prisma del dramma musicale. Tale dramma io non ho voluto, e,
> forse instintivamente, non ho neppure osato scrivere.[1]

It is clear he makes no genuflections in the direction of the shrine at
Bayreuth. The texts of Brueggemann's works are based on Goethe's _Faust_.

The first opera opens with the prologue in heaven. The stage directions call for trumpets backstage with a large chorus. The opening
prelude is quite short. It begins as follows:

Prelude, vocal score, p. 1

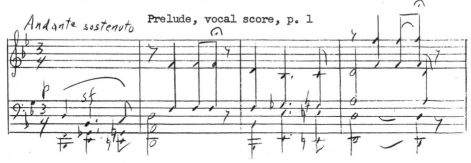

The remainder of the opera takes Faust up to his encounter with Margaret.
The Easter song is sung by a seven-part chorus. SSATTBB. An excerpt
from Faust's aria in Act III will give an idea of his lyric style.

---

[1]Alfredo Brueggemann, _Doctor Faust_ (Leipzig: Ricordi, 1907), p. 1.

Faust, vocal score, p. 141

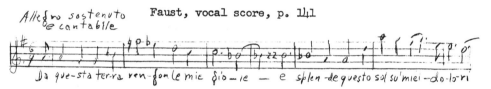

The second opera of the trilogy, <u>Margaret</u>, is divided into four

acts. It makes use of the story from Faust's meeting with Margaret to

the apotheosis. Puccini's influence is evinced here by the frequent

time changes: 2/4, 4/8, 3/8, 4/8, 4/4, and so on. The song of the "King

of Thule" has an interesting melodic twist as it mounts to the G sharp.

Margaret, vocal score, p. 32

The jewel song, which follows, is charming. At the very end of the

opera as the Madonna and Child appear, the angels encourage Margaret

to rejoice in a unisonal chorus. The leap of an eleventh here is sure-

ly unusual.

Chorus, vocal score, p. 200

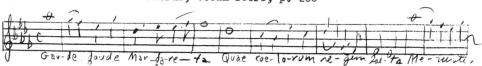

With one act operas entitled <u>Faust et Hélène</u> both Lili Boulanger

(1893-1918) and Claude Delvincourt (1883-) won the <u>Grand prix de Rome</u>

in 1913. The text was a poem by Eugene Adenis fashioned after Goethe's

<u>Faust</u>, Part II. Lili was the first woman to win the <u>Grand prix</u>. She

was ill when she worked on this composition and was advised by her doc-

tor not to attempt it. Her work was performed in Boston in 1917. The

cast is made up of Faust, tenor; Mephistopheles, baritone; and Helène, mezzo-soprano. The instrumentation calls for large orchestra including two harps, celesta, and sarrusophone. The details of interpretation are very carefully marked. For example, near the end we find "<u>mettez vite la sourdine</u>," and trills in the strings are directed to be played "<u>sur la touche</u>."

The opening is awesome and threatening.

Orchestra, vocal score, p. 7

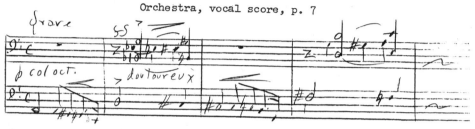

The chromatic nature and richness of the harmony continues until the key changes at (3) to B. It is evening; Faust is stretched out on the grass asleep. Mephistopheles enters (F sharps repeated pp). He addresses the spirits and orders them to continue to fly about Faust, who awakens. This excerpt shows the great care Lili has taken with the vocal line.

Faust, vocal score, p. 12

The next section (8) returns to key of C and is written in arioso style. Mephistopheles mocks Faust for thinking of beauteous Helen. The key changes to C flat at (12) where Faust sings ecstatically about Helen.

Faust, vocal score, p. 17

The music mounts chromatically as Faust summons her. The key changes
to E. Faust repeats the words quietly "Hélène au front de lys" over a
gently undulating accompaniment. Mephistopheles' comments are brusk.
There is a strange leap on "Docteur."

Mephistopheles, vocal score, p. 21

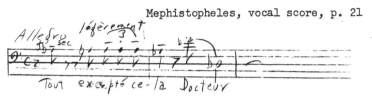

Mephistopheles warns Faust that he is tempting God to want a beauty
who had appeared only once on earth. Faust insists; Mephistopheles re-
signs himself. He draws magic circles as the sun slips over the horizon.
There are horn calls in the music, quietly echoed. The night is filled
with vague rumors. Arpeggio-like figures accompany the melody. Later
the moon rises. Helen appears among the willows. Faust is overwhelmed.
He runs to her. She addresses him, speaking in a halting manner.

Helene, vocal score, p. 28

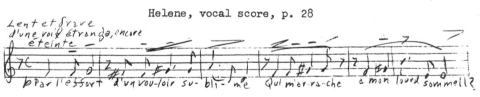

Faust replies that it is eternal desire that has summoned her. She
warns that her beauty is fatal. Then Faust addresses her passionately.
The key changes to the warmth of D flat. She begs him not to force her
to come alive. The key rises to E and Faust renews his passionate outburst. He begs her to remember the hour when she was intoxicated with
ardent kisses. She is awakened by Faust's passionate kiss. They join
in an enraptured duet.

Later storm clouds come up, depicted by typical, chromatic storm music. On the plain and around the base of the mountain a host of wounded warriors gather to the strains of a slow march. Faust is struck with fear. Mephistopheles tells him that they are the warriors of Greece who lost their lives because of her and that they are going to crush him unless he gives up Helen. She attempts to hold him. Mephistopheles summons the phantoms. Faust, Hélène, and Mephistopheles break into an agitated trio. Helen clings to Faust. The spirit of Paris appears, and Faust is overcome with jealousy. Paris seizes Helen. Faust advances towards the spectre and falls under the blow of the warrior's sword. Mephistopheles repeats the words "Sur nous malheur" several times as the music comes to a quiet end. This is, indeed, a powerful work which deserves to be heard.

In the first performance of Claude Delvincourt's one act opera Faust et Hélène the role of Faust was sung by Georges Foix, that of Mephistopheles by Duclos, and that of Hélène by Suzanne Vorska. The work is dedicated to Delvincourt's teacher Charles M. Widor.

The music begins from nothing. Against a sustained F octave a groping figure commences in the bass.

Orchestra, vocal score, p. 17

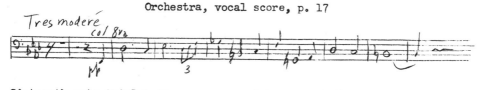

Sixteenth note triplet figures are used to suggest the sylphs. Mephistopheles begins very quietly in short melodic bits. The harmony is quite free and rather Franck-like. The sixteenth note pattern continues

110

through Faust's awakening and acts as a unifying element. More of an attempt is made in this work than in the Boulanger to develop the character of Mephistopheles. Certain phrases are marked to be sung "gaily" and "with irony." The conversational section between Mephistopheles and Faust is in C. When Faust sings his paean of praise to Helène the key changes to D flat. The melody is accompanied by rolled chords.

Faust, vocal score, p. 13

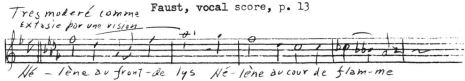

On the repetition of this theme after Mephistopheles' protest that it would be tempting God to summon Helen the key is E flat, a full step higher. Here the accompaniment takes on greater significance with excitement suggested by powerful rhythmic scale passages. There is a stunning climax in the duet when Mephistopheles renews his protest that it would be tempting God. The rhythm is interesting here with Faust in 6/4 and Mephistopheles in 4/4.

Faust and Mephistopheles, vocal score, p. 19

The mood of the time of sunset is suggested by sixteenth note figures weaving back and forth stepwise and later augmented to three note sixth chords weaving back and forth chromatically. Helène's appearance is

handled quite differently from Boulanger. Here she sings a phrase twice
an "ah" before she utters her first words.

Hélène, vocal score, p. 24

Perhaps the Boulanger is the more effective. When Hélène says: "Let us
not add a new crime to the ancient crimes. Love is wicked," and Faust
answers, "Love is divine," the music rises to the key of E. There is a
splendid climax in the duet when Hélène is fully awakened by Faust's
kiss. The following passage sung by Hélène is in the style so characteristic of the impressionists, the melody in the accompaniment, the voice
part in declamatory style.

Hélène, vocal score, p. 39

When the storm section begins the key changes to e. No attempt is
made here to depict the storm. The rhythmic motive suggesting the surging of waves, which accompanies the repeat of the second example, is
sounded twice. Later the rhythm is maintained in an ostinato on G sharp
. The section with the advance of the phantoms is in

G flat and 9/8 and is in the character of a march. Later as they come closer the music is marked _agitato_ 3/4 and this strong rhythmic figure occurs in the bass-- ♪♫♫|♫♫♫ . The music becomes very wild and chromatic. Faust's collapse in Mephistopheles' arms is depicted by descending chromatic triads. The work ends powerfully on the chord of b flat. This composition is quite different from Boulanger's but equally worthy of performance.

In his book _A Short History of Opera_ Donald Jay Grout makes the following comments about Ferruccio Busoni's (1866-1924) opera _Doktor Faust_.

> Busoni's masterpiece, _Doktor Faust_ (completed by Jarnach and post-humously produced in 1925), is, from both the literary and the musical viewpoint, the most significant treatment of this subject in the twentieth century. The highly mystical and symbolical libretto is joined to a score conceived in the same spirit, realized in large forms, worked out with uncompromising musical idealism and logic, but--by reason of these very qualities--lacking the emotional dramatic force which is necessary for wide popular appeal in opera.[1]

It seems that in 1911 Busoni was interested in the idea of a libretto on Leonardo da Vinci and that he discussed this matter with Gabriel d'Annuncio who was not enthusiastic. The poet called Leonardo the "Italian Faust...a skeleton with a torch put in the place of a head."

Busoni made some sketches because he planned to refer to them after a recital but instead of finding them he came across the sketches he had made for _Faust_. He writes in his diary for December 21, 1914.

> Suddenly everything came together like a vision. Five movements. Monologue about studies falls out. Assumed that Gretchen episode is all over. During the past Easter bells ring! Garden festival

---

[1] Grout, op. cit., p. 447.

at the court of Parma, the Duchess betrays her love, in a vision
appears Herod (Salome) and John with resemblance: Duke, Faust.
Three students from Cracow, beginning. Night watchman, end. Query,
Casperle-Intermezzi in front of the curtain, without music, or not?[1]

He finished the libretto December 26, 1915.

He completed the music for the opera up to Faust's final monologue
before his death. It had been settled for some time that the premiere
would take place at Dresden under the supervision of Alfred Reucker. It
was the pressure on the part of Busoni's family that convinced Philipp
Jarnach to undertake to complete the work. It was first performed at
Dresden May 21, 1925. The reception was respectful rather than enthusiastic. About four performances were given.

Busoni recorded the history and theory of his opera in a prologue
in verse which is found in the score. The second stanza gives an idea
of his theory of opera.

> The stage exhibits the gestures of life, but it bears plainly the
> mark of unreality. If it is not to become a distorting mirror, it
> must act fairly and truly as a magic mirror. Grant that the stage
> only lowers the values of what is true, it can then do full justice
> to the incredible, and though you may laugh at drama judging it as
> reality, it will compel you to seriousness if you regard it as mere
> play.[2]

He ends the prologue reminding the auditors that his opera is based
on the puppet plays. The grandiose nature of the opera as well as its
great choral, instrumental and technical demands are sufficient indication
that he never intended it to be performed by puppets. The characters
are restricted to what is necessary and are not permitted to develop

---

[1]Translated in: Edward J. Dent, Ferruccio Busoni: a Biography
(London: Oxford University Press, 1933), p. 295.

[2]Ibid., p. 296.

personalities of their own. Thus, they may seem to be lacking in humanity.

The puppet show idea is impressed on the audience in the stage performance. When the main curtain opens it exposes a second curtain on which a puppet-theater is depicted with the characters of the opera arranged in a row before its tiny proscenium. They appear only as suggestions. The orchestra begins the prelude with a soft suggestion of bells.

Prelude, vocal score, p. 1

A five-part chorus behind the scenes sings the single word "Pax." Their entrances simulate the striking of bells. The rhythm is rather irregular. At the close of this chorus the main curtain opens and reveals the puppet show curtain. An actor rises from a trap in front of this curtain and recites the eighty-two lines of the prologue.

Prelude I. The first scene reveals Faust in his study engaged in an alchemistic experiment. Three students come in with a book, Clavis Astartis Magica.

Wagner, vocal score, p. 17

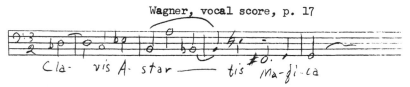

Wagner is excited about this because this is the book he has been seeking. The bass of the students entrance music will give some idea of Busoni's chord clusters.

Orchestra, vocal score, p. 23

Faust urges them to stay but they refuse. Wagner does not see them leave. The brew on the hearth boils over and the whole scene disappears in fumes to the accompaniment of a tremendous c minor chord in the orchestra. Dent says that the stage voices again take up the "Pax" music. The piano score gives no indication of this but says the next scene is to begin without pause. Meanwhile a black curtain has been lowered.

Prologue II. The scene is the same; the time midnight. The exact duration of the rise of the curtain is noted in the score. Faust decides to begin his work of incantation. There is an interesting compositional device used in the orchestra at this point.

Orchestra, vocal score, p. 33

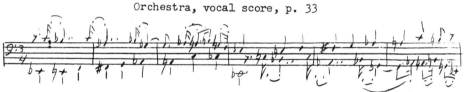

A variation of this material is used as Faust draws a magic circle with a sword and steps into it with the key. He calls upon Lucifer to send his servant, and six spirits appear as flames hovering in the air.

A green light suffuses the room. As Faust is in the process of doing this an unseen chorus under the stage accompanied by trumpets and horns in unison sing out fortissimo "Dein Begehr?" Even the position of the flames is indicated.

*
*   *
*   *   *

The first devil's name is Gravis. He begins singing on low G and rises to G sharp. Faust dismisses all five because they are not swift enough for him. The scene with the six flames is constructed in the form of variations on a theme. The voices rise progressively. Mephistopheles is a high tenor. The chorus comments on the fifth spirit, Megaeros. Faust hardly thinks it worthwhile to question the last spirit. The sixth voice calls to him, a difficult entrance for a singer beginning softly and increasing the volume on high A. Then he calls to him on high B flat. The final call is worth noting.

Mephistopheles, vocal score, p. 62

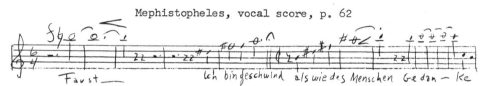

Faust has by this time stepped outside the magic circle and thus the spirit is his master rather than his servant, but Mephistopheles is willing to serve him. On his part Faust must serve Mephistopheles for ever. Faust refuses and wishes to dismiss Mephistopheles. But the devil is shrewd. He tells Faust that his creditors are after him, as well as the brother of the girl he got into trouble, and the priests. This is sung to the accompaniment of a garish waltz. There is a knocking at the door. Faust orders Mephistopheles, "Kill them!" Thus he gives in to the devil. While the devil orders him to sign the pact, an unseen chorus is heard singing the words of the Credo.

After Faust signs the pact he falls senseless to the floor and the double chorus intones a magnificent Gloria to the accompaniment of bells, trumpets and horns. After a pianissimo "Pax" by the choir Mephistopheles

sings out "Gefangen!" on an upward leap of a major seventh and vanishes.
The choirs continues with Alleluia, the morning sun streams through the
window and the curtain falls.

Intermezzo. This is in the form of a rondo. The sound of organ
music is heard. The curtain opens on a Romanesque side chapel in a
cathedral. The organ dominates the episode. A soldier, in armor,
kneels before a crucifix. He is praying that he may find his sister's
seducer. Faust has Mephistopheles, garbed as a monk, get rid of him.
Mephistopheles tells an officer who enters with other soldiers that the
kneeling soldier has killed their captain. They fall upon him and kill
him. This scene is accompanied by martial music.

Main Play, Scene one. Now the main part of the play begins. It
is set in the form of a ballet suite. This scene opens in the court
park at Parma. The music used is very similar to the second of two orchestral studies that Busoni wrote for Faust ("Sarabande and Cortege," op.
51, composed 1918-1919). It is in the tempo of a polacca and is scored
for large orchestra including, bass clarinet, contrabassoon, third
trumpet, two harps and celesta. The theme is announced in the cellos
and basses. The time signature is interesting.

Orchestra, vocal score, p. 123

Dent says Busoni shows his devotion to Bizet in this music.

The curtains do not part until the completion of this piece. The
orchestral music that introduces the wordless chorus has an interesting

five note, <u>ostinato</u> figure in the bass.

Orchestra, vocal score, p. 131

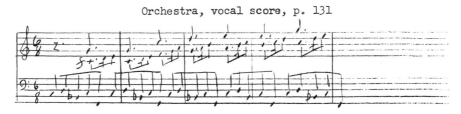

The wedding of the Duke of Parma provides an occasion for pageant and ballet. There is a procession of huntsmen carrying their trophies and a fencing display by little pages. A rustic dance in 2/4 time is followed by a waltz, which Busoni composed in the autumn of 1920. This is followed by a pompous minuet in 3/2.

The master of ceremonies proposes that the Duke and Duchess receive Doktor Faust who enters with Mephistopheles, disguised as a herald, to the strains of martial music and comments from the guests. In turn Faust conjures up Solomon and Sheba, Samson and Delilah, and Salome and John the Baptist. In each case the Duke notices that the male ghost looks like Faust and the female one like his wife. Faust knows that the Duchess loves him, and he urges his attention on her. The Duke brings the performance to a halt and invites Faust to the feast, but Mephistopheles tells him the food is poisoned. Everyone leaves. The Duchess returns and calls to Faust. This aria illustrates Busoni's more lyrical style.

Helen, vocal score, p. 184

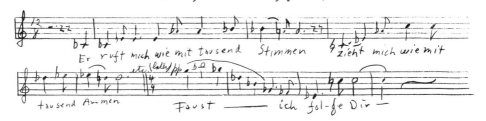

The Duke's chaplain informs him that the Duchess and Faust have ridden away on flaming horses. As the chaplain raises a claw-like hand, we recognize Mephistopheles, who urges the Duke to hush up the matter and marry the Duke of Ferrara's sister.

This is followed by a symphonic intermezzo. Here Busoni makes use of the materials of the first orchestral study, op. 51, the "Sarabande."

The second scene follows. Faust is again in Wittenberg discussing philosophy with his students in a tavern. The introduction is in the style of a rustic minuet. The wine and the arguing result in a fight. Faust manages to quiet them and quotes Luther's famous words, "Wine, women, art and love are to be counted among the best and most consoling things in life." This sets off a musical war between the Catholics and Protestants, in which they praise wine and women in Latin and German, respectively. The Catholics sing a parody of the Te Deum; the Germans break in with "Ein' feste Burg." Faust is lost in thought. There is an echo of the wedding music. Mephistopheles enters with the news that the Duchess of Parma is dead. He brings with him a bundle that turns out to be a little doll made of straw. He burns it, and in the smoke Helen of Troy appears. The scene changes to a classical landscape. The vision disappears as Faust attempts to grasp it. The three students from Cracow return and demand book, key and letter. Faust says he has destroyed them. They tell him his time is up at midnight.

The final scene opens with a funeral march. The first three measures are constructed on a C pedalpoint. The scene is a street in Wittenberg. The voice of the night watchman is heard. A group of students enter. They are congratulating Wagner on his inaugural speech. He has succeeded Faust as rector of the university. One remarks that his speech was worthy of his great predecessor. Wagner says that Faust was a visionary and that his life was deplorable. After Wagner leaves, the students sing a serenade in the tempo of a minuet. The watchman chases them away.

Faust enters and looks up at his home. On the doorstep he notices a beggar-woman with a child and recognizes the Duchess. She hands him the child; it is dead. She vanishes. Strains of the "Dies Irae," sung in German, echo from the church. Faust moves toward the church with the child, but a soldier bars his entrance with a sword. Faust bids the spirit vanish. He kneels and would pray but can think of the words of no prayer. As he looks up at the cross he sees the figure of Helen instead of Christ.

From this point on Jarnach's work begins. Faust lays the dead child on the ground. He steps into the magic circle and by a supreme effort of his will transfers his personality to the child. The child shall continue his existence and unite Faust, as an Eternal Will, with the generations to come. He dies; as the watchman announces the hour of midnight a naked youth rises holding a green bough in his hand. With arms uplifted he strides gaily through the snow into the town.

The watchman lifts his lantern. He sees the body of Faust and carries it off as the curtain falls.

> One cannot apply to Doktor Faust the ordinary standards of opera-
> tic criticism. It moves on a plane of spiritual experience far
> beyond that of even the greatest of musical works for the stage.
> On its first production a German critic said of it that it could
> be compared only with Parsifal...The poem by itself is a literary
> work of extraordinary power and imagination. It clearly shows

how much Busoni owed to the lifelong study of Goethe; it is not Goethe's portrait of Faust, but it is written in Goethe's language. It combines the simplicity of the puppet-plays with something of the concentrated agony of Marlowe.[1]

Busoni stands in direct opposition to the music-drama of Bayreuth. He will not try to describe in music what can be seen by the naked eye. His idea was that an opera should contain everything of which a creative composer was capable.

The "Nocturne Symphonique," op. 43, composed in 1912, and the "Sarabande and Cortege," op. 51, composed 1918-1919, were studies for Doctor Faust. So also was the Second Sonatina, composed in 1912, which becomes clear when its themes are associated with the three students from Cracow. The sound of the orchestra makes clear what was obscure in the piano.

The first performance of Herman Reuter's (1900-) three act opera Doktor Johannes Faust, op. 47, took place in Cologne in 1935. The libretto by Ludwig Anderson is based on the puppet play by Karl Simrock dating from 1846. This follows the Geisselbrecht puppet play rather closely, but it is a synthesis of a number of versions. There are many similarities with Busoni's libretto. The instrumentation calls for a large orchestra including harp. The music is written in continuous style and is reminiscent of the serial technique. If the piano-vocal score is any indication, the orchestration is rather spare.

Cast
Doktor Johannes Faust - baritone
Wagner, his servant - tenor
Mephistopheles - bass
The Duke of Parma - tenor
Bianca, Duchess of Parma - soprano
        appearing in the fourth scene as the goddess Venus

[1] Ibid., p. 304.

Hans Wurst - tenor buffo
Gretel - soprano
The Good Spirit - soprano
    appearing in the third episode as a young maiden and in the
    fourth as another young maiden
The Steward - tenor
    at the court of Parma
Four Topers: Balzer, Rickes, Done, Schambes - two tenors, two basses
Four Market women - two sopranos, two altos
Three Students from Cracow - tenor, baritone, bass
Diabolical Spirits: Auerhahn, Krumpschnabel - tenor, bass
Castle dwellers, students, children, people, good spirits, and evil
    spirits

The figures from the underworld, Mephistopheles, the evil spirits, and the three students, wear masks.

The two scenes of the first act take place in one day; so also the two scenes of Act III twelve years later. The second act lies in the middle: six years after the first and six years before the third.

Act I, Scene i, Faust's study in Mainz. There is a short prelude in the midst of which the curtain rises.

Orchestra, vocal score, p. 1

Faust hears voices from below urging him to take up magic and a voice from above warning him against it. He decides to take his chance with

magic. The infernal beings laugh. Wagner comes in to the accompaniment
of skittish music and says, "Good evening, your magnificence." Some students wish to show Faust a book of magic.

In the next scene Hans Wurst enters and greets the audience with
a lively ditty. Wagner enters and says one must practice patience with
the poor simpleton. Wagner and Hans Wurst sing a duet. Faust summons
the evil spirits. Three appear. Their speed is questioned. Mephistopheles, the third, says he is as quick as thought. There follows a
passage of free declamation with accompaniment. Later, in a beautiful
passage, Faust meditates on the quiet of midnight.

Faust, vocal score, p. 40

Mephistopheles reappears and Faust promises to be his after twenty-four
years. An angel appears and tells Faust he has lost his soul. Hans
Wurst appears again and comments on the fact that the play has not had
a good beginning. His recitative is grotesque and he alternates with
short outbursts from the orchestra. Hans Wurst uses the expression
"perlikke, perlakke" to get rid of the spirits and then does a crazy
dance with many repetitions of these words. Many spirits surround him
and say he will soon be in Parma.

A long orchestral interlude, very chromatic in style, leads to the next scene. Scene iii takes place in the ducal garden in Parma. The Duchess sings a gay song about a mandolin. Later the chorus joins in refrain. This mounts to a big climax. The steward announces that Doktor Faust has arrived. The Duke gives orders to admit him. There is an interesting passage after this when a rustling noise is heard. The colorful ensemble is very lightly accompanied by string tremolo and bits of woodwind. At the end of this section Hans falls into the midst of the surprised courtiers. There is give and take between Faust and Mephistopheles.

In the next scene Faust makes a grand entrance. He is commanded to produce Paris and Helena. They appear on the throne looking like the Duke and Duchess. A chorus of praise is sung in canonic imitation. There is a dance by the arcadian girls and boys. The Count becomes enraged when he sees Faust in the guise of Paris embracing the Countess in the guise of Helena. Hans comes in with a napkin around him. The people are excited because they have seen the devil. The Count warns Faust he will have to flee until his death.

In Act II the scene is laid in the inn. It begins with a waltz-like introduction. The time signature is 3/4, 4/4. Hans and Gretel are drying glasses behind the counter. Gretel says she wants him all to herself. The melody is ornamented in a humorous fashion.

Gretchen, vocal score, p. 132

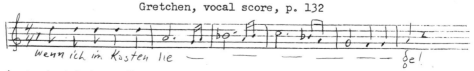

A gay duet between Hans and Gretel follows, "Hei! nun geht ein Leben an!"

There ensues an episode with the four topers. They comment on the fact that Faust is around and discuss some of his deeds. The men's wives appear with brooms and canes. They give their men a bad time. In the next episode a young maiden comes in but does not notice Faust. Faust remarks how wonderful it would be to be loved by such a child. Faust tells the girl that Gretel has become the bride of Hans.

Faust, vocal score, p. 171

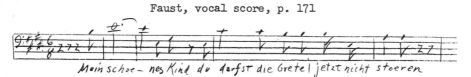

Mein schoe—nes Kind du darfst die Gretel jetzt nicht stoeren

At Faust's request she sings a gay song, "Herr Johann, der war gross und stolz." When Faust tells the girl who he is, she is very frightened. He tells her he loves her, and later they fall into each other's arms. In the next episode Mephistopheles interrupts them. The Countess appears and upbraids Faust for being with the young girl. A lengthy dance episode follows. The dance becomes an orgy. The girl dies in Faust's arms. Mephistopheles is triumphant.

The shrine of our Lady is the setting for Act III. Children are playing before the chapel. After a short orchestral introduction they sing a typical children's song.

Children, vocal score, p. 209

Eins, zwei, drei hicke, hacke Hey, hicke, hacke Haberkorn, der Mueller hat sein Frau

Later they notice Faust in his black mantle. Faust addresses the Mother of God. The music here is very expressive with a syncopated ostinato on F. Mephistopheles appears. Faust asks him if he can return to God.

Mephistopheles says he knows not. Faust says, "Our pact is broken."
In an impassionate outcry he thanks his heavenly mother that he can pray
again. The townspeople gather in the chapel and sing the Angelus.
Mephistopheles tempts him with a vision of Venus who looks like the figure Mary. Faust weakens. He exclaims he has sought Venus all his life.
Venus vanishes as Faust tries to embrace her. Faust is distraught when
he realizes how the devil has tricked him. A powerful unisonal men's
chorus proclaims that he is lost forever. The women continue the Angelus,
"Et verbum caro factum est."

An orchestral interlude makes a bridge to the next episode which
takes place on a street corner in Mainz. Hans is holding a baby and
singing a lullaby. In a duet with Hans, Gretel sings the only florid
passage in the work. The students are heard approaching singing a fine
chorus. They drink some of Hans' wine. In the next episode a chorus
is heard warning Faust to prepare for death. The three students from
Cracow appear again. The tower clock strikes 11:30. The spirits summon
Faust to judgment. The clock strikes twelve. The spirits proclaim that
Faust is condemned. The devils drag Faust down. Hans appears and comments on the stench. He announces to the people what has happened and
says, "If he had taken a wife like I did, all would have been different."
There is a general dance. In my opinion the ending is too drawn out.

Thus we finish our consideration of the operas based on the Faust
theme. Since composers have used both Goethe's version and the old puppet plays, there has been a great deal of variety. Perhaps the only ade-
quate way of dealing with Goethe's poem from an operatic standpoint is to
write a series of operas as Brueggemann did. In the next chapter we shall
consider some important choral compositions inspired by the legend.

CHAPTER VIII

THE CHORAL FAUST

Hector Berlioz (1803-1869), l'enfant terrible of the music world,
published his Huit Scènes de Faust as his opus 1 in 1828. This does
not indicate that it was his first work but rather that it was the first
one he considered fit to publish. He sent a copy to Goethe, who turned
it over to his friend Zelter with results that are worth quoting. Goethe
had requested Zelter to try his hand at making a setting of some sections.
Zelter's awareness of his inadequacy in the matter probably served to fan
the flame of jealousy when he saw Berlioz' score. After his perusal of
the score Zelter wrote Goethe as follows:

> Gewisse Leute koennen ihre Geistesgegenwart und ihren Anteil nur
> durch lautes Husten, Schnauben, Kraechzen und Ausspeien zu verstehen
> geben; von Diesen einer scheint Herr Hector Berlioz zu sein. Der
> Schwefelgeruch des Mephisto zieht ihn an; nun muss er niesen und
> prusten, das sich alle Instrumente im Orchester regen und spuken--
> nur am Faust ruehrt sich kein Haar...[1]

Berlioz tells in his memoirs how he became interested in Faust.

> Another of the most remarkable events of my life was the deep and
> wonderful impression made on my mind by Goethe's Faust, which I read
> for the first time in a French translation by Gerard de Nerval. I
> was fascinated by it instantly, and always carried it about with me,
> reading it anywhere and everywhere--at dinner, in the theater, even
> in the streets.[2]

He goes on to say that he had the scenes he composed printed without

---

[1] Quoted in: Bode, op. cit., p. 291.

[2] Memoires of Hector Berlioz, trans. R. and E. Holmes, revised by
Ernest Newmann (New York: A. A. Knopf, 1932), p. 97.

having heard a note. One of the scenes, the one for six voices called "Concert des Sylphes" was sung by six pupils of the Conservatoire but produced no effect "and was pronounced meaningless, vague, colorless, and wholly devoid of melody."[1] Soon after this Berlioz began work on his Symphonie Fantastique while he was still very much under the influence of Goethe's poem.

Berlioz worked on La Damnation de Faust, op. 24, in 1846 during his travels in Austria, Hungary, Bohemia, and Silesia. The Huit Scènes became the heart of this great work.

He wrote wherever he could. The introduction was written at Passau; the Elbe scene, Mephistopheles' song, Voici des roses, and the sylph's ballet in Vienna. He decided to insert the Rákóczy march which he had previously written in Vienna. One night when he had lost his way in Pesth, he wrote the refrain of the "Ronde des Paysans" by gaslight in a shop. At Prague he arose during the night to set down the melody of the angels' chorus in Marguerite's apotheosis. At Breslau he composed the students' Latin song "Jam nox stillata velamina pandit." The remainder of the score was composed in France. It was finished October 19, 1846. Two performances took place at the Opéra Comique, December 6 and 20, but it unfortunately met with a very cool reception.

Twenty years later Berlioz was invited to direct the work in Vienna.

The rehearsals in Vienna proved almost too much for Berlioz. The strain of thirty hours by railway, the barrier of language and the excitement at rehearsing for the first time in thirteen years the whole of a work which the Parisians had doomed to extinction and which was

---

[1]Ibid., p. 97.

returning to life of itself, made Berlioz irritable and even inadequate on the podium. He knew it and gave up the idea of conducting saying, 'I am sick unto death.' The performance he felt brought him the greatest triumph of his career. He was recalled eleven times, banqueted and toasted...

Although La Damnation is really a dramatic cantata, comprising as it does unconnected episodes based on Goethe's poem, it has been frequently mounted as an opera. It was performed as an opera at Monte Carlo in 1903 and at the Metropolitan in 1906.

Through the courtesy of the curator, Professor Kurt von Faber de Faur, I had the privilege of examining one of the rare full scores of the Huits Scènes, op. 1 in the Speck collection at Yale University. There I compared it with the full score of the later work, La Damnation de Faust, op. 24. Berlioz already demonstrates considerable skill in orchestration in his Op. 1.

Huit Scènes, op. 1.	La Damnation de Faust, Légende dramatique en quatre parties, op. 24.
8 numbers	26 numbers
No. 1. F, C. 4/4. ♩ = 80. Religioso moderato. Chant de la Fête de Pâques. Quote from Shakespeare under title, "Ophelia." "Heavenly powers, restore him." This scene is preceded by lines referring to Faust's last drink. Instrumentation: 2 flutes, English horn, 2 clarinets, 2 horns, 2 bassoons, 2 harps	No. 5. Same key and time. Tempo guide different: 69. Also Religioso moderato assai. Chant de la Fête de Pâques. Orchestration is different: 2 flutes, 2 oboes, 2 clarinets, 4 horns, timpani,

and strings. No part for Faust. The voice divisions of chorus are the same in both, but this opus calls them: Chorus of angels: 1 and 2 sopranos, 1 and 2 altos; and chorus of disciples: 1 and 2 tenors, 1 and 2 basses. Ends with words, "languissent ici bas," and the orchestra rapidly thins out to a few halting notes in the cellos and basses.

strings.

Faust's words, "What do I hesr?," after first choral phrase not in op. 1. Choral material is basically same at, "O, divin maître ton bonheur." The triplet figures played in op. 1 on harps are here done by woodwinds. Before repeat of opening chorus, Faust sings, "O, souvenirs." Dynamics differ from here on. Reprise here mf as opposed to pp of op. 1. In op. 1 Berlioz calls for a more numerous chorus. In the chorus of the disciples from this point on the choral treatment is more restrained because Faust sings. Ends with 3 Hosannas, the final one ppp. This leads directly into a recitative of Faust.

No. 2. Wagner's words precede. He addresses Faust and claims he is the enemy of all that is gross. He says

Not used in op. 24.

they whirl as of possessed and call
it the joy of the dance.

Paysans sous les tilleuls, danse et chant

Again a quote from Shakespeare. Romeo:
"Who'll now deny to dance? She that
makes dainty, I'll swear hath corns."
On side of score: Gaité franche et naïve.
F sharp. 6/8. ♩.= 80. Allegro.
Instrumentation: 2 piccolos, 2 oboes, 2
horns, strings.
Song for soprano or tenor. This is a
rather short gay song with 4 stanzas.

Op. 1, No. 2, full score, p. 20 Allegro

This theme resembles the melody used in
La Damnation, op. 24, no. 16, for the
"King of Thule." Lines spoken by an
old peasant follow this no. 2.

No. 3. Preceded by Mephistopheles'
line, "De vains préparatifs ne sont point
nécessaires, nous voici rassemblés, commen-
cez." Title: "Concert of Sylphes"

This section greatly modified in op. 24.

Mercutio: "True, I talk of dreams which
are the children of an idle brain, begot
of nothing but vain fantasy; which is as
thin of substance as the air, and more
inconstant than the wind." Romeo. Sextet.
3/4. ♩ = 58. Adagio.
Instrumentation: 2 flutes, 2 oboes, 2
clarinets, 2 horns, 2 bassoons, harmonica,
harp, strings and glockenspiel.
Solo voices: soprano 1, soparano 2, contralto,
tenor, baritone, bass.
At side of score: charactère doux et volup-
teux.
Voices enter in recitative style: "Dis-
paraissez arceaux noirs et poudreux." The
recitative, quasi-arioso style, lasts for a
long time. The orchestration is generally
fairly light. A new section begins in 6/8
for voices and woodwinds with a rapid figure
in lower strings. Rhythm here is very interesting. (See illustration, page 97).
An interesting effect very near the close:
4 solo cellos are given the tones of the
D chord to be played with harmonics, truly
a weird and unusual sound. At the end,
Mephistopheles words are given: "He sleeps;

that is good, young spirits of the air,

you have faithfully enchanted him! It

is a concert for which I am in your debt."

No. 4. Brander raps on the table. "Attention! The latest song and repeat the refrain with me good and loud."
Écot de joyeux compagnons, story of a rat.
Hamlet: "How now? A rat? Dead, for a
ducat, dead."
D. 2/8. ♪ = 144. Allegro.
Instrumentation: 4 bassoons and strings.
The 3/4 part refrain is very brief. A
powerful song.
Siebel: "Comme ces plats coquins se re-
jouissent! C'est un beau chef d'oeuvre a
citer que l'empoisonnement d'un pauvre Rat!"

Brander's song is no. 7 in
op. 24.
D. 2/8. ♪ = 125. Allegro.
Instrumentation: flute, oboe,
4 bassoons, strings.
Substantially the same as
in op. 1.

No. 5. Frosch: "Give us a song."
Mephistopheles: "Just as you wish."
Siebel: "But something new." Meph.:
"We have just come from Spain, the be-
loved country of wine and song."
Song of Mephistopheles: "Story of a
flea." Hamlet: "Miching mallecho; it
means mischief."
At side of score: Raillerie amère.

Mephistopheles' song is no. 9
in op. 24.
F. 3/4. ♪ = 168. Allegretto
con fuoco.
Instrumentation: piccolo, 2
oboes, 2 clarinets, 4 horns,
2 trumpets, 4 bassoons,
timpani, strings.
The musical material is sub-

F. 3/4. ♩. = 72. <u>Allegro</u>.

Instrumentation: 2 clarinets, 2 horns, 2 bassoons, timpani, strings.

In the course of the number, he calls for ophicleide with the second bass. Siebel, at end: "And so be it with all fleas."

stantially the same. At the words: "<u>Mais ce qui fut bien pire</u>," he calls for small orchestra and strings <u>sul ponticello</u>.

No. 6. Marguerite: "A chill runs through my body . . . Ah! I am a woman most foolishly sad."

The "King of Thule," Gothic song.

Ophelia: "He is dead and gone; At his a grass-green turf, At his heels a stone."

G. 6/8. ♪. = 72. <u>Andante con moto</u>.

There is a note at the bottom that the singer should make no attempt to inflect the verses. Marguerite is preoccupied with her own thoughts.

Instrumentation: 2 clarinets, 4 horns, no violins, solo viola, violas, cellos and basses.

Marguerite's song is no. 16 in op. 24.

F. 6/8. ♪. = 56. <u>Andantino con moto</u>.

Instrumentation: 2 flutes, 2 clarinets, 4 horns and strings as follows: 1 viola solo, 6 violas, 2 first cellos, 2 second cellos, 4 basses with 4 strings, other basses.

There are eight measures of breathless introduction based on the viola theme; the score has the directions: <u>Elle chant en tressant ses cheveux</u>.

Except for minor changes, and the key change, the two are the same.

Op. 24, No. 16, vocal score, p. 191

Andantino con moto

Once in far Thule famed of old

There lived a monarch loy-al-heart-ed,

No. 7. Romance of Marguerita. Romeo:
"Ah me! sad hours seem long."
F. 3/4. ♩ = 58. <u>Lento</u>.
Instrumentation: English horn, **strings**.
At side of score: <u>Sentiment mélancholique</u>
<u>et passioné</u>.
Three part chorus is very effective.
Note at end of chorus: "Although in Goethe's
drama the soldiers chorus is far removed
from Marguerita's romance, I have nevertheless joined together these two pieces
thinking that the contrast resulting from
the juxtaposition of two such different
characters would augment the effect of the
one and the other."

No. 21.
F. 3/4. ♩ = 50. <u>Andante un</u>
<u>poco lento</u>.
Instrumentation: 2 flutes, 2
clarinets, English horn, third
and fourth horns, strings.
Identical until entrance of
soldiers' chorus. Treatment
of beginning more imaginative
where a wisp of the chorus is
first heard at a distance.
Words are different. The
chorus is quite brief in op.
24.
Some of the music is the same.

No. 8. Mephistopheles: "While the sky
full of stars scintillates, you are
going to hear a true masterpiece; I will
sing her a moral song, which will surely
seduce her."
At side of score: <u>Effronterie</u>.
Mephistopheles is accompanied only by
guitar.
E. 3/4. ♩. = 72. <u>Allegro</u>.
At the end, lines spoken by Valentine ad-

No. 19. Introductory text of
op. 1 here sung as recitative:
"Now we will sing for a certain
beauty a moral song which will
surely bring about her ruin."
B. 3/4. ♩. = 72. <u>Allegro</u>,
<u>mouvement de valse</u>.
Instrumentation: flute and
piccolo, 2 oboes, 2 clarinets,
4 bassoons, 4 horns, 3 trombones,

vancing: "Qui leurres tu la? Par le feu!   strings.

maudit preneur de Rats! . . . Au diable   Four-part male chorus of

d'abord l'instrument! Et au diable ensuite   will-o-the-wisps. Same melody

le chanteur."   is used. A marvelous piece.

Felix Mendelssohn (1809-1847) began his composition of Die erste

Walpurgisnacht, op. 60, in Rome and completed it in its first form in

Milan in 1831. On September 9, 1831, Goethe had written Mendelssohn re-

garding the symbolic nature of his poem and its depiction of the triumph

of indestructible enthusiasm over hatred. No doubt Mendelssohn tried to

capture this quality in his music. He revised the score in 1842. It was

performed in Leipzig in its revised form in 1843 with great success. The

score calls for soprano, alto, tenor, and bass solos, chorus and orchestra.

After a lengthy and mildly interesting overture, which has a curi-

ous recitative-like section in the middle of it, the work proper begins

with a solo and chorus.

Tenor (a Druid), vocal score, p. 2

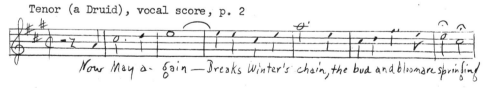

The writing is grateful for the soloists and there is good contrast

between the slow and more rapid sections. No. 6, "Come with torches

brightly flashing," is an effective and rousing chorus. The work closes

with an eight part chorus, "Thy light shall shine for ever."

Robert Schumann (1810-1856) composed his Scenes From Goethe's Faust,

for solo voices, chorus and orchestra over a period of nine years, from

1844 to 1853. The dates for the various sections are: 1844, a large part of the epilogue; 1847, the final chorus; 1848, "A noble ray of Spirit-life"; 1849, the garden scene, the cathedral scene, Margaret's prayer to the Mater Dolorosa, the scene of Ariel and Faust; 1850, the midnight scene and Faust's death; 1853, the overture.

The work was composed when Schumann's powers were waning. He describes his condition in a letter to Dr. E. Krueger.[1]

> Leipzig, October, 1844
> ...You may not perhaps know that I have had a serious nervous illness for the past three months, and was, in consequence, forbidden every exertion, mental or physical, by my doctor. I am now a little better, and can see some brightness in life, some return of hope and confidence. I think I did too much music. My music to Goethe's Faust occupied me very much lately, and in the end mind and body both gave way...During this time I have not been able to hear a note of music, for it was like a knife to my nerves...[2]

Five weeks later he wrote to Krueger from Dresden as follows:

> ...My Faust music still makes great demands on my time. What should you say to using the whole material for an oratorio? Is it not a bold and happy idea? But I must content myself with thinking of it for the present.[3]

In a letter to Franz Brendel,[4] Schumann comments on the paltry success his Faust music had when it was performed at Leipzig on the centenary of Goethe's birth, August 29, 1849.

> Dresden, September 18, 1849
> I am delighted with all your notices of Faust. I knew before the performance what the effect on the public would be, and was, therefore, not surprised; but I knew also that my music would appeal to individual

---

[1] Dr. Eduard Krueger (1805-1885), the co-rector at Emden, was a composer and critic. Later Schumann broke off his friendship with him because of his criticism of his opera Genoveva.

[2] The Letters of Robert Schumann, trans. Hannah Bryant (New York: E. P. Dutton & Co., 1907), p. 246f.

[3] Ibid., p. 247.

[4] Karl Franz Brendel (1811-1866), writer and critic, took over the post of editor of Schumann's Neue Zeitschrift fuer Musik, 1844.

hearers. I have never been satisfied with the final chorus as you heard it, and have written a second and far more satisfactory version. But as the parts of the new one were not written out, I chose the other. The second version will certainly be sung at the next perform- ance at Leipzig, when I hope to include some of the first part of Faust in the programme...[1]

In his setting Schumann picks only the sections from Goethe's <u>Faust</u> that especially appeal to him without regard for continuity. The over- ture begins with a strong dissonance. A b flat chord is imposed above an A pedal.

After the short, solemn introductory section a march-like theme is introduced marked <u>poco piu animato</u>, in which three-measure phrases are used. Overture, vocal score, p. 2

Following a quiet section marked <u>dolce</u> and a brief reference to the up- ward striving motive of the opening the key changes to D and a powerful march theme is introduced.

Overture, vocal score, p. 6

Part I, no. 1 consists of the garden scene with a duet between Faust and Margaret. It is treated in <u>arioso</u> style. In no. 2, Margaret's prayer to the <u>Mater Dolorosa</u>, we find a description of the setting: "On the ramparts, in a recess in the wall is a shrine of the <u>Mater Dolorosa</u>." There is also a short stage direction, "Margaret places fresh flowers

[1]Bryant, op. cit., p. 263.

in the vases." Perhaps Schumann had the staging of these scenes in mind. The prayer opens with a sobbing figure in the accompaniment. The song is made up of short phrases.

Orchestra, vocal score, p. 15   Margaret, vocal score, p. 15

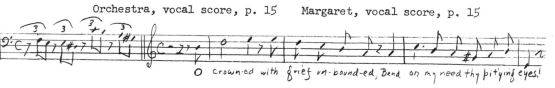

Near the end of the song the time signature is changed to 6/4. After a dramatic outburst punctuated by heavy chords on the words, "Help! save me ere in shame I die," there follows a subdued echo of the opening words that will be quite a hurdle for most sopranos.

Margaret, vocal score, p. 18

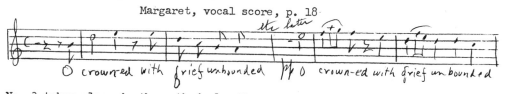

No. 3 takes place in the cathedral. Here again are found stage directions. After a short introduction that is based on an inversion of the opening material of the overture the evil spirit begins to torment Margaret. The Gregorian melody is not used for the "Dies Irae." The chorus is powerfully treated, now in unison, then in parts, then with the women and the men alternating.

Part II opens with Ariel's song from Goethe's Faust, Part II. Again stage directions are included. The chorus is divided into SSA and TTB. At first they alternate. Then they sing together. The opening music played by harp and strings sets the mood admirably. Faust's long mono-logue becomes tiresome because it is treated in recitative fashion to a large extent. In the next section, midnight, no. 5, the chattering of

the four women is followed by a rather dull conversation between Faust
and Care. Part II concludes with no. 6, Faust's death. Here the recitative, aria, choral and orchestral elements are effectively combined.

Part III is the most effective section of the work. It is a setting of the entire closing section of Goethe's Part II. Here Schumann
succeeds in suggesting the airy, incorporeal world of the heavenly crea-
tures. Solo sections alternate with a variety of choral settings.
There are two versions of the closing Chorus Mysticus. The first is
more concise and thus more effective.

Schumann's complete Faust music would probably not be well received by the public today. But surely sections are worthy of occasional
presentation.

Henry Litolff (1818-1891) composed his Scenen aus Goethes Faust,
op. 103, for soloists, chorus and orchestra about 1850. They were intended for concert, not stage, performance. There are four scenes: Faust in
his study, before the city gate, Margaret in church, and the prison scene.
I was only able to examine the first two. Faust is a speaking part. The
part of the evil spirit is to be sung by a baritone. The instrumentation
calls for full orchestra.

The introduction to the first scene is quite short. The restless
upward surging figure begins quietly in the cellos and basses.

Andante   Orchestra, full score, p. 1

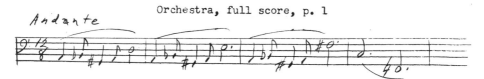

Then Faust begins declaiming, "O saehst du, voller Mondenschein." His declamation is usually free, but on page seven there is a note that the conductor must beat to each line of the declamation. After Faust's words:

> Umsonst, dass trocknes Sinnen hier
> Die heil'gen Zeichen dir erklaert:
> Ihr schwebt, ihr Geister, neben mir,
> Antwortet mir, wenn ihr mich hoert.

there follows a lengthy, wild orchestral passage which eventually quiets down to a charming lyrical theme.

Orchestra, full score, p. 35

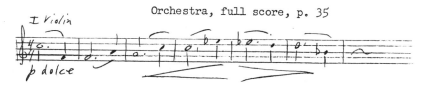

A little later on, the orchestra accompanies Faust's declamation, "Es weht ein Schauer vom Gewoelb'herab und fasst mich an! Ich fuehl's du schwebst um mich; erflehter Geist. Enthuelle dich!" The orchestra carries on violently and harshly till the spirit enters with a scream. What an entrance for a singer! There is repartee between the two, Faust speaking; the spirit singing. Faust repudiates the spirit. The thematic material is quite strong considering its accompanimental nature.

Mephistopheles sings, "Du gleichst dem Geist den du begreifst, nicht mir!" Faust replies speaking, "Nicht dir? wem denn? ich Ebenbild der Gottheit! und nicht einmal dir!" There is a long orchestral passage which uses material from the first section including the second musical example. Toward the end of the section Faust re-enters with "Nun komm herab, kristallne reine Schale! Hervor aus deinem alten Futterale an die ich viele Jahre nicht gedacht."

In the next part, after several introductory measures for harps, cellos and basses, the chorus of angels sings the Easter song which is augmented from one to three parts. This is lightly accompanied by winds. On the fourth repetition of "erstanden" there is an outburst from the full orchestra. The violins and violas are muted. This is followed by an expressive chorus for the contraltos. "Christ ist erstanden" is repeated. A chorus of youths follows.

Chorus of youths, full score, p. 122

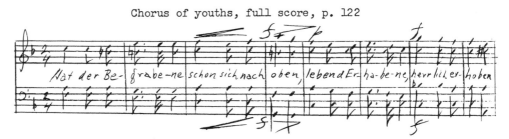

Later the angels' chorus, the women and the youths sing together. A very important climax develops. After a short interlude the cellos and basses play powerfully rasped out thirty-second note figures which subside to p when the upper strings enter with a variant of the second example. The movement is brought to an impressive conclusion by the choruses.

In the second scene, before the city gate, the instrumentation is the same except that one oboe and the cymbals drop out. Over a restrained open fifth in the strings the first theme is introduced in the clarinet and echoed by the English horn. This is expanded for quite some length: . Then the beggar enters with an unaccompanied solo followed by an imitation in the bassoon three measures later.

Beggar, full score, p. 21

This is succeeded by a rapid 2/4 dance. The soldiers' song follows.

Soldiers song, full score, p. 28

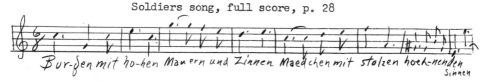

A brief, rapid passage in 2/4 leads to the next section, a four part

chorus of townspeople, "Der Schaefer putzte sich zum Tanz." A charming

melody is imposed over a droning fifth in the strings, clarinets and

bassoon. The women introduce the gay theme and they sustain it, when the

tenors enter, with a modified form. The scene ends with a repitition

of the quiet music of the opening somewhat altered.

Wilhelm Berger's (1861-1911) oratorio, Euphorion, op. 74, based

on Goethe's Part II, was composed about 1905. It is a richly romantic

work for soloist, chorus and orchestra. The soloist alternates with

the chorus throughout.

Chorus, vocal score, p. 35

The <u>Faust Cantata</u> by Hans Stieber (1886-), composed about 1930, requires a bass soloist, chorus, and orchestra. The instrumentation is for
full orchestra. There are six sections. In the Prooemion, the chorus begins with the words "<u>In Namen dessen, der sich selbst erschuf</u>" unisonally
and then breaks into parts. In the second section, <u>Muetter</u>, the basses
have an eerie beginning with their recitative on low D sharp. Later the
soloist and the remainder of the chorus enter. The basses conclude the
number alone. The <u>Erdgeist</u> is an impressive section. It is a canon and
fugue. It is introduced by a short dissonant passage. The soloist's
line is worth noting for its atonal quality.

Bass, full score, p. 12

Ihr In-stru-men-te frei-lich spottet mein mit Rad und Kae-men, walz und Buegel.

The fourth section, <u>An den Mond</u>, consists of a rather simple
chorus. The time signature changes freely, 4/4, 6/4, 3/2, 3/4, 3/2,
3/4, 6/4, etc.

No. 5, <u>Leben</u>, is a passacaglia. After quite a long orchestral
passage the altos enter: "<u>Entbehren sollst entbehren. Das ist der
ewige Gesang.</u>"

No. 6, <u>Schaffer</u>, begins with the basses alone. Later chorus and
soloist alternate. The rhythm is again very free. This is a very interesting composition.

CHAPTER IX

THE GREAT FAUST SYMPHONIES

Berlioz acquainted Franz Liszt (1811-1886) with Goethe's _Faust_ when
they met in December, 1830. The subject appealed to Liszt right away.
Although he was further stimulated by the performance of Berlioz' _Damna-_
tion in 1846, he had misgivings about undertaking a work on the subject
himself. Shortly before starting work on the symphony he wrote Princess
Sayn-Wittgenstein, "Anything to do with Goethe is dangerous for me to
handle."[1] It took him some time to absorb the real significance of
Faust in such a way as to germinate his creative sources so that, in
producing his great _Faust Symphony_,[2] he would at the same time, in a
sense, produce a musical portrait of himself. For surely no one needs
convincing that this titan, this musical blood-relative of Paganini, was
a nineteenth century Faust. Yes, he was Mephistopheles too. And his
affairs of the heart certainly prepared him au plus haut point for the
melting loveliness of his symphonic Gretchen. He wrote the symphony,
one of his very best works, in the short space of two months (August -

---

[1]Quoted in: Humphrey Searle, _The Music of Liszt_ (London: Williams
& Norgate, Ltd., 1954), p. 76.

[2]On Monday, December 12, 1949 I had the thrill of conducting this
work with the St. John's University Symphony Orchestra. What a struggle
it was to bring the work to a fairly satisfactory performance pitch! To
give the final electric spark to set off the musical conflagration, we
imported for the first time several members of the Minneapolis Symphony
Orchestra. The choral ending was used. The program commemorated the
Goethe bicentennial. Selections from Gounod's _Faust_ were also performed.

146

October, 1854). In a letter to Bernhard Cossman, dated Weimar, September 8, 1854, he says, "On your return I shall pretty nearly have finished my Faust Symphony, at which I am working like being possessed."[1]

The symphony has three movements: Faust, Gretchen, Mephistopheles. The work resembles the sonata in that the first and third movements are related. The first movement has a long exposition, a brief development, a rather short recapitulation, and a coda. There are five main themes, each expressing a different facet of Faust's character. The opening measures comprise a precis of the entire work with the surety and unsureness of the string opening followed by the gentle, sorrowful moan of the oboe.

Faust, theme 1, full score, p. 3   Theme 2, full score, p. 3

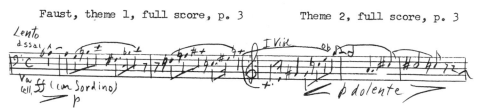

The first theme has great importance as a unifying element in the whole structure. After the short introduction the allegro begins with a hesitant, impetuous upward rushing figure in the violins. Later a martial theme is hammered out in the brass.

The utterly beautiful Gretchen movement begins with some sweet and tentative murmurings in the flutes and clarinets. The main theme is finally introduced in the oboe.

---

[1]La Mara (ed.), Letters of Franz Liszt, trans. Constance Bache (London: H. Grevel & Co., 1894), I, p. 207.

Gretchen, full score, p. 138

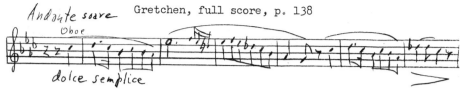

The three part song form is used. There is a little interlude depicting
the scene where Gretchen plucks the petals of a flower, "He loves me..."

For the _finale_ Liszt conceived the brilliant idea of using the
Faust themes but all twisted and turned in caricature fashion. They suggest Mephistopheles, the spirit of negation, who can only destroy. It
is surprising to find upon examining the score what a scrappy appearance
the music makes on the page. This is probably some of the most piquantly
annoying and unpleasant music ever written.

Mephistopheles, full score, p. 183

Liszt originally planned to end the work with the disappearance of
Mephistopheles and a suggestion of the Gretchen and Faust themes. Three
years later he added the solemn tones of the _Chorus Mysticus_. This deeply felt music makes a splendid summation for one of the finest symphonies
ever written. The chorus begins indistinctly on low C. The tenor solo
that follows has some lovely moments. What a pity that this work is so
neglected!

Liszt was inspired by Lenau's _Faust_ to write two compositions: _Der_
naechtliche Zug (The Nocturnal Procession) and the _Tanz im Dorfschenke_
(The Dance in the Village Inn). The former is almost never heard and the

latter is very well known in either its orchestral or pianistic dress as the Mephisto Waltz. "The Nocturnal Procession" interprets a Faustian episode not found in Goethe's poem. The nightingales are singing in the warm spring night. Faust lets his horse saunter along quietly. A religious procession passes singing the Pange Lingua. An interesting practice in this number is the insertion of a quatrain every so often between the various sections. The piece rises to a tremendous climax. The Mephisto Waltz is one of the most brilliant pieces in the repertoire. Faust and Mephistopheles enter the inn in search of amusement. Mephistopheles seizes a violin and after some pretentious tuning sets the crowd to some wild dancing. The lilting offbeat effect of the melody in the middle section is very charming.

Liszt wrote another Mephisto Waltz for orchestra in 1880-1881. Searle says of this work:

> It is a most powerful and effective piece, with a characteristic ending; after building up a big climax in E flat, the main key throughout most of the waltz, the music suddenly falls on to the tritone B natural F, and so ends the piece in an entirely unexpected and startling manner.[1]

Gustav Mahler (1860-1911) was very fond of Goethe's Faust and carried a battered copy around with him protruding from his coat pocket.

His monumental Symphony of the Thousand, no. 8, for seven soloists, double chorus of mixed voices, children's chorus, organ and a tremendous orchestra was composed 1906-1907. It was given its first performance in Munich September 13, 1910 under the composer's direction. The first part is based on the Latin hymn "Veni, Creator Spiritus" and

---

[1]Searle, op. cit., p. 117.

Mahler, Symphony of the Thousand, no. 8, Choruš mysticus, p. 215.

150

the second part is based on the closing scene of Goethe's *Faust*, Part II. Only the second scene will be considered.

In a letter from Amsterdam presumably to Alma Mahler, his wife, he comments on the great conductor Mengelberg's favorable reaction to his symphony. He expresses surprise that perhaps his most important work would be the most easily understood.

In her earlier book on Mahler, Alma Mahler describes in her rather perfervid manner the reception of the work in Munich, September 12, 1910.

> The whole of Munich as well as all who had come there for the oc-
> casion were wrought up to the highest pitch of suspense. The dress-
> rehearsal provoked rapturous enthusiasm, but it was nothing to the
> performance itself. The whole audience rose to their feet as soon
> as Mahler took his place at the conductors desk; and the breathless
> silence which followed was the most impressive homage an artist could
> be paid...
> And then Mahler, god or demon, turned those tremendous volumes of
> sound into fountains of light. The experience was indescribable.
> Indescribable too the demonstration which followed. The whole audi-
> ence surged toward the platform...[1]

The Faustian part of the <u>Symphony of the Thousand</u> begins with a masterstroke, a delicate clash of the cymbals plus an accented entrance of the first violins <u>tremolando</u> followed by a rapid <u>diminuendo</u>. A mysterious, germinal theme follows in the cellos and basses played <u>pizzicato</u>. This is immediately answered by a beautiful phrase played by the clarinet.

First and second themes, piano score, p. 104

The woodwind theme will be a unifying element throughout the movement.

---

[1]Alma Mahler, <u>Gustav Mahler</u>, trans. Basil Creighton (London: John Murray, 1946), p. 151.

The alternating three part choruses of male voices enter very quietly
on the words "Waldung, sie schwankt heran." The song of the Pater
ecstaticus (six measures after /327) is based on the woodwind motive
and passages of the Chorus Mysticus.

Pater ecstaticus, piano score, p. 115

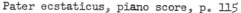

At the entrance of the Pater profundus /39/ (tiefe Region) there is an
interesting mark connecting the tenth. Perhaps Mahler wishes portamento
to be employed.

Pater profundus, piano score, p. 117

At the point /56/ where the choir of angels enters with the unisonal
chorus, "Geretet ist das edle Glied der Geisterwelt vom Boesen," the key
changes to B after a rich orchestral interlude built on the woodwind
theme. The tempo becomes allegro deciso.

There follows a lengthy passage of trilling and twittering, those
bird-like sounds so dear to Mahler's heart. When the young angels sing
their "Jene Rosen aus den Haenden" the key changes to E flat after having been briefly in G. There is an interesting pedal point on D at /75/.

Orchestra, piano score, p. 130

At /81/ there is a beautiful chorus for SSAA. The key changes to G and

the Doctor Marianus enters at /84/. Mahler directs that he shall not

obtrude himself upon the choir. When the Doctor Marianus addresses the

Queen of the Heavens there is a modulation to E /89/.

Doctor Marianus, piano score, p. 143

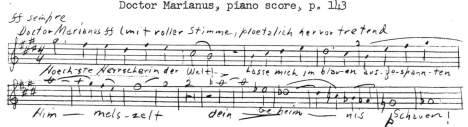

The singer is called upon to assert himself suddenly. Mahler warns in

a footnote, "Darf vorher unter keinen Umstaenden auffallen!" At /106/

the key returns to E at the descent of the Mater Gloriosa. The harmonium

is introduced here. Five measures after /114/. Margaret, in the guise

of Una Poentitentium, has begun to sing her plea. She is joined by a

choir of twenty penitents. At /120/ when Mary Magdelene refers to her

hair drying the holy limbs the key changes to E flat. The song of the

Mulier Samaritana at /121/ is in choral style. The Chorus Mysticus is

a magnificent piece of choral writing. The final "hinan" of the chorus

is followed by a powerful orchestral coda.

The movement is composed in Mahler's usual dark style with rich

chromatic harmonies that obscure the notion of a clear-cut tonality much

of the time. The music is deeply felt and highly colored. The mood of

the text is admirably captured. A tremendous variety of dynamics is

called for.

In his book on Mahler, Richard Specht also speaks of the tremendous

effect this work has on audiences.

...Als die 'Achte' in Muenchen zum erstenmal erklang--und auch jedesmal nachher--hat sie derart in siedenden Taumel, in ungemessene Trunkenheit der Begeisterung gerissen, wie kein anderes Mahlersches Werk und auch wie wenig andere zuvor. Wer Mahler dort oben stehen sah, wohl eine halbe Stunde lang umdraengt von lachenden und weinenden Maennern und Frauen, die mit traenenueberstroemten Wangen ihm ihren Dank entgegenriefen, und sah, wie er mit frohem Laecheln, mit einem Leuchten auf dem blassen Antlitz und mit einem tief in sich hinein- und zurueckschauenden Blick auf die tuecherwehenden stammelnden, haendeklatschenden Menschen unten im Saal hinabsah, der musste das Gehuehl haben, ihn auf dem Hohepunkt seiner Existenz und in der Stunde seines hoechsten Triumphes zu sehen.[1]

There is no question that participation in this great work whether as auditor or performer would be a shattering emotional experience. Mahler has somehow succeeded in bringing to full realization the words of an unknown poet on a card given me by my old music teacher, Sister Agnesia, many years ago, "Music is the only art of heaven given to earth and the only art of earth we take to heaven."

---

[1]Richard Specht, Gustav Mahler (Berlin: Schuster & Loeffler, 1922), p. 267.

CHAPTER X

FAUST IN INSTRUMENTAL AND VOCAL MUSIC

It was during a miserable winter spent in Paris 1839-1840 when
Richard Wagner (1813-1883) was forced to write cheap dance tunes and make
all sorts of arrangements of other composers music that he composed the
"Faust Overture." It was originally intended as the first movement of
a Faust symphony. He was working on the opera The Flying Dutchman at
the time, and some of its dark and mysterious character has spilled over
into the overture. The overture was performed in Dresden in 1844 but
was not successful. In 1854 when Wagner heard that Liszt was busy on
his Faust Symphony, he decided to rework his overture. The work in
general has a tautness of texture that is quite unusual for Wagner.

Many shorter orchestral works have been inspired by the Faust
theme. Karl Schulz wrote an overture for Klingemann's Faust. Emilie
Mayer's (1821-1883) overture on this theme is an ambitious composition.
Edmond von Mihalovich's (1842-1929) Faust Phantasie is a heavily or-
chestrated but well-written work. In his Mephisto Triumphiert Erwin
Nyiregyhazi has written a rather bombastic work. It was composed in
1919. Occasionally he employs chord clusters, but for the most part
the harmony is conventional. The thematic material is undistinguished.
An interesting work is the "Oberturo para el Fausto criollo" by the
Argentinian composer, Alberto Finastera (1916-), composed in 1943. A
peasant attends a performance of Gounod's Faust and tells his friends

Manuscript of the first version of Wagner's "Eine Faust Ouvertuere," measures 61ff.

about it when he returns home. Some tunes from Gounod's work are used.

The Faust story has inspired many ballet scores. One of the most recent is Abraxas by Werner Egk (1910-), which is made up of five scenes from Faust. There was a scandal at the first performance in 1947.

A great deal of stage music has been written for performances of various versions of the Faust drama. There have been many settings for Goethe's play such as the effective one by Prince Radziwill (1775-1833) written in 1819, the one by Henry Pierson (1816-1873) for the second part and the one by Hermann Simon (1886-1943) for the first part written about 1940. As can be seen by an examination of the list at the end of the dissertation, a great many composers have tried their hand at the task. In general they tend to stay with the requirements that Goethe has indicated in his play. One of the longest and most carefully worked out settings is that by Felix Weingartner.

There have been many parodies and burlesques on the Faust theme. Several of them are parodies of Gounod's opera like those of Hervé and Salingré. Most of them are not worthy of serious consideration.

The number of songs with the "King of Thule" or the exploits of the rat or the flea as their theme are legion. Most of the famous composers and many but little known have set texts from Goethe's Faust. Famous settings have been written by Beethoven and Schubert. At the Library of Congress, I examined the manuscript of the Erdgeist scene which Edward MacDowell (1861-1908) began but did not complete.

A very interesting contemporary work is <u>Mephisto's Cantata</u> for bass
and string quartet by Jean Françaix (1912-).

Thus we see that there has been a truly amazing number of compositions of every conceivable variety inspired by some phase of the <u>Faust</u>
story. Perhaps one reason why it has remained so popular is that all
men see themselves in Faust. Faust, and especially the Faust of Goethe,
will undoubtedly continue to be a creative force in the arts for a long
time to come.

APPENDIX I

The widely-renowned puppet play: The Tragical History of Doctor Faustus

DOCTOR FAUSTUS

Dramatis Personae in Order of Appearance

JOHANNES FAUSTUS: Far-famed Doctor of Theology, Philosophy. Magnifico of the University of Wittenberg, later traveling Sorcerer and young cavalier
Wagner: Famulus to Dr. Faustus
KASPER: Traveling Rogue, later Servant to Dr. Faustus, still later Night Watchman of Wittenberg
Porcusculus:
Auerhahn: Devils of the lowest order
Arraxas:
Alcadazur: A gigantic Demon, Lucifer's messenger
Phryne: Ghost of a famous Courtesan
Thrax: One of the Lemures attached to Phryne
Mephistopheles: Devil of the Highest Order
Belisario: Captain of the Guard at the Court of Parma
Niccolo: Herald with Trumpet
Hectore: Duke of Parma
Eleonora: His Wife, Duchess of Parma
Il Biondo: Famed Rhenish Singer at the Court of Parma
Liese: An ubiguitous Herbalist and Beggar Woman (who should have been inserted after Wagner)
Helen of Troy: Ghost of the famous Queen Sir Paris took to Dardania
Vitzliputzli: Devil of the lowest order
Buhur: A Hellish Dragon
Fredegonde: Witch, passing by, she molests and frightens Kasper
Fritz: Spirit of the deceased Night Watchman of Wittenberg
Pui: Pui and Hui (should be after Mephistopheles), menial
Hui: servants of Mephistopheles
Wumburz: Gehennor's Helpers
Cinghiale: more dreadful than Wumburz
Gehennor: A dreadful Monster from the banks of the River Styx, sent to kill Faustum and to carry him to Lucifer

SCENES

I and II Fausti Study - III Ruins in the Vicinity of Wittenberg - IV Graveyard near Wittenberg - V Fausti Study - VI A Terrace of the Ducal Palace in Parma - VII A Room in the Palace - VIII Street near the Piazza del Duomo in Parma - IX A Room in the Palace - X In the Netherworld, in front of Helen's Palace - XI Fausti Study - XII Fausti Study with Kasper's bed in it - XIII Fausti Study - XIV Street in front of Fausti House

The following Horrifying and Edifying Scenes will be shown:

1. Faustus concocting poison in his alchemistic retorts 2. The horrible Book "Clavis Astartae de Arte Magica" will be carried on the Stage by Wagner 3. The Conjuring up of Devils from a Magic Circle 4. Mephistopheles will appear from and dive into Hell on the open Stage. Item: He draws blood from Fausti Hand. Item: Bags of Gold are brought to him by the Devils Pui and Hui. Item: He transports Faustum through the Air to Parma 5. A most tender Love Scene which will particularly please the young Demoiselles 6. A vicious and prolonged Sword Fight which will particularly please the young Cavaliers. 7. A precious Egyptian Mummy Case will be on exhibition on the Stage. 8. Hell Fire will burst out of the Ground 9. Gehennor will kill Faustum on the open Stage and cast him into it.

THE AUDIENCE IS REQUESTED NOT TO INSULT MEPHISTOPHELES OR TO TRY IN ANY WAY TO WARN FAUSTUM OF THE CONSEQUENCES OF HIS TRAFFICKING WITH DEVILS.

BABES IN ARMS AND UNACCOMPANIED DEMOISELLES CANNOT BE ADMITTED, THERE BEING TOO MUCH EVIL ON THE STAGE. ITEM: SPECTATORS ARE REQUESTED NOT TO SUP ON THE THEATRE PREMISES.

WE THANK THE MAGISTRATES FOR THE PERMISSION TO PERFORM IN THIS ILLUSTRIOUS TOWN.

The Director[1]

---

[1]I am grateful to Dr. Meno Spann for permission to reproduce the handbill circulated at his delightful puppet show presented in 1959.

BIBLIOGRAPHY

Books and Articles

Aber, Adolf. "Faust-Musik bis zu Goethes Tod," Die Musik-welt (Hamburg), Vol. VI, No. 4.

Abert, Hermann. Goethe und die Musik. Stuttgart: Engelhorns Nachfolge, 1922.

Abraham, Gerald (ed.). Schumann: A Symposium. London: Oxford University Press, 1952.

Adams, W. H. D. Witch, Warlock and Magician. London: Chatto, 1889.

Albini, Eugenia. "Goethe e la musica," Revista Musicale Italiana, Vol. XXXVI (1932).

Alpenburg. "Goethe und die Musik," Deutsche Musik-zeitung (Cologne), Vol. XXXIII, No. 10.

Ammon, Hermann. Daemon Faust. Berlin and Bonn: Ferd. Duemmlers Verlag, 1932.

Appia, Adolphe. Goethes Faust Erster Teil als Dichtung Dargestellt. Emsdetten: H. & J. Lechte, 1929.
     Contains simple designs for stage settings.

Atkins, Stuart. "The Evaluation of Romanticism in Goethe's Faust," Journal of English and Germanic Philology, LIV, 9-38.

Atkins, Stuart. "Goethe, Aristophanes, and the Classical Walpurgis-night," Comparative Literature, VI, 64-78.

Atkins, Stuart. "Goethe, Calderon, and Faust: Der Tragoedie zweiter Teil," Germanic Review, XXVIII, 83-98.

Atkins, Stuart. Goethe's Faust--A Literary Analysis. Cambridge: Cambridge University Press, 1958.

Atkins, Stuart. Irony and Ambiguity in the Final Scene of Goethe's Faust. See Merkel, G. F. (ed.).

Atkins, Stuart. "The Mothers, the Phorcides and the Cabiri in Goethe's Faust," Monatshefte, LXV, 289-96.

Atkins, Stuart. "The Prologues to Goethe's Faust, and the Question of Unity: A Partial Reply," Modern Language Review, XLVIII, 193-94.

Atkins, Stuart. "A Reconsideration of Some Misunderstood Passages in the "Gretchen Tragedy" of Goethe's Faust," Modern Language Review, XLVIII, 421-34.

Atkins, Stuart. "A Reconsideration of Some Unappreciated Aspects of the Prologues and Early Scenes in Goethe's Faust," Modern Language Review, XLVII, 362-73.

Atkins, Stuart. "Some Lexicographical Notes on Goethe's Faust," Modern Language Quarterly, XIV, 82-97.

Bacher, Otto. Die Geschichte der Frankfurter Oper im 18. Jahrhundert. Frankfurt: Englert & Schlosser, 1926.

Baer, Der. Jahrbuch von Breitkopf und Haertel auf das Jahr 1925. Den Manen Goethes gewidmet. Leipzig: Breitkopf & Haertel, 1925.

Baetz, Ruediger. Schauspielmusiken zu Goethes Faust. Dissertation. Leipzig: University of Leipzig, 1924.

Baeumer, Gertrude. Die drei goettlichen Komoedien des Abendlandes: Wolframs Parsifal, Dantes Divina Commedia, Goethes Faust. Muenster: Regensburg, 1949.

Bagge, Selmar. "Robert Schumann und seine Faust-Scenen," Waldersee, Sammlung musikalischer Vortraege (Leipzig), I (1879), 121-40.

Ballo, Ferdinando. Arrigo Boito. Torino: Arione, 1938.

Bangs, John K. Mephistopheles, a Profanation. New York: DeWitt, 1899.

Barrett, F. The Magus or Celestial Intelligencer. London: Lackington, 1801.

Bartels, Adolf. Chronik des Weimarischen Hoftheaters 1817-1907. Weimar: H. Boehlau's Nachfolge, 1908.

Bartscherer, Agnes. Paracelsus, Paracelsisten und Goethes Faust. Dortmund: F. W. Ruhfus, 1911.

Barzun, Jacques. Berlioz and the Romantic Century. 2 vols. Boston: Little, Brown & Co., 1950.

Baumgart, Herrmann. Goethes Faust als einheitliche Dichtung erlaeutert. Koenigsberg: W. Koch, 1893.

Belmonte, C. "Goethe und Beethoven," Wiener Fremdenblatt, No. 237 (1899).

Berlioz, Hector. Memoires. Paris: 1870. Translated by R. and E.
Holmes. Annotated and translation revised by Ernest Newman. New
York: A. A. Knopf, 1932.

Berlioz, Hector. Les Soirées de l'orchestre. Paris: M. Lévy, 1871.
Translated as: Evenings in the Orchestra. New York: A. A.
Knopf, 1929.

Beutler, Ernst. Faust und Urfaust. Bremen: C. Schuenemann, 195-.

Beutler, Ernst. "Der zweite Teil von Goethes Faust," Goethe-Kalender,
XXX (1937), 68-108.

Bevan, F. "Design for Faust," Theatre Arts, XXXIII (July, 1949), 51ff.

Beyerlein, F. A. "Goethe als Operntextdichter," Die Musik-welt (Hamburg),
Vol. VII, No. 10.

Bezold, Karl. "Goethe und die Oper," Baden-Badener Buehnenblatt, Vol.
VIII, No. 64.

Bianquis, Geneviève. Faust à travers quatre Siècles. Paris: Librairie, E. Droz, 1935.

Bickermann, Joseph. Don Quijote y Fausto. Barcelona: Aratuce, 1932.

Bielschowsky, Albert. Goethe: Sein Leben und seine Werke. Munich:
C. H. Beck, 1919.

Biggs, Charles. The Clementine Homilies. Oxford: Studia Biblica, Oxford University Press, 1890.

Birnbaum, M. "Briefwechsel zwischen Goethe und Zelter," Goethe Jahrbuch
(Frankfurt), No. 27, p. 245.

Blaschke, J. "Goethes musikalisches Leben," Musikalisches Wochenblatt
(Leipzig), No. 1 (1904), p. 40.

Blechschmidt, K. Goethe in seinen Beziehungen zur Oper. Dissertation.
Frankfurt: University of Frankfurt, 1937.

Blessinger, K. "Goethes musikalische Persoenlichkeit," Die Ernte (Hannover), No. 9 (1932).

Blume, Friedrich. Goethe und die Musik. Kassel: Baerenreiter Verlag,
1949.

Bock, Alfred. "Goethe als Musiker," Frankfurter Zeitung, Abendblatt No.
183 (April 7, 1895).

Bock, Alfred. "Goethe und Fuerst Radziwill," Allgemeine Zeitung, No.
252, supplement (1894).

Bock, W. von. Goethe in seinem Verhaeltniss zur Musik. Berlin: Schneider & Co., 1871.

Bode, Wilhelm. Goethes Gedanken. Berlin: E. S. Mittler & Sohn, 1907.

Bode, Wilhelm. Goethes Schauspieler und Musiker. Berlin: E. S. Mittler & Sohn, 1912.

Bode, Wilhelm (ed.). Stunden mit Goethe. 10 vols. Berlin: E. S. Mittler & Sohn, 1905-1921.
    Goethe als Theaterdirektor. Von Karl Eberwein. VIII, 31-44.
    Die Musik zum Goetheschen Faust. Von Karl Eberwein. VIII, 45-55.

Bode, Wilhelm. Die Tonkunst in Goethes Leben. 2 vols. Berlin: E. S. Mittler & Sohn, 1912.

Boehm, Wilhelm. Faust der Nichtfaustische. Halle: M. Niemeyer, 1933.

Boetscher, Elmar. Goethes Singspiels. Dissertation. Marburg: University of Marburg, 1912.

Bois, Jules. Le Satanisme et la Magie. Paris: Chailley, 1895.

Bolt, K. F. "Goethe inspiriert die Musiker," Die Tonkunst, Vol. XXXVI, No. 12.

Borgese, Giuseppe A. Saggio sul "Faust". Milan: Fratelli Treves, 1934.

Boschot, Adolphe. "A propos du centenaire de La Damnation de Faust," Revue Musicale, XXII (February-March, 1946), 11-14.

Boschot, Adolphe. Le Faust de Berlioz. Vol. I: Collection des grandes oeuvres musicales. Paris: René Dumasnil, 1927.

Boschot, Adolphe. Une Vie romantique; Hector Berlioz. Paris: Librarie de France, 1927.

Boutarel, Amédée. "Une lettre de Berlioz à Goethe," Menestrel, LXIX (1903), 52f., 59f.

Boutarel, Amédée. La vraie Marguerite et l'interprétation musicale de l'âme féminine, d'apres le "Faust" de Goethe. Paris: Heugel & Cie., 1900.

Boutet, Frédéric. Mages Noirs, Messes Noires, No. 51. Paris: Les Oeuvres Libres, 1925.

Boyesen, Hjalmar H. Goethe and Schiller: Their Lives and Works. New York: Charles Scribner's Sons, 1879.
    A commentary on Goethe's Faust is included.

Brandes, Georg. Goethe. 4th ed. Berlin: E. Reiss, 1922.

Bricht, Balduin. "Goethe und die Musik," Volkszeitung (Vienna), March 17, 1932.

Bricht, Balduin. "Musikalisches von der Goethe-Ausstellung," Volkszeitung (Vienna), April 30, 1932.

Brock, Klaus. Goethes Faust auf dem Weimarer Theater. Dissertation. Jena: Jena University, 1934.

Brooke, C. F. Tucker (ed.). The Works of Christopher Marlowe. Oxford: Clarendon Press, 1929.

Brown, Rev. J. Wood. An Inquiry Into the Life and Legend of Michael Scot. London: D. Douglas, 1897.

Bruford, Walter H. Theatre, Drama, and Audience in Goethe's Germany, pp. 343-63. London: Routledge & Paul, 1950.

Brukner, Fritz and Hadamowsky, Franz (eds.). Die Wiener Faust-dichtungen von Stranitzky bis zu Goethes Tod. Vienna: Wallishausser, 1935.

Buchwald, Reinhard. Fuehrer durch Goethes Faustdichtung. Stuttgart: Kroener, 1949.

Buelow, Hans von. Briefwechsel mit Liszt. Collected and edited by LaMara. Leipzig: Breitkopf & Haertel, 1898.

Buelow, Paul. "Ein Faustjubilaeum aus dem Schaffenskreise R. Wagners," Zeitschrift fuer Musik, XCIX, 324f.

Buelow, Paul. "Hans Wildermanns "Faust-Wirklichkeiten"," Zeitschrift fuer Musik, Vol. XCIX, No. 3.

Buelow, Paul. "Musik und Musiker um Goethe," Boersenblatt fuer den deutschen Buchhandel (May 19, 1932).

Buelow, Paul. "Musikalische Schicksalstage im Leben Goethes," Deutsche Oberschule (Frankfurt), VI (1932-1933), 35.

Burdach, Konrad. "Faust und die Sorge," Deutsche Vierteljahrsschrift fuer Literaturwissenschaft und Geistesgeschichte, Vol. I (1932).

Burdach, Konrad. Goethe und sein Zeitalter. Vol. II: Vorspiel. (Deutsche Vierteljahrsschriften, Buchreihe Vol. 3a). Halle/Saale: 1926.

Burdach, Konrad. "Das religioese Problem in Goethes Faust," Euphorion, XXXIII (1932), 3-83.

Burkhardt, C. A. H. Das Repertoire des Weimarischen Theaters unter Goethes Leitung 1791-1817 Theater-geschichtliche Forschungen, Vol. I. Hamburg und Leipzig: Berthold Litzmann, 1891.

Busoni, Ferruccio. "Nota bio-bibliografica su Ferruccio Busoni," Rassegna Musicale, XIII (1940), 82-8.

Busoni, Ferruccio. Ueber die Moeglichkeiten der Oper und ueber die Partitur des Doktor Faust. Leipzig: Breitkopf & Haertel, 1926.

Butler, Eliza M. Vol. I: The Myth of the Magus. Vol. II: Ritual Magic. Vol. III: The Fortunes of Faust. Cambridge: University Press, 1948, 1949, 1952.

Calderon, de la Barca, Pedro. El Magico Prodigioso. Madrid: Castilla, 1948.

Castle, E. "Goethe und Schiller als Vorlaeufer R. Wagners," Chronik der Wiener Goethe-Vereins, XXXVIII, 27-35.

Cauzons, Th. de. La Magie et la Sorcellerie en France. 4 vols. Paris: Dorbon-aine, 1910-1911?

Caxton, William. The Golden Legend or Lives of the Saints as Englished by William Caxton. Vol. IV, pp. 14-20; Vol. VI, pp. 254-64. London: Longmans, 1900.

Chantavoine, Jean. Musiciens et poètes: Goethe Musicien. Paris: F. Alcan, 1912.

Clément, Félix and Larousse, Pièrre. Dictionnaire des opéras. Paris: Administration du grand dictionnaire universel, 1905.

Coeuroy, A. "Climat musical de Goethe," La Revue Musicale, Vol. XIII, No. 125.

Coleridge, A. D. (trans.). Goethe's Letters to Zelter, with Extracts of Those of Zelter to Goethe. Selected and Annotated. London: George Bell & Sons, 1887.

Comparetti, D. Vergil in the Middle Ages. Translated by Benecke. London: Sonnenschein, 1908.

Constant, A. L. [Levi, Eliphas]. History of Magic. Translated by A. E. Waite. London: W. Rider, & Son, 1922.

Corte, Andrea (Della). La vita musicale di Goethe. Torino: G. B. Paravia, 1932.

Crass, E. Goethes Beziehungen zur Tonkunst und den Tonkuenstlern seiner Zeit. Sechs Studienabende der Ortsgruppe Leipzig der Goethe-Gesellschaft. Leipzig: Goethe Ges., 1944.

Crawford, F. Marion. Zoroaster. London: Macmillan & Co., 1885.

Creizenach, Wilhelm. Die Buehnengeschichte des Goetheschen Faust. Frankfurt: Lit. Anst., 1881.

Creizenach, Wilhelm. Versuch einer Geschichte des Volksschauspiels vom Doctor Faust. Halle: M. Niemeyer, 1878.

Daur, Albert. Faust und der Teufel. A Commentary on Goethe's Faust. Heidelberg: Carl Winter, 1950.

Davies, J. "The Earliest Musical Setting to Goethe's Faust," The Journal of English and Germanic Philology (Illinois, Leipzig), XXV (1926), 517-30.

Dédéyan, Charles. Le thème de Faust dans la litterature européene. Paris: Lettres modernes, 1954.

Delehaye, S.J., Hippolyte. Analecta Bollandiana, Vol. XXXIX. Brussels: Société des bollandistes, 1921.

Dent, Edward J. "Busoni's Doctor Faust," Music & Letters, VII (1926), 196-208.

Dent, Edward J. Ferruccio Busoni: A Biography. London: Oxford University Press, 1933.

Dhalla, Maneckji N. History of Zoroastrianism. New York: Oxford University Press, 1938.

Dingelstedt, Franz. Eine Faust-Trilogie. Dramaturgische Studie. Berlin: Paetel, 1876.

Dorn, Otto. "Goethe in seinem Verhaeltnis zur Musik und zu Musikern," Theater- und Musikzeitung (Koenigsberg), Vol. I, No. 1 (1904).

Dubitzky, Fr. "Schillers und Goethes Werke als Opern," Buehne und Welt, X, Nos. 20-21 (1908), 901-909.

Eberwein, Karl. "Erinnerungen eines Weimarischen Musikers," Weimarer Sonntagsblatt (July 6, 13, 20, 1856), pp. 225-48.

Eberwein, Karl. "Die Musik zum Goetheschen Faust," Europa, Chronik der Gebildeten Welt, No. 43 (1853), p. 337ff.

Edwards, Henry Sutherland. The Lyrical Drama. 2 vols. London: W. H. Allen & Co., 1881.

Ehrenhaus, Martin. "Die Operndichtung der deutschen Romantik; ein Beitrag zur Geschichte der Deutschen Oper," Breslauer Beitraege zur Literaturgeschichte (Breslau), New Series 19, Heft 29 (1911).

Eitner, R. "K. F. Zelter," Allgemeine deutsche Biographie, XLV, 46-52.

Elliot, J. H. Berlioz. New York: Farrar & Strauss, 1949.

Engel, Karl D. L. Das Volksschauspiel Doktor Johann Faust. Vol. I: Deutsche Puppenkomoedien. Oldenburg: Schulzesche Bb, 1876.

Engel, Karl D. L. Zusammenstellung der Faust-Schriften vom 16. Jahrhundert bis Mitte 1884. Oldenburg: A. Schwartz, 1885.

English Faust Book. British Museum text reprinted in 1900. Fascicle 24 in Recueil de Travaux, University of Ghent.

Enrst, Alfred. L'Oeuvre dramatique de Berlioz. Paris: Levy, 1884.

Ettinger, Max. "Goethes Beziehungen zur Musik," Das Prisma, II, No. 17, 177-81.

Fairley, Barker. A Study of Goethe. Oxford: Clarendon Press, 1947.

Fiedler, H. G. Textual Studies of Goethe's Faust. Oxford: Oxford University Press, 1948.

Fischer, Kuro. Goethes Faust. 2 vols. Stuttgart: J. G. Cotta Nachfolge, 1893.

Floch, Siegfried. Goethe und die Musik. Vienna: Verlag der Wochenschrift fuer Kunst und Musik, 1904.

Floessner, Franz. Goethes Beziehungen zur Musik und zu den Musikern seiner Zeit. Das Goethe-Jahr 1932. Frankfurt: Goethe-Verlag, 1932.

Foos, Alphonse. "Musik nach Goethe," Musical Quarterly (April, 1939).

Foos, Alphonse. Musik und Goethe. Esch-Alzette: Imprimerie Cooperative Luxembourgeoise, 1932.

Frank, Grace (ed.). Rutebeuf, Le Miracle de Theophile. Paris: E. Champion, 1925.

Frank, Rudolf (ed.). Wie der Faust entstand; Urkunde, Sage und Dichtung. Berlin: Borngraeber, 1912.

Frazer, James G. The Golden Bough. Abridged edition. New York: Criterion Books, 1959.

Freher, Marquard. Johannis Trithemii opera historica. 2 vols. Frankfort: Typis Wechelianis apud Claudium Marnium, 1610.

Friedlaender, Max. "Goethe und die Musik," Jahrbuch der Goethe-Gesellschaft (Weimar), Vol. III.

Friedlaender, Max. "Goethes Lyrik in Vertonungen," Goethe-Gesellschaft (Weimar, 1896, 1916).

Friedlaender, Max. "Musikerbriefe zu Goethe," Goethe-Jahrbuch (Frankfurt), Vol. XVII.

Fuchs, A. "Goethe und die Musik," Schweizerische Musikzeitung, Vol. XVII, No. 1 (1902).

Gallwitz, S. D. "Der musikalische Goethe," Die Hilfe, XXXVII (1931), 284.

Garçon, M. and Vinchon, J. The Devil. Translated by Haden Guest. New York: Dutton, 1929.

Garland, M. A. Storm and Stress. London: Harrap, 1952.

Gatti, Guido Maria. "The Stage Works of Ferruccio Busoni," Musical Quarterly, XX (1934), 267-77.

Geiger, L. Goethe und Zelter: Briefwechsel in den Jahren 1799-1832. Mit Einleitung und Erlaeuterungen. 3 vols. Leipzig: Reclams Universal-Bibliothek, 1902-1904.

Geisler, Horst W. Gestaltungen des Faust; die bedeutendsten Werke des Faustdichtung seit 1587. Munich: Parcus & Co., 1927.

Geoffrey of Monmouth. Vita Merlini. Edited by Parry. University of Illinois Studies in Language and Literature. Champaign: University of Illinois Press, 1925.

Gerhard, C. "Goethe und die Musik," Supplement to Das Blatt der Hausfrau (Vienna), Vol. IX, No. 24 (1899).

Gerhard, C. "Mendelssohn bei Goethe," Frankfurter Nachrichten, No. 254 (1897).

Giannini, R. C. "Il simbolo nel Faust di Goethe e l'opera di A. Boito," Rivista d'Italia (Rome), Vol. IV, No. 2.

Gillies, Alexander. Goethe's Faust—An Interpretation. Oxford: B. Blackwell, 1957.

Givry, Grillot de. Witchcraft, Magic and Alchemy. Translated by Courtenay Locke. London: Harrup, 1931.

Gluecksmann, Heinrich. Goethe als Theaterleiter. Vienna: Eisenstein, 1932.

Godwin, William. Lives of the Necromancers. London: Chatto, 1876.

Goedeke, Karl. Grundriss zur Geschichte der deutschen Dichtung aus den Quellen. 2 vols. Dresden: Ehlermann, 1862.

Goethe, Johann W. von. Conversations of Goethe with Eckermann. Translated by John Oxenford. London: George Bell & Sons, 1874.

Goethe, Wolfgang von. Faust: die urspruengliche Gestalt nach der Handschrift des Fraeuleins Luise v. Goechhausen (der Urfaust). In: Wie der Faust Entstand, edited by Frank Rudolf, pp. 242-368. Berlin: Borngraeber, 1912?

Goethe Centuries, The. 1749-1949--An Exhibition Commemorating the Bicentennial of the Birth of Johann Wolfgang von Goethe. Washington, D.C.: Library of Congress, 1949.

Goethes Werke. Faust, Vols. XIV and XV. Herausgegeben in Auftrage der Grossherzogin Sophie von Sachsen. Weimar: Boehlau, 1877, 1888. This is the standard text.

Goetz. "Goethe - Loewe - Wagner," Der Chorleiter (Cassel), I, 8ff.

Goldschmidt, Helene. Das deutsche Kuenstlerdrama von Goethe bis Richard Wagner. Weimar: A. Duncker, 1925.

Golther, Wolfgang. "Richard Wagner und Goethe," Goethe Jahrbuch (Weimar), XXVI, 203-224.

Goslich, Siegfried. Beitraege zur Geschichte der Deutschen romantischen Oper zwischen Spohrs Faust und Wagners Lohengrin. Leipzig: Kistner & Siegel, 1937.

Gounod, Charles. Autobiographical Reminiscences, with Family Letters and Notes on Music. Translated by W. Hely Hutchison. London: Heinemann, 1896.

Gounod, Charles. Memoires d'un artiste. Translated by A. E. Crocker. New York: Rand McNally & Co., 1895.

Graef, H. G. Goethe ueber seine Dichtungen. Vol. II, No. 2, pp. 59-121. Frankfurt: Lit. Anst., 1904.

Graf, Arturo. The Story of the Devil. Translated by E. N. Stone. New York: Macmillan, 1931.

Gregor, Josef. Weltgeschichte des Theaters. Zuerich: Phaidon-Verlag, 1933.

Grimm, Herman. Goethe-Vorlesungen. 2 vols. 7th edition. Stuttgart: J. G. Cotta, 1903.

Grout, Donald Jay. A Short History of Opera. Reprint of 1947 edition. New York: Columbia University Press, 1956.

Gruenwald, L. "Goethe und die Musik," Die Muse des Saitenspiels, XIV (1931), 29, 45, 61, 77.

Grunsky, K. "Goethes tragisches Verhaeltniss zur Musik," Zeitschrift fuer Musik, XCIX (1932), 185.

Gundelfinger, Friedrich [Gundolf, Friedrich]. Goethe. Berlin: G. Biondi, 1920.

Gundelfinger, Friedrich [Gundolf, Friedrich]. Paracelsus. Berlin: G. Biondi, 1927.

Guttmann, Alfred. Musik in Goethes Wirken und Werken. Wunsiede: Dt. Musikliteratur-Verlag, 1949.

Guttmann, Oskar. "Goethes Stellung zur Musik," Musikalische Jugend, II (1930), 6f.

Hagen, Benno von. "Fausts Hellas Fahrt. Goethe," Vierteljahrsschrift (Weimar), V (1940), 39.

Harnack, A. Geschichte der altchristlichen Literatur. 2 vols. Leipzig: J. C. Hinrichs' Verlag, 1893, 1904.

Hartwig, Hellmut A. (ed.). The Southern Illinois Goethe Celebration— A Collection of Nine Papers. Carbondale: Southern Illinois University, 1949.

Hefele, Hermann. Goethe's Faust. Stuttgart: Fromann, 1931.

Heffner, R-M. S., and others. Goethe's Faust: A Complete German-English Vocabulary. Boston: D. C. Heath & Co., 1950.

Heffner, R-M. S., Rehder, Helmut, Twaddell, W. F. Goethe's Faust. 2 vols. Boston: D. C. Heath & Co., 1954, 1955.
    This is a student edition of the German text with lengthy introduction and copious notes.

Heid, Ph. "Goethe und der Chorgesang," Der Chormeister, VI (1932), 38.

Heilborn, A. "Mendelssohn und Goethe," Gegenwart, Vol. XXXVIII, Nos. 5, 6 (1909).

Heine, Heinrich. Der Doktor Faust, ein Tanzpoem. Hamburg: Hoffmann & Campe, 1851.

Heintz, A. "Goethes Ausspruch zur Rechtfertigung der Oper als Kunstwerk," Allgemeine Musikzeitung, Vol. XVII (1891-1892).

Heller, Otto. Faust and Faustus: A Study of Goethe's Relation to Marlowe. Washington University Studies, Language and Literature, No. 2. St. Louis: Washington University Press, 1931.

Henkel, Arthur. "Die Rettung Gretchens," Marburger Theaterblaetter, No. 2 (1949), p. 3ff.

Hernried, Robert. "Goethe und die Musik," Das Orchester, Vol. IX, No. 5.

Hernried, Robert. "Goethe und die Orchestermusiker," Das Orchester, Vol. IX, No. 5.

Herrmann, Helene. "Faust, der Tragoedie Zweiter Teil: Studien zur inneren Form," Zeitschrift fuer Aesthetik, Vol. XXII (1917).

Herrmann, Helene. "Goethe und die Komponisten," Deutsche Militaermusikerzeitung, Vol. LIV, No. 41.

Hertz, G. W. Natur und Geist in Goethes Faust. Frankfurt: Diesterweg, 1931.

Heuss, Alfred. "Goethe und die Musik," Mitteldeutsche Monatshefte (1926), p. 49.

Heywood, T. The Life of Merlin... London: Lackington, Allen & Co., 1813.

Hirschberg, L. "K. Loewes Faustkompositionen," Neue Musikzeitung, XXXIV (1913), 447-50.

Hirschberg, L. "Spohr, Goethe und Beethoven," Allgemeine Musikzeitung, LVI, 1055ff.

Hirschberg, W. "Faust in der Musik," Signale fuer die musikalische Welt (1925), p. 1231.

Hoechst, Coit R. Faust in Music. Dissertation. Gettysburg: Gettysburg Compiler Print, 1916.

Hoffman, R. St. "Goethe und die Musik," Anbruch, V (1932), 69-72.

Hohenstein, F. A. Goethe. Die Pyramide. Dresden: W. Jess, 1928.

Hohlfeld, A. R. Fifty Years with Goethe 1901-1951. Collected Studies. Madison: University of Wisconsin Press, 1953.

Hohlfeld, A. R., Joos, Martin, Twaddell, W. F. Wortindex zu Goethes Faust. Madison: University of Wisconsin Press, 1940.

Hollaender, A. "Goethes Verhaeltnis zur Musik," Zeitschrift fuer Musik, Vol. XC (1932).

Holle, Hugo. Goethes Lyrik in Weisen Deutscher Tonsetzer bis zur Gegenwart. Dissertation. Munich: Wunderhornverlag, 1914.

t'Hooft, B. H. van. Das hollaendische volksbuch vom Doktor Faust. Haag: Martinus Nijhoff, 1926.

Hort, F. J. Notes Introductory to Study of Clementine Recognitions: Lectures. London: Macmillan, 1901.

Hueben, H. H. "Mendelssohn-Erinnerungen aus der Goethe-Zeit," Kleine Blumen, kleine Blaetter (Dessau, 1925), pp. 25-39.

Hughes, H. Stuart. Oswald Spengler--A Critical Estimate. New York: Charles Scribner's Sons, 1952.

Huschke, K. "Beethoven, Schumann und Goethes Faust," Propylaeen (Munich), XXXI (1934), 371.

Ilwof, F. "Goethe und das unsichtbare Orchester," Chronik der Wiener Goethe-Vereins, XI, 4f., 14.

Imbert, Hugues. Etudes sur Faust. Portraits et Etudes. Paris: Fischbacher, 1894.
      Contains article on Schumann's Faust.

Ishikura, K. "Goethe und die Musik," Goethe-jahrbuch zur Jahrhundertfeier (Weimar, 1932).

Istel, Edgar. "Fuenf Briefe Spohrs an Marschner. Festschrift..." Liliencron (Leipzig, 1910), pp. 110-115.

Istel, Edgar. "Goethe and Music," Musical Quarterly (New York), Vol. XIV, No. 2.

Jachimecke, Zdzislaw. Od pierwazej do ostatniej muzyki do Fausta. Krakow: 1932. Publisher unknown.

Jacobskoetter, Ludwig. Goethes Faust im Lichte der Kulturphilosophie Spenglers. Berlin: E. S. Mittler & Sohn, 1924.

Jantz, Harold. "Goethe's Faust as a Renaissance Man," Comparative Literature, I (1949), 337-48.

Jockers, Ernst. "Faust und die Natur," Publications Modern Language Association, LXII (1947), 436-71, 707-32.

Jockers, Ernst. "Faust und Meister: Zwei polare Gestalten," Germanic Review, Vol. XXI (1946).

John, Hans. Goethe und die Musik. Dissertation. Jena: University of Jena, 1926.

Jullien, Adolphe. Goethe et la musique. Paris: Fischbacher, 1880.

Jullien, Adolphe. Hector Berlioz, sa vie et ses oeuvres. Paris: Fischbacher, 1888.

Kahle, A. "Goethe und die Musik," Norddeutsche Allgemeine Zeitung (Berlin), Supplement No. 201a (August 28, 1899).

Kahlert, A. "Goethes Verhaeltnis zur Tonkunst," Der Freihafen (Altona), No. 4 (1838), pp. 174-212.

Kaminski, Heinrich. "Goethe-Musik," Rheinische Musik- und Theaterzeitung, Vol. XVIII, Nos. 15-16.

Katalog der Sammlung Kippenberg. 2 vols. and Registerband. 2d edition. Leipzig: Insel-Verlag, 1928.

Katalog von Goethevertonungen. Leipzig: Breitkopf & Haertel, 1932.

Keller, O. Faust and Faustus, a Study of Goethe's Relation to Marlowe. St. Louis: Washington University Press, 1931.

Keller, W. "Goethe und Schiller in ihren Beziehungen zur Musik," Schweizerische Musikzeitung, Vol. LXI, No. 3f.

Kelly, J. A. "Musical Settings of Goethe's Poems in America," Germanic Review, VI (1931), 233-43.

Kiesewetter, Carl. Faust in der Geschichte und Tradition. Leipzig: M. Spohr, 1893.

Kilian, Eugen. Goethes Faust auf der Buehne. Beitraege zum Problem der Auffuehrung und Inszenierung des Gedichtes. Munich: G. Mueller, 1907.

Kinsky, G. "Zeitgenoessische Goethe-Vertonungen," Philobiblon (Vienna), V (1932), 91-9, 131-37.

Kleiboemer, Georg. "Goethes Theaterleitung," Die Staette (Deutsche Buehne, Hamburg), Nos. 17-18 (March, 1926), pp. 1-9.

Klein, John W. "Boito and His Two Operas," Music & Letters, VII (1926), 73-80.

Klett, Ada M. Der Streit um "Faust II" seit 1900. Jena: Frommann, 1939.
    Condensations of existing literature.

Kling, H. "Goethe et Berlioz," Rivista Musicale Italiana, XII, No. 4 (1905), 714-32.

Kommerell, Max. "Faust und die Sorge," Goethe-Kalender auf das Jahr 1939, pp. 89-130.

Korff, H. A. Faustischer Glaube: Versuch ueber das Problem humaner Lebenshaltung. Leipzig: J. J. Weber, 1938.

Kossmann, E. F. Das niederlaendische Faustspiel des siebzehnten Jahrhunderts. (De Hellevaart van Dr. Joan Faustus.) Haag: Martinus Nijhoff, 1910.

Krause, H. "Goethe in der Vertonung lebender Komponisten," Das Orchester, Vol. VII, No. 22.

Kretschman, L. V. "Mendelssohn in Weimar," Deutsche Rundschau, LXIX, 304-308; LXXV, 431.

Krogmann, Willy. "Zum Ursprung der Gretchentragoedie," Germanisch-Romanische Monatsschrift, XVII (1929), 193-204.

Krueger, Karl-Joachim. "Die Bedeutung der Musik fuer Goethes Wortkunst," Goethe Vierteljahrsschrift (Weimar), I (1936), 204-220.

Kube, K. H. Goethes Faust in franzoesischer Auffassung und Buehnendarstellung. Berlin: E. Ebering, 1932.

Kuechler, Ferdinand. Goethes Musikverstaendnis. Leipzig: Gebr. Hug & Co., 1935.

Landormy, Paul C. Faust de Gounod. Paris: P. Mellottée, 1922.

Landormy, Paul C. "Goethe, the Musician," The Chesterian (London), Vol. XIV, No. 105.

Landry, Lionel. "Goethe et Schumann," La Revue Musicale, Vol. XIII, No. 125.

Lang, A. Myth, Ritual and Religion, 2 vols. London: Longmans, 1887.

Lang, W. "Goethe und die Musik," Im neuen Reich, II (1880), 313.

Langhans, W. "Goethe und Mendelssohn," Neue Berliner Musikzeitung, XLV, 350-53.

Langton, E. Satan, a Portrait. London: Skeffington, 1946.

Lasserre, Pierre. Portraits et discussions. L'unite du Faust de Goethe. Paris: Merovre de France, 1914.

Lauer, M. (trans.). Des Faustus von Byzanz Geschichte Armeniens. Cologne: M. Du Mont-Schauberg, 1871.

Lehmann, A. Aberglaube und Zauberei. Translated by Petersen. Stuttgart: F. Enke, 1898.

Leifs, A. "Goethe und unsere Zeitwende," Zeitschrift fuer Musik, Vol. XCVI.

Lenau, Nicolaus. Faust, No. 614. Berlin: Meyer's Volksbuecher, 1888.

Levin, L. W. "Goethe and Music," Contemporary Review, CLXXVI (October, 1949), 225-30.

Lienhard, F. "Goethe und die Musik," Wege nach Weimar (July, 1908), p. 189f.

Lillie, Arthur. The Worship of Satan in Modern France. London: Sonnenschein, 1896.

Lippman, O. v. "Zu Baukunst--erstarrte Musik," Goethe Jahrbuch (Frankfurt), XXVII, 249.

Lobe, Johann Christian. Aus dem Leben eines Musikers. Leipzig: Weber, 1859.

Loescher, F. H. "Goethe in seinem Verhaeltnis zur Musik, besonders zur geistlichen Musik und Dichtung," Der Kirchenchor, XLIII (1932), 22-6.

Loewe, Carl. Autobiographie. Berlin: W. Mueller, 1870.

Loewenberg, Alfred. Annals of Opera, 1597-1940. 2d ed. Revised and corrected by Frank Walker. Geneva: Societas Bibliographica, 1955.

Loewy, Siegfried. Deutsche Theaterkunst von Goethe bis Reinhardt. Vienna: P. Knepler, 1932.

Logeman, Henri (ed.). English Faustbook of 1592. Gand: H. Engelcke, 1900.

Lohmann, Peter. Ueber Robert Schumann's Faustmusik. Leipzig: Kahnt, 1860.

Loiseau, H. "Goethe et la Musique," Revue de l'enseignement des langues vivantes (Paris), XLII (1926), 1-201, 253-58.

Long, M. F. Recovering the Ancient Magic. London: Rider, 1936.

Lowie, R. H. Primitive Religion. London: Harrap, 1936.

Lualdi, Adriano. "Arrigo Boito, un' anima," Revista Musicale Italiana, XXV (1918), 524-49.

Lunacharskii, Anatolli V. Faust and the City. In: Three Plays. Translated by L. A. Magnus and K. Walter. London: George Routledge & Sons, 1923.

Macdowall, H. C. "The Faust of the Marionettes," Macmillan's Magazine, LXXXVII (January, 1901), 1981ff.

Maecklenburg, A. "Goethe und Mendelssohn," Die Harmonie, Vol. XXIII, No. 2.

Maecklenburg, A. "Goethes Musikanschauung," Schweizer musikpaedagogische Blaetter, XXI (1932), 81-5.

Magnette, Paul. Les traducteurs du "Faust" de Goethe en musique. Liege: C. Fromenteau-Olivier, 1908.

Magre, M. The Return of the Magi. Translated by R. Merton. London: P. Allan, 1931.

Malory, Thomas. Le Morte D'arthur. 4 vols. Caxton's text. London: Lee Warner, 1906.

Mann, Thomas. Doktor Faustus. 1st American edition. New York: A. A. Knopf, 1948.

Mann, Thomas. Freud, Goethe, Wagner. New York: A. A. Knopf, 1937.

Marix-Spire, Thérèse. "Gounod and His First Interpreter, Pauline Viardot. Part I," Musical Quarterly, XXXI (1945), 193-211.

Marlowe, Christopher. The Tragical History of D. Faustus. In: The Works of Christopher Marlowe. Edited by C. F. Tucker Brooke. Oxford: Clarendon Press, 1910.

Marr, Wilhelm. "Wie Goethes Faust auf die Buehne kam," Gartenlaube, No. 41 (1875), p. 1694ff.

Marschner, K. W. "Goethe und Mendelssohn," Die Post, Sunday supplement, No. 4 (1909).

Marsop, Paul. Faust-Musik. Musikalische Essays. Berlin: E. Hofmann & Co., 1899.

Martell, E. "Goethe und die Musik," Gegenwart, LVIII (1929), 129-34.

Marx, Henry. "Thomas Mann and Music," Music News, XLI (April, 1949), 14.

May, Kurt. "Zur Einheit in Faust II," Germanisch-Romanische Monatschrift, XVIII (1930).

Mayer, Dorothy. The Forgotten Master. The Life and Times of Louis Spohr. London: Weidenfeld & Nicolson, 1959.

Meek, Harold George. Johann Faust: The Man and the Myth. London: Oxford University Press, 1930.

Meessen, H. J. (ed.). Goethe Bicentennial Studies by Members of the Faculty of Indiana University. Humanities Series No. 22. Bloomington: Indiana University, 1950.

Meissinger, K. A. Helena. Schillers Anteil am Faust. Frankfurt: Schulte-Bulmke, 1935.

Meister, Richard. "Goethes Stellung zum Musikdrame," Bayreuther Blaetter, Vol. LVI (1934).

Melchinger, Siegfried. Dramaturgie der Sturm- und Drangzeit. Gotha: L. Klotz, 1929.

Mello. "Goethe im Verkehr mit Meistern der Tonkunst," Deutsche Musikerzeitung, Vol. LXIII, No. 12.

Mendelssohn-Bartholdy, Karl. Goethe und Felix Mendelssohn-Bartholdy. Leipzig: Hirzel, 1871.

Menth, A. "Faust-Kompositionen," Deutsche Musikerzeitung, Vol. LXIII, No. 14.

Merbach, P. A. "Goethe und K. F. Zelter," Daheim, Vol. LX, No. 48 (1924).

Merkel, G. F. (ed.). On Romanticism and the Art of Translation, pp. 7-28. Princeton: Princeton University Press, 1956.

Metz, Adolf. "War schon im Urfaust die Rettung des Helden vom Dichter beabsichtigt? Ein Loesungsversuch," Jahrbuch der Goethe-Gesellschaft (Weimar), VII (1920), 45-95.

Meyer, Kathi. "Schumanns Faust Musik," Frankfurter Zeitung (March 10, 1926).

Meyer, Wilhelm. Nuerhberger Faustgeschichten. Reprint of original: Abhandlung d.I. Classe d. K. Akademie d. Wiss. XX. Bd. II Abth. Munich: 1895.

Michelet, Jules. Satanism and Witchcraft. New York: Citadel Press, 1946.

Mies, Paul. "Musikauffassung und Stil der Klassik," Zeitschrift fuer Musikwissenschaft, Vol. XIII.

Milchsack, Gustav. Historiad. Johannis Fausti. Wolfenbuettel: J. Zwissler, 1892.

Miller, Ronald Duncan. The Meaning of Goethe's "Faust." Cambridge: W. Heffer & Sons, 1939.

Milligen, S. "Goethe en de muziek," Caecilia, Vol. LXII, No. 6.

Milligen, S. "Goethe...tot de muziek," Caecilia, Vol. LXXIV, No. 1.

Minor, Jakob. Goethes Faust. Entstehungsgeschichte und Erklaerung. 2
vols. Stuttgart: J. G. Cotta, 1901.

Mojsisovics, R. "Faust in der Musik," Zeitschrift fuer Musik, XCIX,
194-97.

Mojsisovics, R. "Problem einer Faust-Musik," Neue Musikzeitung, Vol.
XLII, No. 15.

Morgan, Bayard Q. A Critical Bibliography of German Literature in English Translation, 1461-1927. Palo Alto: Stanford University
Press, 1938.

Morgenroth, Alfred. "Goethes Faust in der Musik," Die Szene (Berlin),
Vol. IX, Nos. 11-12.

Morgenroth, Alfred. "Zelter." Unpublished dissertation, Berlin, 1922.

Morold, Max. "Goethe und Richard Wagner," Musikalisches Wochenblatt,
Vol. XXXVI, Nos. 34-36 (1905).

Moser, Hans Joachim. "Goethe im juengsten Jahrhundert der Musik," Der
Tag (Berlin), May 29, 1931.

Moser, Hans Joachim. Goethe und die Musik. Leipzig: C. F. Peters, 1949.

Mueller, Friedrich (Mahler). Fausts Leben. Heilbronn: Hinninger, 1881.

Mueller-Blattau, Joseph. Geschichte der deutschen Musik. Berlin: Lich-
terfelde, 1938.

Mueller-Blattau, Joseph. Goethe und die Kantate. Jahrbuch der Musik-
bibliothek Peters. Leipzig: C. F. Peters, 1931.

Mueller-Blattau, Joseph. "Zur Musikuebung und Musikauffassung der
Goethe-Zeit," Euphorion, Vol. XXXI.

Musiol, Robert. "Franz Liszt als Goethe-Komponist," Neue Zeitschrift
fuer Musik, LXIX (1902), 302-303, 318-20.

Musiol, Robert. "Goethes "Faust" und der Maennerchorgesang," Saenger-
halle (Leipzig), Vol. XL, Nos. 30-31ff.

Musiol, Robert. "Der Koenig in Thule," Neue Zeitschrift fuer Musik
(1900), pp. 17-19.

Musiol, Robert. "Lortzing als Faust-Komponist," Neue Zeitschrift fuer
Musik (1901), pp. 322-24.

Musiol, Robert. "Eine neue Faustmusik," Tonkunst, Vol. XIII, No. 6 (December 15, 1882).

Nardi, Piero (ed.). Collected Writings of Arrigo Boito. Milan: Mondadori, 1942.

Neissen, Artur. "Musikalisches vom Goethe-Tag," Allgemeine Musikzeitung (Berlin), Vol. XLIII, No. 26.

Nettl, Paul. "Musiciens de Goethe et musique Goethienne," La Revue Musicale, Vol. XIII, No. 125.

Nettl, Paul. "Thomas Mann's Novel Dr. Faustus," Music News, XLI (January, 1949), 28.

Neubert, Franz. Goethe und sein Kreis, erlaeutert und dargestellt in 651 Abbildungen. Leipzig: J. J. Weber, 1922.

Neubert, Franz. Vom Doktor Faustus zu Goethes Faust, mit 595 Abbildungen. Leipzig: J. J. Weber, 1932.

Newman, Ernest. Musical Studies. Faust in Music, pp. 71-103. London: J. Lane, 1914.

Niedermeier. "Der Fauststoff in der Musik," Allgemeine Musikzeitung, Vol. LIX, No. 40.

Olliver, Charles W. An Analysis of Magic and Witchcraft. London: Rider & Co., 1928.

Ollone, Max d'. "Gounod et l'opera-comique," La Revue Musicale, XIV (November, 1933), 303-308.

Orel, Alfred. Goethe. Vienna: K. Wach, 1932.

Orel, Alfred. "Goethe und die Musik," Akademikerzeitung (Vienna), Vol. XXIV, Nos. 7-9 (1932).

Oster, O. "Goethe und der Geist der Musik," Muenchner Neueste Nachrichten (November 29, 1932).

Pagano, Luigi. "Arrigo Boito: l'artista," Revue Musicale Italiana, XXXI (1924), 199-234.

Palmer, Philip Mason and More, Robert Pattison. The Sources of the Faust Tradition - From Simon Magus to Lessing. New York: Oxford University Press, 1936.

Pannain, Guido. "Il Dottor Faust," Rassegna Musicale Italiana, XIII (1940), 20-29.

Paschal, Roy. "Four Fausts From W. S. Gilbert to Ferruccio Busoni," German Life & Letters, New Series 10 (1956-1957), pp. 263-74.

Pasque, W. Goethes Theaterleitung in Weimar. 2 vols. Leipzig: J. J. Weber, 1863.

Pautrier, C. "Goethe et la musique," Correspondant, Vol. I (1881).

Peacock, Ronald. Goethe's Major Plays: An Essay. New York: Hill & Wang, 1959.

Peter, F. Die Literatur der Faustsage bis Ende des Jahres 1848. Halle: Schmidt, 1851.

Peters, Andre. Goud uit oude legenden. 's-Gravenhage: W. P. van Stockum, 1951.

Petersen, Julius. Goethes Faust auf der deutsche Buehne. Leipzig: Quelle & Meyer, 1929.

Petsch, Robert. "Die dramatische Kunstform des 'Faust'," Euphorion, XXXIII (1932), 211-44.

Petsch, Robert. Einfuehrung in Goethes "Faust." Hamburg: 1949.

Petsch, Robert. Gehalt und Form. Dortmund: F. W. Ruhfus, 1925.

Petsch, Robert. Goethes Faust. A Commentary. Leipzig: Bibliographisches Institut, 1923.

Petsch, Robert. "Goethe's Faust. Der Tragoedie II. Teil," Germanisch-Romanische Monatsschrift, XI (1913), 336ff.

Petsch, Robert. "Der historische Doktor Faust," Germanisch-Romanische Monatsschrift, II (1910), 99ff.

Petsch, Robert (ed.). Lessings Briefwechsel mit Mendelssohn und Nicolai ueber das Trauerspiel. Leipzig: Verlag der Duerrschen buchhandlung, 1910.

Petsch, Robert. Lessings Faustdichtung. Heidelberg: Carl Winter, 1911.

Petsch, Robert. Theophilus, Mittelniederdeutsches Drama in drei Fassungen. Heidelberg: Carl Winter, 1908.

Petsch, Robert. Das Volksbuch vom Dr. Faust, zweite Auflage. Halle: M. Niemeyer, 1911.

Petsch, Robert. Zur Tongestaltung in der Dichtung. Festschrift fuer Petersen, pp. 1-22. Leipzig: 1938.

Pfitzer, Nicolaus. Faustbuch. Revision of 1674 Widman edition. Stuttgart: A. von Keller, 1880.

Pfordten, H. v. "Goethes Stellung zur Musik," Deutsche Volksbildung, VII (1931), 23-6.

Philostratus. Life of Apollonius of Tyana. Translated by F. C. Conybeare. New York: Macmillan, 1912.

Pizzetti, Ildebrando. "Il Faust della leggenda, della poema e della dramma musicale," Revista Musicale Italiana, XIII (1906), 1-49.

Plenzat, Karl. Die Theophiluslegende in den Dichtungen des Mittelalters. Germanische Studien. Berlin: E. Ebering, 1926.

Pohl, R. "Liszt's Faust-Symphonie," Neue Zeitschrift fuer Musik (Leipzig), Vol. IV, Nos. 1, 2, 4-6, 20, 21 (1862).

Pougin, Arthur. "Gounod ecrivain," Revista Musicale Italiana, XVII (1910), 590-627; XVIII (1911), 747-68; XIX (1912), 239-85, 637-95; XX (1913), 453-86, 792-820.

Pourtalès, Guy de. Goethe en musique. Les affinités instinctives. Paris: Les editions de France, 1934.

Preussner, E. "Goethes Anschauungen von der Musik," Die Musikpflege, VIII, No. 1 (April, 1937), 15-20.

Prieberg, Fred K. Lexikon der Neuen Musik. Freiburg: Karl Alber, 1958.

Priest, George M. (trans.). Faust by Johann Wolfgang von Goethe. New York: A. A. Knopf, 1941.

Pringsheim, Klaus. "The Music of Adrian Leverkuehn," Musicology, II, No. 3 (April, 1949), 255-68.

Pringsheim, Klaus. "Thomas Mann und die Musik," Schweizerische Musikzeitung, XCV (July, 1955), 286-90.

Prod'homme, J.-G. "Goethe et les musiciens francais," Revue Franco-Allemande, Vol. I, No. 18 (1899).

Prod'homme, Jacques Gabriel. Gounod. 2 vols. Paris: C. Delagrave, 1911.

Prod'homme, Jacques Gabriel. "Miscellaneous Letters by Charles Gounod," Musical Quarterly, IV (1918), 630-53.

Prod'homme, Jacques Gabriel. "Spontini et Ch. Gounod," Zeitschrift der internationalen Musik Gesellschaft, XI (1909-1910), 325-8.

Proelss, Robert. "Goethe und die Musik," Schlesische Zeitung (January 1-7, 1885).

Prost, A. Les sciences et les arts occultes au XVI. siecle. Corneille Agrippa, sa vie et ses oeuvres. Paris: Champion, 1881-1882.

Pruefer, Arthur. Musik als toenende Faust-Idee. Leipzig: Steingraeber, 1920?

Prunieres, Henry. "Goethe et la musique," La Revue Musicale, Vol. XIII, No. 125.

Rademacher, J. "Griechische Quellen zur Faustsage. Sitzungs Berichte der Akademie der Wissenschaften in Wien," Phil.-hist. Kl., Vol. CCVI, Abhandlung 4 (1927).

Raphaël, Alice (trans.). Faust. A Tragedy by Johann Wolfgang von Goethe. New York: Cape & Smith, 1930.

Rayye, Selmar. "Robert Schumann und seine Faustszenen," Sammlung musikalischer Vortraege (Leipzig), Vol. I, No. 4 (1874).

Read, John. Through Alchemy to Chemistry. London: George Bell & Sons, 1957.

Refardt, Edgar. "Goethe in Schweizerischen Kompositionen," Schweizer Musikzeitung und Saengerblatt, LXXII, Nos. 14-15, 16-17 (1932), 472-76, 506-511.

Reuper, Julius. "Goethe und Zelter," Neue Freie Presse (Morgenblatt), Nos. 6484, 6485 (1882).

Reuter, O. "Musik waehrend der Weimarer Goethe-Woche," Signale fuer die musikalische Welt, XC (1932), 363.

Richard, August. "Goethe im Verkehr mit musikalischen Zeitgenossen," Gegenwart, No. 34 (1911), p. 35.

Richards, Alfred E. Studies in English Faust Literature. Berlin: E. Felber, 1907.

Rickert, Heinrich. "Fausts Tod und Verklaerung," Deutsche Vierteljahreschrift fuer Literaturwissenschaft und Geistesgeschichte, III, No. 1 (1925), 1-74.

Rickert, Heinrich. Goethes Faust. Die dramatische Einheit der Dichtung. Tuebingen: Mohr, 1932.

Riehl, Wilhelm H. Musikalische Characterkoepfe. 2 vols. Stuttgart: J. G. Cotta, 1899.
    Contains essays on opera composers of early 19th century.

Riemann, Hugo. Opern-Handbuch. Leipzig: C. A. Koch, 1887.

Rintel, W. C. F. Zelter. Berlin: Janke, 1861.

Rittmeyer-Iselin, D. J. "Goethe und die Musik," Garbe (Basel), XV (1932), 348.

Roberts, Alexander and Donaldson, James (eds.). Ante-Nicene Christian Library. Vol. III: The Writings of Tatian, Theophilus and Jacobus de Varagine; and the Clementine Recognitions. Vol. VIII: The Writings of Cyprian, Bishop of Carthage. Vol. XVI: Apocryphal Books. Vol. XX: The Works of Gregory Thaumaturgus, Dionysius of Alexandria, and Archelaus. 24 vols. Edinburg: T. & T. Clark, 1867, 1868-1869, 1870, 1871.

Roentz, W. "Goethe und Zelter," Jahrbuch des deutschen Saengerbundes (Dresden, 1932), p. 73.

Rohde, R. Das englische Faustbuch und Marlowes Tragoedie. Pamphlet. Halle: M. Niemeyer, 1910.

Rohmer, Sax. The Romance of Sorcery. London: Methuen, 1914.

Rolland, Romain. "Goethe musicien," Europe (Paris), No. 23 (1929), pp. 324-53, 498-516.

Rolland, Romain. "Goethe's Interest in Music," Musical Quarterly, Vol. XVII, No. 2.

Roos, Carl. Faust problemer. Kopenhagen: Gyldendal, 1941.
    A good part of this study repudiates theories about the order of composition.

Rose, William. Doctor John Faustus 1592. London: George Routledge & Sons, n.d.
    This is a modernization of the English Faust Book.

Rothes, W. "Goethe und die Musik," Allgemeine Rund-Schau (Munich, 1932), pp. 79-82.

Ruetzel, M. "Goethe ueber die Oper," Rheinische Musik- und Theaterzeitung, IV (1903), 344f.

Runes, Dagobert. Goethe, a Symposium. New York: Roerich, 1932.

Russo, Wilhelm. Goethes Faust auf der Berliner Buehnen. Vol. XXXII of Germanische Studien. Berlin: E. Ebering, 1924.

Salburg, Edith. Ludwig Spohr. Leipzig: Hasse & Kohler, 1936.

Saminsky, Lazare. "More About Faustus," Modern Music, V, No. 1 (November-December, 1927), 38-9.

Sandor, Max. Sterne der Buehne...Mappe: Faust. Vienna-Leipzig: Augarten-Verlag, 1935.

Schade, R. "Goethe und die Musik," Germania (August 22, 1921).

Schaefer, Albert. Historisches un systematisches Verzeichnis saemtlicher Tonwerke zu den Dramen...Schillers, Goethes, Shakespeares, Kleists und Koerners, p. 86. Leipzig: Merseburger, 1886.

Schallaboeck, Karl. Der Komponist Ph. Chr. Kayser und seine Beziehungen zu Goethe. Dissertation. Vienna: University of Vienna, 1911.

Schaudorfer, E. "Die drei Erzengel in Goethes Faust und in Haydns Schoepfung," Musica Divina (Vienna, 1937), p. 91-4.

Scheible, J. Kloster. 12 vols. Stuttgart: The Author, 1845-1849.

Schletterer, Hans Michael. "Ludwig Spohr," Waldersee, Sammlung musikalischer Vortraege (Leipzig), III (1879-1898), 127-62.

Schmidt, Erich. Faust und das sechzehnte Jahrhundert. Charakteristiken I. Berlin: Weidmann, 1886.

Schmidt, Erich. "Faust und Luther," Berichte der Berliner Akademie, XXV (1896), 567ff.

Schmidt, Ora Lydia. "Thomas Mann and the Musical Element in His Works." Unpublished Master's thesis, University of Wisconsin, 1932.

Schneider, Hermann. Urfaust? Eine Studie. Tuebingen: H. Laupp, 1949.

Schneider, Reinhold. Faust Rettung. Taschenbuch fuer junge Menschen. Berlin: 1946.

Schoenberg, Arnold. "Further to the Schoenberg-Mann Controversy," Music Survey, II, No. 2 (Autumn, 1949), 77-80.

Schoenberg, Arnold. "Letters to the Editor: Doctor Faustus Schoenberg?" Saturday Review (January 1, 1949), p. 22.

Scholz, Hans. "Hector Berlioz zum 50. Todestage," Zeitschrift fuer Musikwissenschaft, I (1918-1919), 328-51.

Schorn, H. "Goethes Faust und die Musik," Neue Musikzeitung, Vol. XXXVIII (1917).

Schorn, H. "Wie stand Wagner zu Goethe," Schwalbennest (Erfurt), Vol. XIV, No. 7.

Schreiber, Carl F. The William A. Speck Collection of Goethiana. No. 3 of Collections of Yale University. New Haven: Yale University Press, n.d.

Schrickel, Leonhard. Geschichte des Weimarer Theaters von seinen An-
faengen bis heute. Weimar: Panses Verlag, 1928.

Schroeer, Karl J. Die Auffuehrung des ganzen Faust auf dem Wiener Hof-
burgtheater. Wien: Henninger, 1883.

Schroeer, Karl J. Faust von Goethe. Mit Einleitung und fortlaufender
Erklaerung. Heilbronn: Henninger, 1881.

Schuchard, G. C. "Julirevolution, St.-Simonismus und die Faustpartien
von 1831," Zeitschrift fuer deutsche Philologie, Vol. LX (1936).

Schuchard, G. C. L. "The Last Scene in Goethe's Faust," Publications of
the Modern Language Association, Vol. LXIV (1949).

Schuenemann, G. "R. Wagners Komposition zu Goethes Faust," Frankfurter
Zeitung (March 6, 1917).

Schuh, W. "Die fruehesten Schweizer Goethe-Vertonunger," Neue Zuercher
Zeitung (March 20, 1932).

Schulte-Strathaus, Ernst. Goethes Faust-fragment. Zurich: Corona,
1940.

Schuurmann, M. "Goethes Verhaeltnis zur Tonkunst," Goetheanum, XII
(1932), 255.

Schwebsch, E. "Goethe und Wagner," Bayreuther Blaetter (1919), pp. 105-
129, 149-75.

Searle, Humphrey. The Music of Liszt. London: Williams & Norgate,
1954.

Segnitz, Eugen. Goethe und die Oper in Weimar. Langensalza: H. Beyer
& Sohn, 1908.

Segnitz, Eugen. "Goethe und die Tonkunst," Allgemeine Musikzeitung,
Nos. 59, 60 (1911).

Seidlin, Oscar. "Is the Prelude in the Theatre a Prelude to Faust?"
Publications of the Modern Language Association, LXIV (1948),
445-61.

Seidlin, Oscar. Southern Illinois Goethe Celebration. A Collection of
Nine Papers. Carbondale: Southern Illinois University Press, 1950.

Seligmann, Kurt. The History of Magic. New York: Pantheon Books,
1948.

Sengle, Fr. "Goethes Verhaeltnis zum Drama," Neue deutsche Forschungen
(Berlin), Vol. CXVI (1937).

Silbergleit, Richard. "Goethe und die Mendelssohns," Die juedische Frau, II, 7f.

Simon, James. Faust in der Musik. Berlin: Bard & Marquardt, 1906.

Simon, James. "Goethe und die Musik," Geisteskultur (Berlin), XLI (1932-1933), 193-97.

Sittard, Joseph. "Faust, Musik-Drama von H. Zoellner," Studien und Charakteristiken, Vol. III (1884).

Soubies, Albert and Henri de Curzon. Documents inédits dur le Faust de Gounod. Paris: Fischbacher, 1912.

Specht, Richard. Gustav Mahler. Berlin: Schuster & Loeffler, 1922.

Specht, Richard. Gustav Mahler's Eighth Symphony. Thematic analysis. Leipzig: Universal Edition, 1912.

Spengler, Oswald. The Decline of the West - Form and Actuality. 2 vols. Translated by Charles F. Atkinson. New York: A. A. Knopf, 1945.

Spiess, Helmut. Goethe, Eckermann und Faust auf der Buehne. Dissertation. Jena: 1933.

Spitta, Philipp. "Die aelteste Faust-Oper und Goethes Stellung zur Musik," Zur Musik (Berlin, 1892), pp. 199-234.

Spohr, Louis. Louis Spohr's Selbstbiographie. 2 vols. Cassel: Wigand, 1860-1861.

Stawell, F. M. and Dickinson, G. L. Goethe and Faust. New York: Dial Press, 1929.

Stege, Fritz. "Bilder aus der deutschen Musik-Kritik von deutsche Musik," (Regensburg), Vol. L.

Stein, Jack M. "Adrian Leverkuehn as Composer," Germanic Review, XXV (December, 1950), 257-74.

Stein, K. "Goethes Stellung zur Musik," Musikerziehung, VII (1930), 379-82.

Stein, William B. Hawthorne's Faust. Gainesville: University of Florida Press, 1953.

Steiner, Olga. Das Zeitgeschichtliche Element in den Faustgestaltungen der Stuermer und Draenger. New York: New York University Press, 1946.

Sternfeld, Frederick W. "Goethe and Music." Unpublished doctoral dissertation, Yale University, 1943.

Sternfeld, R. "H. Berlioz und seine Faustmusik," Westermanns Illustrierte Deutsche Monatshefte (1904), pp. 485-92.

Stettner, Th. "Goethe und Zelter," Pauliner-Zeitung (Leipzig), XLVI (1934), 65.

Stockdale, Gretchen. "Faust's Gretchen." Unpublished thesis, Yale University, 1951.

Stockmann, S.J., Aloys. "Eine neue Faustkommentar," Stimmen der Zeit, Vol. CVII (Februarheft, 1925).

Stoecklein, P. "Fausts Kampf mit der Sorge," Dichtung und Volkstum, Vol. XLIII (1944).

Stoessinger, F. "Musik und Goethe," Vossische Zeitung (March 17, 1932).

Stuart, Hannah. "Goethe's Influence on Music," Publications of the English Goethe Society, New Series, XII (1935-1937), 65-81.

Suares, Andre. "Goethe et la musique," La Revue Musicale (Paris), Vol. XIII, No. 125.

Suares, Andre. "Pensees sur la musique," La Revue Musicale (Paris), XII (1931), 237-40.

Summers, Montague. The Geography of Witchcraft. London: Keagan Paul, 1927.

Summers, Montague. The History of Witchcraft and Demonology. London: Keagan Paul, 1926.
    Contains a fine bibliography.

Summers, Montague. Witchcraft and Black Magic. London: Rider, 1946.

Tabori, Paul. The Natural Science of Stupidity. Philadelphia: Chilton Co., 1959.

Tanner, André. "Faust et les musiciens. Les germaniques: Wagner, Liszt, Schweitzer musik-paedagogische," Feuillets de pedagogie musicale (Zuerich), XLIII, No. 4 (1955), 155-63.

Taylor, Bayard (trans.). Faust, a Tragedy by Johann Wolfgang von Goethe. New York: Random House, 1950.

Theens, K. Doktor Johann Faust. Geschichte der Faustgestalt vom 16. Jahrhundert bis zur Gegenwart. Meisenheim am Glan: West Kulturverlag, 1948.

Thomasberger, Karl. "Schumann und Goethe," Neue Freie Presse (June 3, 1937).

Thompson, Oscar. "If Beethoven Had Written Faust," Musical Quarterly, X (1924), 13-20.

Thorndike, Lynn. A History of Magic and Experimental Science During the First Thirteen Centuries of Our Era. 2 vols. London: Macmillan, 1923.

Tiersot, Julien. "Charles Gounod; a Centennial Tribute," Musical Quarterly, IV (1918), 409-39.

Tiersot, Julien. "Le Faust de Goethe et la musique," Guide Musical (Brussels), No. 48 (1899-1900).

Tiersot, Julien. "Gounod's Letters," Musical Quarterly, V (1919), 40-61.

Tiersot, Julien. "Hector Berlioz and Richard Wagner," Musical Quarterly, III (1917), 453-92.

Tille, Alexander. "Die Bilder zu Goethes Faust," Preuss. Jahrbuecher, LXXII, No. 2 (1893), 264-99.

Tille, Alexander. Die Faustsplitter in der Literatur des Sechzehnten bis achtzehnten Jahrhunderts. Berlin: E. Felber, 1900-1904.

Torchi, L. Robert Schumann e le sue "Scene tratte dal Faust di Goethe." Torino: Bocca, 1895.

Tornius, V. "Goethe und die Musik," Illustrierte Zeitung (Leipzig), No. 4547 (1932).

Towers, John. Dictionary-Catalogue of Operas and Operettas Which Have Been Performed on the Public Stage. Morgantown: Acme Publishing Co., 1910.

Trench, A. Life and Genius of Calderon. London: Macmillan, 1880.

Trimz, Erich. Faust. Hamburg: C. Wegener, 1949.
This is one of the best German editions.

Tschirch, O. "Radziwill und seine Faustmusik," Mitteilungen des Vereins fuer Geschichte Berlin (1907), pp. 229-34.

Twardowski, Juljusz. "Goethe z muzyka," Muzyka, Vol. IX, Nos. 3-4.

Ulbrich, Franz. Radziwills Privatauffuehrungen von Goethes Faust in Berlin. Ein Abschnitt aus der Buehnengeschichte des Goetheschen Faust. Studien zur Literaturgeschichte. Albert Koester zum 7. November, 1912, ueberreicht, pp. 193-220. Leipzig: Inselverlag, 1912.

Unger, Max. "Goethe und die Musik," Der Musikalienhandel (Leipzig), Vol. XXXIV, No. 5.

Unger, Max. "Goethe und die Musik seiner Zeit," Skizzen (Berlin), No. 4 (1932).

U.S. Library of Congress. Division of Music. Catalogue of Opera Librettos Printed Before 1800. Prepared by O. G. T. Sonneck. Washington, D.C.: Government Printing Office, 1914.

U.S. Library of Congress. Division of Music. Dramatic Music... Catalogue of Full Scores. Compiled by O. G. T. Sonneck. Washington, D.C.: Government Printing Office, 1908.

Valera, Juan. Sobre el Fausto de Goethe. Sevilla: Imprenta Akmana, 1883.

Valery, Paul. "Mon Faust." Paris: Gallimard, 1946.

Vietor, Karl. Goethe the Poet. Translated by Moses Hadas. Cambridge: Harvard University Press, 1949.

Vittadini, Stefano. Il primo libretto del Mefistofele di Arrigo Boito. Milan: Gli amici del museo teatrale alla scala, 1938.

Von Faber du Faur, Curt. German Baroque Literature. A Catalogue of the Collection in the Yale University Library. New Haven: Yale University Press, 1958.

Waetzold, Paul. Carl Friedrich Zelter als Chordirigent. Pritzwalk: Koch, 1932.

Wahr, Fred B. "Form and Proportion of Goethe's Dramas," Germanic Review, Vol. VII (1932).

Waite, A. E. Devil Worship in France. London: Redway, 1896.

Waite, A. E. Lives of Alchemystical Philosophers. London: Redway, 1888.

Waite, A. E. The Mysteries of Magic. London: Redway, 1897.

Walker, Ernest. "Goethe and Some Composers," The Musical Times, No. 1072 (1932), pp. 497-502.

Wallner, B. A. "Goethe und die Musik," Ausstellung in Muenchen, Zeitschrift fuer Musik, Vol. XCIX, No. 9.

Walz, U. "An English Faustsplitter," Modern Language Notes, XLII (1927), 353ff.

Walz, U. "A German Faust Play of the Sixteenth Century," Germanic Review, III (1928), 1f.

Warkentin, R. Nachklaenge der Sturm- und Drangperiode in Faust-dichtungen. Munich: Forschungen zu neuern Litteratur-Geschichte, 1896.

Wasiliewski, W. J. von. Goethes Verhaeltnis zur Musik. Sammlung musikalischer Vortraege. Leipzig: Breitkopf & Haertel, 1880.

Wassermann, Rudolf. Ludwig Spohr als Opernkomponist. Rostocker dissertation. Munich: University of Munich, 1909.

Wattenbach, Wilhelm. Deutschlands Geschichtsquellen in Mittelalter. 3
vols. Weimar: H. Boehlaus, 1952-1957.

Weingartner, Felix. Buffets and Rewards; a Musician's Reminiscences.
Translated by Marguerite Wolff. London: Hutchinson & Co., 1937.

Weiser, Karl. Goethes Faust. Neue Weimarer Einrichtung. Leipzig:
Universal Bibliothek, 1908.

Weiss, Anton. "Zelter," Volkszeitung (Vienna), May 9 and 23, 1932.

Wendriner, Karl G. Die Faustdichtung vor, neben und nach Goethe. 4
vols. Berlin: Morawe & Scheffelt, 1913.

Wheatley, H. B. (ed.). Merlin; or the Early History of King Arthur.
London: K. Paul, Trench, Truebner & Co., 1899.

Wieruszowski, Helene. "Das Mittelalterbild in Goethes Helena," Monatshefte, XXXVI (1944), 81.

Wilbrandt, Adolf. Faust. Tragoedie von Goethe. Fuer die Buehne in
drei "Abenden" eingerichtet. Vienna: Rosner, 1895.

Williams, Charles. Witchcraft. London: Faber & Faber, 1941.

Williams, S.J., Joseph J. Voodoos and Obeaks. London: Allen & Unwin,
1933.

Winterfeld, A. von. "Goethe on Music," Music Review (Chicago, 1893).

Winterfeld, A. von. "Goethe und Mendelssohn," Salon, No. 8 (1890).

Witkop, Philipp. Goethe. Leben und Werk. Stuttgart: J. G. Cotta,
1931.

Witkowski, Georg. "Goethe als Opernregisseur," Der Anbruch, XVII (1935),
230.

Witkowski, Georg. Goethes Faust. A Commentary. 2 vols. Leipzig:
Duerr & Weber, 1924.

Witkowski, Georg. "Goethes Faust auf dem deutschen Theater," Buehne
und Welt (Berlin), Vol. 4, Nos. 1-3.

Witkowski, Georg. "Der historische Faust," Deutsche Zeitschrift fuer Geschichtswissenschaft (Freiburg, Leipzig), VII (1896-1897), 298-350.

Witkowski, Georg. Die Walpurgisnacht im I. Teile von Goethes Faust. Leipzig: F. W. v. Biedermann, 1894.

Wolff, Eugen. Faust und Luther; ein Beitrag zur Entstehung der Faust-dichtung. Halle: M. Niemeyer, 1912.

Woltereck, K. "Goethe und Wagner," Goethe Jahrbuch, p. 34.

Wraxall, L. Remarkable Adventures and Unrevealed Mysteries. 2 vols. London: Bentley, 1863.

Wright, T. Narratives of Magic and Sorcery. 2 vols. London: Bentley, 1851.

Wustmann, G. "Clara Schumann bei Goethe," Die Grenzboten (1897), p. 508f.

Yates, Peters. "Leverkuehn and the Magician," Saturday Review (February 26, 1949), pp. 47-8.

Zahn, T. Cyprian von Antiochien und die deutsche Faust- sage. Frlan-gen: Deichert, 1882.

Zant, Ludwig. "Eine verschollene Komposition zu Goethes 'Faust'," Chronik des Wiener Goethes-Vereins (Vienna), LVIII, No. 42 (1954), 69.

Ziegler, Hans Severus. Das Theater des deutschen Volkes. Ein Beitrag zur Volkserziehung und Propaganda. Leipzig: Voigtlaender, 1933.

Zuckerhandl, Victor. "Die Musik des Doktor Faustus," Neue Rundschau, LVIII (Winter, 1948), 203-214.

MUSICAL COMPOSITIONS

Below the names of some of the composers will be found an indication * of the source I have used. This is not intended to preclude
the possibility that the compositions may be found elsewhere.

Operas

Bandini, Primo (1857- ?). Fausta. Produced in Milan, September, 1886.
Had a good success.

Béancourt (? - ?). Faust. Text by Théaulon and Gondelier. Presented
in Paris at the Nouveauté Theatre, October 27, 1827. The music
was taken from various French operas. Newspaper accounts dub text
as laughable. Clement says Théaulon made it into an opera pas-
tiche but that Béancourt's music is magnificent and powerful.

Bernhardi, E. (1838-1900). Faustina.

Bertin, Angelique L. (1805-1877). Faust, a semi-serious opera in four
(B)   acts. Text adapted from Goethe. Paris: Janet & Cotelle, 1831.
Presented in Paris at the Italian Theater, March 8, 1831. Not a
success but according to Loewenberg not unworthy of its great
subject.

Boito, Arrigo (1842-1918). Mefistofele, opera in four acts with pro-
(N)   logue and epilogue. Text by the composer after Goethe. Milan:
Ricordi, 1878.

Boulanger, Lili (1893-1918). Faust et Helène, one act opera. Poem by
(B)   Eugene Adenis (pseud. for E. F. A. Colombeau). Paris: Societé
(C)   Anonyme des editions Ricordi, 1913.

Brueggemann, Alfredo (1873-). An opera cycle: I. Der Doktor
(C)   Faust. II. Gretchen. III. Faust und Helena, Faust's Verklae-
(P)   rung (Faust and Helena, Faust's Redemption). Text after Goethe.
Leipzig: Ricordi, 1907, 1909.

---

*(B) - A. A. Brown Collection, Boston Public Library
 (C) - Library of Congress
 (N) - Newberry Library, Chicago, Illinois
(NU)- Northwestern University, Evanston, Illinois
 (P) - New York Public Library
 (S) - Speck Collection, Yale Library, New Haven, Connecticut

Busoni, Ferruccio (1866-1924). Doktor Faust. Text by the composer.
  (N) Final Scene completed from Busoni's materials by Philip Jarnach.
       Leipzig: Breitkopf & Haertel, 1926. Performed in Dresden, May
       21, 1925.

Cereceda, Guillermo (1844-1919). Mefistofeles, zarzuela (comic opera)
       in three acts. Presented in Madrid.

Conti, Carlo (1796-1868). Mefistofele. 1853?

Cordella, Giacomo (1783-1847). La Faustina.

Delvincourt, Claude (1888-   ). Faust et Hélène, one act opera. Text
  (B) by E. F. A. Colombeau after Goethe's Faust, Part II. Paris: Le-
       gouix, 1914.

  Egk, Werner (1901-   ). Die Zaubergeige, a folk opera. Text after
       the marionette play by Franz von Pocci. Composed, 1935; revised,
       1954.

Engelmann, Hans U. (1921-   ). Doktor Faust's Hoellenfahrt (Doctor
       Faust's Journey to Hell), chamber opera. Composed, 1949.

Freitas-Gazul, Francisco de (1842-   ). A damnacao do Fausto. 1860?

Gordigiani, Luigi (1806-1860). Il Fausto. Presented in Florence at the
       Pergola Theater. Could not win a following because of the wretch-
       ed text.

Gounod, Félician Charles (1818-1893). Faust (often called Margarethe
       in Europe). Text by Jules Barbier and Michel Carré after Goethe.
       Full score. New York: Mapleson Music Publications, n.d. First
       performance in Paris at Theatre-Lyrique, March 19, 1859.

Hennebert, Porphiré D. (? - ?). Faust, opera in three acts. Text by
       Théaulon. Performed at Luettich, 1835.

Hoffmann, E. T. A. (1776-1822). Faust (Faustine). Text by Z. Werner.
       1804?

Kauer, Ferdinand (1751-1831). Das Faustrecht in Thueringen.
  (P)

Kistler, Cyrill (1848-1907). Faust, opera in four acts. Completed,
  (C) 1905.

Kugler, V. (? - ?). Faust. 1832?

Lachner, F. (1803-1890). Faust. Vienna: A. Diabelli, 18--?
  (C)

Lickl, Georg (1769-1843). Leben, Thaten, und Hoellenfahrt des Dr. Faust
(Dr. Faust's Life, Deeds, and Journey to Hell). Text after Max
Klinger's novel of the same title. Performed in Vienna at the
Schikaneder Theater, 1815.

Methfessel, Friedrich (1771-1807). Doctor Faust. Text by Johann F.
Schink. Left a fairly complete version at his death.

Meyer, Carl H. (1784-1837). Faust. Text after August Klingemann's tragedy.

Mueller, Wenzel (1767-1835). Doktor Faust, singspiel. Bruenn: 1784.

Pellaert, Baron von (1793-1876). Faust, opera in three acts. Text by
Théaulon. Presented in Brussels, February, 1834, where it was
very successful.

Raimondi, P. (1786-1853). Il Fausto Arrivo. Performed in Naples, c.
1837.

Reutter, Herman (1900-   ). Doktor Johannes Faust, opera in three
(P) acts, op. 47. Libretto by Ludwig Andersen (pseud.) based on Karl
Simrock's version of the puppet play Dr. Faust. Mainz: B.
Schott's Soehne, c. 1936. World premiere at Cologne, 1935.

Roliczek (? - ?). Twardowski (Faust). Text by Joh. Kaminski. Lem-
berg: 1825.

Ruta, Michele (1827-1896). Faust.

Sauchay, Marc-Andre (? -   ). Faust and Helena, opera in a prelude
(S) and three acts. Text after Goethe's Faust, Part II. Stuttgart:
Kohlhammer, 1940 (text).

Spohr, Ludwig (1784-1859). Faust, grand opera, op. 60. Text by J. C.
(C) Bernard (pseud.). Leipzig: Peters, 1840? Written for Vienna,
(N) 1813. First performance in Frankfurt, 1818.

Strauss, Joseph (1793-1866). Leben und Thaten Faust's (Faust's Life and
Deeds). Performed in Vienna, 1814.

Terrasse, Claude (1867-1923). Faust en ménage, lyric fantasy in one
act. Text by Albert Carré. Paris: Choudens, 1923.

Valente, G. (? - ?). Fausto. 1814?

Walter, Ignaz (1759-1822). Doktor Faust, opera in four acts. Text by
Schmieder after Goethe. Composed, 1797. First opera on Goethe's
poem. Score now in the Koenigl. Hochschule fuer Musik, Berlin.

Werstowsky, Alexie N. (1799-1862). Pan Twardowski (Faust). Text by
Zagostin. Composed, 1828. First performance in Moscow, 1831.

Zaitz, J. von (? - ?). Twardowski (Faust). Text by C. Tomic. First performance in Agram, 1880.

Zoellner, Heinrich (1854-1941). Faust, music drama with prelude and
(B) four acts. Text after Goethe's Faust, op. 40. Leipzig: Siegel,
(N) 1886. Written, 1892. First performance in Munich, October, 1887. This composition is the first attempt to set the actual text of Goethe's poem in the form of an opera.

Large Choral Works

Ambrosius, Hermann (1897- ?). Chorwerk, symphonic poem for soprano, baritone, mixed chorus and orchestra. Performed by Fritz Busch, 1923.

Baussnern, Waldemar von (1866-1931). Kantate "Steigt hinan zu Hoeherm Kreise" (Cantata "Ascend to the Higher Circle").

Berger, Wilhelm (1861-1911). Euphorion (from Faust II) Oratorium, op.
(S) 74. Berlin: Bote & Bock, 1899? Composed, c. 1905.

Berlioz, Hector (1803-1869). Huit Scenes de Faust, Tragedie de Goethe
(S) (Eight Scenes from Faust, Tragedy by Goethe), op. 1. Translated by Nerval. Paris: Schlesinger, 1829. Written, 1828-1829. Berlioz considered the work a complete failure and destroyed all copies he could find. Later he incorporated some of the music into—

Berlioz, Hector (1803-1869). La damnation de Faust. Légende Dramatique
(N) en quatre parties, avec texte francais et allemande (The Damnation
(NU) of Faust. Dramatic Legend in Four Parts, with French and German
(S) Text), op. 24. Paris: Richault et Cie., n.d. Written, 1846. Often given as an opera, the work is made up of unconnected episodes and is really a dramatic cantata.

Cohen, Henri (1808-1880). Faust et Marguerite, poeme lyrique. Text by Victor Doinet after Goethe. Paris: chez tous les editeurs de musique, 1847. Performed in Paris, April 15, 1846.

Dachauer, Louis (1837-1878). Faust, symphonische Dichtung fuer Soli, Chor und Orchester (Faust, symphonic poem for soloists, chorus, and orchestra). Performed by the Philharmonic Society in New York, 1872.

Draeseke, Felix (1835-1913). Osterszene (Easter Scene), op. 39. Written, c. 1870.

Enden, Johann van den (1844- ?). Cantate "La derniere nuit de Faust" (Cantata "The Last Night of Faust"). Performed in Brussels, October, 1869.

Geisler, Paul (1856-1919). Walpurgisnacht. Posen, c. 1890.

Groenland, Petersen (1761-1834). Die erste Walpurgisnacht. (Teilkomp.)

Hensel, Fanny (1805-1847). Choere zum zweiten Theil von Goethes Faust
(Choruses for the Second Part of Goethe's Faust). Manuscript.
Felix Mendelssohn's sister married the painter Hensel in 1829;
died in Berlin, May 4, 1847 during a rehearsal of her Faust music.

Litolff, Henry Charles (1818-1891). Scenen aus Goethes Faust, mit Or-
(B) chester. Scene I. Faust in seinem Studirzimmer (Faust in his
(C) study), for orchestra, soprano, baritone and chorus with declamation, op. 103, no. 1. Scene II. Vor dem Thore (Before the Gate),
for orchestra, tenor, bass and chorus, op. 103, no. 2. Scene III.
Gretchen in der Kirche (Marguerite in the Church), for orchestra,
organ, soprano, bass and chorus, op. 103, no. 3. Scene IV. Ker-
ker (Prison), for orchestra, soprano and chorus with declamation,
op. 103, no. 4. Braunschweig: printed by his own publishing
house, n.d.

Loewe, Carl (1796-1869). Die erste Walpurgisnacht.

Mendelssohn, Felix (1809-1847). Walpurgisnacht. London: Novello, n.d.
(NU)

Meyerbeer, Giacomo (1791-1864). Die "Kirchenscene" des ersten und das
"Hosianna der Cherubim" des zweiten Theils aus Goethes "Faust"
(The "Church Scene" of the first and the "Hosannah of the Cheru-
bim" of the second part of Goethe's Faust). Manuscript.

Mojsisovics, Roderich von (1877-   ). Chorus mysticus, op. 4, 2 Soprano, alto, Doppelchorus, orchestra.

Roda, Ferdinand von (1818-1876). Faust, Musikdrama nach Goethe's Dichtung fuer Concert-Auffuehrung (Faust, music drama after Goethe's
poem for concert performance). Performed in Rostock, March 7,
1872.

Schumann, Robert (1810-1856). Scenen aus Goethes Faust fuer Solostim-
(N) men, Chor und Orchester (Scenes from Goethe's Faust for solo voi-
(NU) ces, chorus and orchestra). Leipzig: C. F. Peters, 187-? Writ-
ten, 1844-1850.

Speidel, Wilhelm (1826-1899). Geisterchor aus Faust von Goethe, fuer
Maennerchor (Chorus of spirits from Goethe's Faust for men's chorus), op. 40. Leipzig: Kahnt.

Stiober, Hans (1886-   ). Faust Cantata. Heidelberg: Sueddeutscher
(C) Musik-verlag, 1955.

Striecher, Theodor (1874-1940). Scenen und Bilder (Scenes and pictures),
for baritone, mixed chorus and orchestra. Written, 1911.

Taubert, Wilhelm (1811-1891). Geisterchor aus Goethe's Faust (Chorus of spirits from Goethe's Faust), op. 26, no. 6. Berlin: Schlesinger (R. Lienau). In: Zehn Lieder fuer Sopran, Alt. Tenor, und Bass. 2 Lieferung.

Wolfurt, Kurt von (1880-   ). Rhapsodie aus "Faust" (Chorwerk). Performed in Munich, 1909.

Small Choral Works

Mixed Chorus

Banck, Carl (1809-1889). Peasants' Dance and Song, op. 31, 1 for Soprano, clarinet, and mixed chorus. Faust I, 2, v. 949. Leipzig: Kistner.

Bleyle, Leo (1880-   ). Chorus mysticus, op. 19, for mixed chorus, harmonium, and clarinet. Faust II, V, 7, v. 12 104.

Boettcher, Georg (1889-   ). Das ist der Weisheit letzter Schluss (The last result of wisdom stamps it true), cantata for baritone, orchestra, and chorus. Faust II, V, 6, v. 11 574. Wie alles sich zum Ganzen webt (How each of the whole its substance gives), cantata 11. Faust I, v. 447. Chorus mysticus, cantata 19. Faust II, V, 7, v. 12 104. Lynkeus' Tower Song, cantata 24. Faust II, V, 4, v. 11 288.

Buechter, Fritz (1903-   ). Lynkeus' Tower Song, cantata op. 11, 1. Faust II, V, 4, v. 11 288.

Clemens, Adolf (1909-1942?). "Sprich aus der Ferne" (Voice from the distance) - Lynkeus' Tower Song, for soprano and mixed chorus. Faust II, V, 4, v. 11 288.

Haydn, Franz J. (1732-1809). Du musst verstehn (See, thus it's done). Faust I, 6, v. 2540.

Hoeffer, Paul (1895-1949). Der reiche Tag (The rich day), oratorio. Faust I, 2, v. 949. Composed, 1938.

Hummel, Ferdinand (1855-1928). The King of Thule, op. 111, 3. Faust I, 8, v. 2759.

Knab, Armin (1881-1951). Peasants' Dance and Song. Faust I, 2, v. 949.

Lendvai, Erwin (1882-1949). Die Sonne Toent nach alter Weise (The sun-orb sings, in emulation), comic cantata for mixed chorus and orchestra, op. 50, 3. Faust I, Prologue in heaven, v. 243.

Messchaert, Johs. (1857-1922). The King of Thule. Faust I, 8, v. 2759.

Schlottmann, Louis (1826-1905). The King of Thule, op. 34, 2. Faust I,
8, v. 2759. Berlin: Challier & Co.

Schumann, Robert (1810-1856). The King of Thule, op. 67, 1. Faust I,
8, v. 2759. Leipzig: Whistling.

Sehlbach, Erich (1898-   ). Lynkeus' Tower Song, op. 60. Faust II, V,
4, v. 11 288.

Streicher, Theodore (1874-1940). Angels' Easter Chorus. Faust I, 1,
v. 737. Leipzig: Breitkopf & Haertel.

Taubert, Wilhelm (1811-1891). The King of Thule, op. 81, 1. Faust I,
8, v. 2759. Leipzig: Breitkopf & Haertel.

Thate, Albert (1908-   ). Lynkeus' Tower Song. Faust II, V, 4, v. 11
288.

Unger, Hermann (1886-   ). Angels' Easter Chorus, for mixed chorus or
women's chorus, and small orchestra, op. 56. Faust I, 1, v. 737.

Wennerberg, Gunnar (1817-1901). Scenes from Goethe's Faust for solo
voice and chorus. Vol. I: Auerbach's Cellar in Leipzig. Stockholm: Hirsch.

Zoellner, Carl Fr. (1800-1890). Soldiers' Song, for mixed chorus, clarinet and winds. Faust I, 2, v. 884.

Men's Chorus

Herbeck, Johann (1831-1877). Soldiers' Chorus from Goethe's Faust. No.
37 in "Sammlung von Choeren und Quartetten fuer Maennerstimmen."
Vienna: Gloeggl.

Horn, August (1825-1893). Auerbach's Keller, op. 58. Poem by Mueller
(S) von der Werra. Leipzig: Breitkopf & Haertel, 1891?

Just, J. (? - ?). Soldiers' Chorus - Burgen mit hohen Mauern und Zinnen (Castles with lofty ramparts and towers). Faust I, 2, v. 884.
Vocal quartets, Vol. III. Frankfurt: Fischer.

Lemcke, H. (? - ?). Soldiers' Song from Faust, op. 12, 1. Bonn:
Simrock.

Liszt, Franz (1811-1886). Soldiers' Song from Goethe's Faust. Brander's
Song "Es lebt eine Ratt" (There lived a rat). Faust I, 5, v. 2126.
Mainz: B. Schott's Soehne.

Moehring, Ferdinand (1816-1887). Die Maulbronner Fuge, op. 89. Poem
by J. B. Scheffel. Men's chorus with bass solo. Offenbach-am-
Main: Andre.

Ochs, Siegfried (1859-1929). Die Maulbronner Fuge, op. 3, for baritone and men's chorus. By J. B. von Scheffel. Berlin: Rabe & Plothow.

Schachner, Rudolf J. (1815-1896). Die Maulbronner Fuge, op. 37, 1. From "Gaudeamus" by Victor von Scheffel. Vienna: Haslinger.

Schubert, Franz (1797-1828). The King of Thule. Faust I, 8, v. 2759. Set for men's chorus by Robert Musiol. Vienna: Schreiber.

Veit, Wenzel H. (1806-1864). The King of Thule, op. 37, 4. Faust I, 8, v. 2759. Leipzig: Breitkopf & Haertel.

Woehler, Gotthard (? - ?). The King of Thule, op. 27, 1. Faust I, 8, v. 2759. Pest: Kugler.

Women's Chorus

Hermann, Hans (1870-1931). Chorus of Spirits - Himmlischer Soehne (Heaven's own children). Faust I, 3, v. 1457.

Liszt, Franz (1811-1886). Angels' Chorus from Faust II. Leipzig: Schuberth & Co., 1875.

Unger, Hermann (1886-   ). Christ ist erstanden (Christ is risen), Angel's chorus, op. 56. Faust I, 1, v. 737.

Orchestral Works

Symphonies

Albrecht, Max R. (1890-   ). Faustsinfonie.

Heidingsfeld, Ludwig (1854-1920). Triumph-Sinfonie ueber Faust's Rettung (mit Bezug auf die Goethe'sche Tragoedie), fuer Orchester und Chor (Triumphal Symphony over Faust's redemption (with reference to Goethe's tragedy), for orchestra and chorus). 1. Theil (fuer Orchestra). Triumphspiel (Triumphal music). Empfindungen bei der Erinnerung an Gretchen (Emotions experienced at the recollection of Marguerite). 2. Theil (fuer Orchester). Von ewiger Liebe (Of eternal love). 3. Theil (fuer Orchester und Chor). Choere der Engel (Angelic Choruses). 4. Theil (Orchester und Chor). Chorus mysticus. Presented in Glogau at the Sing-Akademie, November 18, 1882.

Liszt, Franz (1811-1886). Eine Faust-Symphonie in drei Charakterbildern
(N)   (nach Goethe) (A Faust Symphony in three character sketches (after
(NU) Goethe). I. Faust (allegro). II. Gretchen (andante). III. Mephistopheles (scherzo und finale) mit Schlusschor fuer grosses Orchester und Maennerchor (with closing chorus for men's chorus and orchestra). Leipzig: J. Schuberth, 1866.

Mahler, Gustav (1860-1911). Symphony of the Thousand, no. 8, for chorus
(N)   and orchestra. Text for part 1 - Veni Creator Spiritus. Text for
(NU) part 2 - closing scene of Faust, part II, pp. 75-218. Vienna:
(S)   Aktiengesellschaft, c. 1911.

Raspe, Dr. (? - ?). Symphonie nach Motiven aus Goethe's Faust (Sym-
       phony after motives from Goethe's Faust). Performed in Rostock,
       January, 1875.

Symphonic Poems and Fantasies

Heidingsfeld, Ludwig (1854-1920). Faust, symphonic poem.

Hirschbach, Hermann (1812-1888). Faust's Spaziergang (Faust's Prome-
       nage). Fantasie fuer Orchester, op. 27. Heraustritt in die Natur.
       Innere Stimme. Von ferne herueber. Beim Sonnenuntergang (Going
       out among nature. Inner voice. From a distance. At sunset).

Mihalovich, Edmund von (1842-1929). Eine Faust-Phantasie fuer grosses
(B)   Orchester. Arrangement for piano, four hands, made by the compo-
(C)   ser. Leipzig: Breitkopf & Haertel.

Muenchheimer, Adam (1831-1904). Faust, symphonic poem.

Nyiregyházi, Erwin. Mephisto Triumphiert, fantasy no. 1, for large or-
(C)   chestra. Kristiania (Norway). Piano reduction published by the
       composer, 1920.

Rabaud, Henri (1873-1949). La Procession Nocturne Poème symphonique
(N)   d'après Nicholas Lenau, op. 6. Paris: Durand, c. 1910.

Overtures

Bierey, Gottlob (1772-1840). Ouvertuere zu Faust von Klingemann. Man-
       uscript. Schlesisches Tonkuenstler-Lexicon, Vol. I, pp. 16-21.
       Breslau: Koaamaly & Carlo, 1864.

Ginastera Alberto E. (1916-   ). Oberturo para el "Fausto" criollo.
       Buenos Aires: Barry & Cia., 1951. Written, 1943.

Hiller, Ferdinand (1811-1885). Faust Overture. Ouvertuere zu Goethe's
       Faust. Manuscript. The work was written in his youth.

Mayer, Emilie (1821-1883). Faust Overture, op. 46 (fuer grosses Orches-
(B)   ter). Stettin: Witte, 187-?
(C)

Schubert, Franz (1797-1828). Ouvertuere zu Goethe's Faust. Manuscript.
       Performed at the "Euterpe" concert, December 18, 1841.

Schulz, Karl (? - ?). Faust Ouverture, op. 8. Leipzig: Hofmeister,
(C) n.d.

Taubert, Wilhelm (1811-1891). Ouvertuere zu Goethe's Faust. Manuscript.

Wagner, Richard (1813-1883). Eine Faust-Ouvertuere. Leipzig: Breit-
(N) kopf & Haertel, 1890.
(NU)

Occasional Pieces

Foerster, Adolph (1854-1927). Prelude to Goethe's Faust, op. 48. New
(P) York: C. Fischer, 1915.

Frankel, Benjamin (1906- ?). Mephistopheles' Serenade and Dance, a
(C) caricature for orchestra, op. 25. London: Augener, 1953.

Graener, Paul (1872-1943). Tuermerlied, op. 107. Orchestral Variations.

Liszt, Franz (1811-1886). Zwei Episoden aus Lenau's Faust (Two episodes from Lenau's Faust). I. Der naechtliche Zug (The Nocturnal Procession). II. Der Tanz in der Dorfschenke (Mephisto-Wal-
zer) (Dance in the village inn). Leipzig: Schuberth & Co., 187-?
This music was transcribed by the composer for piano, two and four
hands.

Ballet Scores

Adam, Adolph (1803-1856). Music for the ballet "Faust." Performed in
London at the King's Theater, 1856.

Dunkel, Friedrich (? - ?). Music for the pantomime ballet, "Doktor
Faust," by Ruth. Presented in Dresden, 1809.

Egk, Werner (1910- ?). Abraxas, ballet on the Faust theme in five episodes: The Pact, The Snare, The Pandemonium, The Dream, The Solution. Composed, 1947.

St. Lubin, Leon de (1805-1860). Music for the pantomime "Dr. Faust's
Nephew." Presented in Berlin, 1832. This may be an operetta.

Panizza, Giacomo (1804-1860). "Faust." Ballo fantastico by Giulio
(P) Perrot adapted from Goethe's Faust. Milan: Ricordi, 1848? Pre-
(S) sented in Milan, 1848.

Pugni, Caesar (1810-1870). Music for the fantastic ballet "Faust" by
Julius Perrot. St. Petersbourg: Glasounoff & Co., 1854.

Reuner, Carl (1778-1830). Music for the ballet "Faust". (Weber remarks that there are a number of substantial compositions in this ballet). Posthumous Writings, Dresden (1828) II, 26.

Ronzani, Domenico (? - ?). Faust: A grand fantastic ballet, in three
(B) acts and ten tableaux. Translated and adapted by C. M. Richings. Philadelphia: Rullman, 1857 (words only).

Skvor, Frantisek (? - ?). Faust ballet. 1926.

Waldmueller, Ferdinand (? - ?). Faust Ballet fantastique, op. 79.
(P) Bouquet of melodies for piano. Vienna: Pietro Mechetti, 1850.

Incidental Music for the Play

Arnim, Bettina von (born Brentano) (1785-1859?). Attempted a musical setting of Faust.

Artus, M. (? - ?). Music to the French fantastic drama Faust by Adolphe D'Ennery after Goethe.

Blum, Carl (1786-1844). Music for the folk melodrama, Faust the Wonder Working Magician of the North, by K. von Holtei. First performance in Berlin at the Koenigstaedtische Theater, January 10, 1829.

Bondeville, Emmanuel (1898- ?). Illustrations for Faust. Concert
(N) version. After Goethe's Faust Part I. Translated and adapted by Pierre Sabatier. Paris: Durand, c. 1955.

Brahms, Johannes (1833-1897) with Dessoff and Hellmesberter. Stage music. Vienna: c. 1875.

Bungert, August (1846-1915). Stage music, op. 58. 2 vols. Leipzig:
(C) C. F. Leede, 1903.

Cadou, Andre P. (1885- ?). Incidental music for Faust tragedy by
(C) Goethe transposed into a prologue, seventeen tableaux and an epilogue. Paris: Coutan-Lambert, 1937.

Coleridge-Taylor, Samuel (1875-1912). Stage Music. Incidental Music
(C) to Stephen Phillips and J. Comyns Carr's version of Goethe's drama. London: Boosey & Co., 1908.

Conradi, August (1821-1873). Music to the fairy tale Faust and Beautiful Helena, op. 131. Berlin: Bote & Bock.

Damcke, Berthold (1812-1875). Music for Goethe's Faust. Manuscript.

Eberwein, Karl (1784-1868). Music for the first act of Faust, Part II by Goethe. Composed in Weimar, 1829. Performed in Weimar, June 24, 1856.

Fritze, Wilhelm (1842-1881). Music to Goethe's Faust. For concert performance. With explanation of the unity of the composed parts by G. v. T. (1871).

Gregoir, Edouard (1822-1890). Music for the play.

Grelinger, Charles (1873- ?). Incidental Music for Fausta; verse play
(P) in four acts with prologue. Text by Paul Sonnies. Paris: P. Ollendorff, 1899. First performance in Paris at Nouveau-Theatre, May 16, 1894.

Hatton, John L. (1809-1886). Ouverture und Entr'actes zum Drama: Faust et Marguerite. Manuscript.

Herbeck, Johann (1831-1877). Music to Goethe's Faust. Manuscript.

Kienlen, Johann Christoph (1784-1830). Music for the play.

Kreutzer, Konradin (1780-1849). Music for the play.

Lassen, Eduard (1830-1904). Music for Goethe's Faust, Parts I and II,
(S) op. 57. After the version of Otto Devrient. Hainauer: Breslau, 1876. This work was presented for the first time on the commemoration of Goethe's coming to Weimar.

Lassen, F. (? - ?). Faust's Tod und Entsuehnung aus Goethes Faust, Part II, Acts 4 and 5. Berlin: O. Dreyer, 1925.

Lazzari, Sylvio (? - ?). Faust. Incidental music for Goethe's dra-
(C) ma. Transcribed for small orchestra by Godfroy Andolfi. Paris: Buffet-Crampon, 1925.

Lindpaintner, Peter Joseph von (1791-1856). Music for the Faust trage-
(C) dy by Goethe, op. 83 (1832?). Leipzig: Peters. Presented in Stuttgart at the Hoftheater, March 2, 1832. Overture published under op. 80. Leipzig: C. F. Peters, n.d.

Lothar, Mark (1902- ?). Music for the play.

Petzold, Eugen Karl (1813-1889). Music for the play.

Pembaur, Karl Maria (1876-1939). Music for the Weimar production of Part I under Ernst Hardt, 1920.

Piccini, A. (? - ?). Music for the French drama by Anthony Bérard after Goethe. Paris: Chassaignon, 1828. Presented at the theatre de la Porte-Saint-Martin, October 29, 1828.

Pierson, Henry H. (1816-1873). Music for the second part of Goethe's
(B)   Faust. German and English text. Mainz: B. Schott's Soehne,
      187-? Performed in Hamburg at the Stadttheater, March 25, 1854.

Radziwill, Anton H., Fuerst von (1775-1833). Compositions for Goethe's
(N)   Faust. Completed, 1819. First performance in Berlin at the Sing-
      akademie, 1835. Commissioned by J. Trautwein, Berlin. It is a
      deluxe edition with illustrations by Biermann, Cornelius, Hensel,
      Hosemann, Prince Ferdinand Radziwill, E. Schulz, and Zimmerman.
      His work is supposed to be far above that of a mere dilettante.

Reichardt, Johann Friedrich (1752-1814). Music to Goethe's Faust. Man-
      uscript. Performed or composed, c. 1790.

Reichwein, Leopold (1878- ?). Music for the play.

Reissiger, Carl Gottlieb (1798-1859). Music for the entr'acte Helena
      from Goethe's Faust. In Gutzkow's version a fragment from the
      second part of Goethe's Faust with the title "The Rape of Helena"
      with Reissiger's music was performed in Dresden as a festival
      play, 1849, on the centenary of Goethe's birth.

Rietz, Julius (1812-1877). Music for the Witches' Kitchen (Hexenkueche)
      scene in Goethe's Faust. Leipzig: C. F. Kahnt. Performed in
      Duesseldorf, c. 1836.

Salmhofer, Franz (? - ?). Stage music. Vienna: Universal edition,
      1928.

Schillings, Max von (1868-1933). Music for the play.

Schloesser, Louis (1800-1886). Music for the First Part of Goethe's
      Faust. First performance in Darmstadt at the court theater, Feb-
      ruary 11, 1838.

Schulz, Christian Johann Philipp (1773-1828). Music for the tragedy
      Faust by Klingemann. Overture is op. 8. Leipzig: Hofmeister.

Seyfried, Ignatz X., Ritter von (1776-1828). A Dramatic Legend, music
(B)   for the tragedy Faust by Klingemann. Leipzig: Breitkopf & Haer-
      tel. Written for Vienna, 1820. Remaining in manuscript for the-
      atrical performance. Orchestral parts for overture.

Simon, Hermann (1896-1948). Music for the First Part of Goethe's Faust.
(C)   Berlin: Bote & Bock, c. 1941. Written or performed, c. 1932.
(S)

Stone, Gregory (? -   ). Music for the Max Reinhardt production of
      Faust. Composed for presentations in America, 1938.

Tomachek, Johann (1774-1850). Music for the First Part of Goethe's
Faust. Manuscript in the Bohemian Museum-Library in Prague.
Songs only.

Trantow, Herbert (1903- ?). Stage music for Urfaust. Performed in
Dresden, 1948.

Weigmann, Friedrich (? - ?). Music for Goethe's Faust, Part I. Berlin: B. Scheithauer, 1901.

Weingartner, Paul Felix von [Edler von Muenzberg] (1863-1942). Stage
(B) music for Goethe's Faust, op. 43. Leipzig: Breitkopf & Haertel, 1907.

Music for Burlesques, Musical Comedies,
Parodies, and Puppet Plays

Arnold, Samuel (1740-1802). Harlequin and Faustus.

Barbier, Frederic E. (1829-1889). Le Faux Faust (The False Faust).
Parody in three acts. Presented in Paris at the "Folies nouvel-
les," 1858.

Bishop, Henry R. (1786-1855). Faust a musical romance. T. Cooke and
C. E. Horn assisted in the composition. London: Goulding &
D'Almaine, 1825. Presented at the Theatre Royal Drury Lane, 1825.

Buechel, A. (? - ?). Music for Margaretha; or, the Parodied One.
Theater manuscript. This is a parody of Gounod's Faust with
song, dance and music in five acts and four entr'actes. Breslau:
Freund.

Clarke, James Hamilton Smee (1840-1912). Faust, operetta?

Galliard, Johann Ernst (1687-1749). Music to The Necromancer, or Harlequin Doctor Faustus. Farce by W. Mountfort.

Genée, Richard and Storch, A. M. (1823-1895). Music to the comedy of
magic Ein moderner Faust (A Modern Faust). Comedy with a prelude
and four acts by P. F. Trautmann. (Theater-Commissions-Geschaeft
von H. Michaelson in Berlin). London: 1715. Riemann says this
is the oldest musical-dramatic version.

Goodwin, ? (? - ?). Harlequin Faustus, Operetta. Text by Preston.

Grétry, André Ernest Modeste (1741-1813). La fausse magie (The False
(N) Magic). Comedy in one act. Text by J. F. Marmontel. Paris:
Houbaut, 1782. First performance in Paris, February 1, 1775.

Halford, John (? - ?). Faust and Marguerite; or, The Devils Draught. A grand operatic extravaganza. A "free and easy" adaptation of Goethe's Faust. London: T. H. Lacy, 18--?

Hanke, Carl (1754-1835). Music for the comedy Doktor Faust's Leibguertel (Doctor Faust's Waistband). Written for the theater in Flensburg, 1794.

Hebenstrait, P. (? - ?). Doctor Faust's Zauber Kaeppchen (Magic Hat). Vienna: 1843.

Hervé, Florimond Ronger, known as (1825-1892). Le petit Faust (The Little Faust). Opera-bouffe in three acts and four tableaux. Words
(N) by Cremieux and Jaime. Paris: Heugel. First performance in Paris at the Folies Dramatiques, April, 1869. Parody on Gounod's opera.

Homann, W. (1894- ?). Music for the parody Faust and Marguerite. Text by C. Schultze and L. Schoebel. Theater manuscript in the Carl Schultze-Theater in Hamburg.

Hopp, Julius (? - ?). Music to the comic opera-burlesque Faust and Grete. Five acts after Barbier and Carré. Text by Quidam and Hopp. Theater manuscript. Vienna: Spina (now Alwin Cranz).

Lang, Adolph (? - ?). Music for the one act dramatic comedy Faust
(B) und Gretchen. Text by Ed. Jacobson. Theater-manuscript. Berlin: A. Heinrich, 186-? Margaretha. Solo scene with piano. Parody on Gounod's opera. Text by Salingré. Berlin: Bloch.

Levenston, P. M. (? - ?). Doctor Faust. Produced in Dublin, May, 1892.

Lutz, Wilhelm Meyer (1892-1903). Faust up to Date, burlesque opera.
(B) Text by George R. Sims and Henry Pettitt. 9th ed. Ascherberg
(C) & Co., 1889.

Moreau, Max (? - ?). Faust 1944, opera in three acts. Paris: Edi-
(S) tions Marion, 1944. Probably a parody of Gounod's opera.

Mueller, Wenzel (1767-1835). Music for the comedy of magic Doctor Faust's Mantel. Text by Ad. Baeuerle. Vienna: Haslinger. Performed in Vienna, 1818. Music to the magic play The Shadow of Faust's Wife. Text by Ad. Baeuerle.

Phanty, ? (1766- ?). Musikdirector der Tillyschen Schauspieler-gesellschaft im Jahre 1785; hat die Operette Doktor Faust's Leibguertel nebst einigen Balleten in Musik gesetzt. Leipzig: 1792.

Redstone, Willy (? -   ) and Gideon, Melville (? -   ). Faust on
(C) Toast. A gaiety burlesque. Written by F. Firth Shephard and Adrian Ross. London: B. Feldman & Co., 1921.

Stephan, M. (? - ?). Le Faux Faust, operette-bouffe. Presented at the Folies-Nouvelles, November, 1858.

Thiele, Richard (1847-1903). Faust and Gretchen, a comic sketch. Li-
(S) bretto by W. Koehler. Adapted by Adrian Rose. London: Joseph Williams, 1898? Original edition published, 1886-1891.

Wolf, Walter (? -   ). Music for the old puppet play Dr. Johann Faust. Arranged for hand puppets by R. A. Stemmle. Berlin: E. Bloch, 1928.

Songs
(with piano unless otherwise designated)

Alvensleben, G. von (? - ?). Opus 2. Six Songs for Alto or Baritone. No. 4, Der Koenig in Thule (The king of Thule). Faust I, viii, 2759.

Anonymous. Faust Lied. Comical round song. Berlin: E. Bloch, n.d.

Arnim, Bettina von (born Brentano) (1785-1859). Seven Compositions. No. 2, O schaudre nicht (O do not shudder). Faust I, xii, 3188. No. 5, Herbst Gefuehl (Autumn mood). Leipzig: Breitkopf & Haer-tel.

Banck, Karl (1809-1899). Bauer, Buerger, Bettelmann, op. 31, No. 1.
(S) Tanzreigen aus Faust. Leipzig: Fr. Kistner, 1839.

Barbier, Frederic E. (1829-1889). Faust et Marguerite, a little comic play in the Spanish manner. Words by Baumaine and Blondelet. Paris: Feuchot.

Baussnern, Waldemar von (1866-1931). Es war ein Koenig in Thule (The king of Thule), op. 3, 5. Faust I, viii, 2759. Steigt hinan zu hoeherm Kreise (Upward rise to higher borders). Faust II, V, vii, 11 918.

Beer, Max Joseph (? - ?). Gretchen am Spinnradl (Margaret at the spinning wheel), op. 2. Meine Ruh' ist hin (My peace is gone). Faust I, xv, 3374. Vienna: Buchholz & Diebel.

Beethoven, Ludwig van (1770-1827). Flohlied (Song of the flea). Es war einmal ein Koenig (There was a king once reigning), op. 75, no. 3. Faust I, v, 2211. Gretels Warnung (Margaret's warning), op. 75, no. 4. Leipzig: Breitkopf & Haertel.

Behrends, F. W. (? - ?). Der Koenig von Thule (The king of Thule). Faust I, viii, 2759.

Boettcher, Georg (1889- ?). Cantata No. 21 for soprano, clarinet and
    orchestra. Neige, neige, du Onnegleiche (Incline, O Maiden, with
    mercy laden). Faust II, V, vii, 12 069.

Bordese, Luigi (1815-1886). Faust et Mephistopheles, duet. Words by
(B) L. de Peyre. Paris: Schonenberger. Faust, Scene dramatique.
    Words by Edouard Plouvier. Paris: Choudens, 186-?

Breu, Simon (1858-1933). Es war ein Koenig in Thule (There was a king
    in Thule), op. 65, 1. Faust I, viii, 2759.

Bruyck, Carl Debrois van (1828-1902). Drei Lieder Gretchens (Three of
    Margaret's Songs). Ich gaeb was drum, wenn ich nur wuesst (I'd
    something give, could I but say). Faust I, viii, 2678. Wie konnt
    ich sonst so tapfer schmaehlen (How scornfully I once reviled).
    Faust I, xvii, 3577. Ach neige, du Schmerzen reiche (Incline, O
    Maiden, Thou sorrow-laden). Faust I, xviii, 3587. Leipzig:
    Breitkopf & Haertel.

Buelow, Hans von (1830-1894). Der Koenig von Thule (The king of Thule).
    Faust I, viii, 2759. Munich: Aiblinger.

Busoni, Ferruccio (1866-1894). Mephisto's Flohlied (Song of the flea),
    op. 49, 2. Faust I, v, 2211.

Canthal, A. M. (? - ?). Three Lieder aus Goethe's Faust. Hamburg:
    Boehme.

Carstens, C. (? - ?). Der Koenig von Thule (The king of Thule).
    Faust I, viii, 2759.

Cassimir, Heinrich (1873- ?). Die Sonne toent nach alter Weise (The
    sun-orb sings, in emulation). Faust I, prologue in heaven, 243.
    Leipzig: Schuberth & Co.

Commer, Franz (1813-1887). Mein Ruh' ist hin (My peace is gone), op.
    19, 3. Faust I, xv, 3374. Berlin: Bote & Bock.

Curschmann, Friedrich (1805-1841). Meine Ruh' ist hin (My peace is
    gone), op. 11, 5. Faust I, xv, 3374. Berlin: Schlesinger.

Dessauer, Josef (1798-1876). Gretchen im Faust. Ach neige, du Schmer-
    zen reiche (Incline, O Maiden, Thou sorrow-laden). Faust I,
    xviii, 3587. Leipzig: Hofmeister.

Deurer, Ernst (? - ?). Der Koenig von Thule (The king of Thule), op.
    11, 2. Faust I, viii, 2759. Leipzig: R. Seitz.

Dixon, Thomas B. (? - ?). Margaret's Gebet, for voice and orchestra.
    Privately printed by the composer, 1901. This is an effective
    part of a larger projected work.

Draeske, Felix (1835-1913). Der Koenig in Thule (The king of Thule), op. 26, 6. Faust I, viii, 2759.

Dreszer, A. A. (? - ?). Der Koenig in Thule. For bass. Manuscript. Faust I, viii, 2759.

Eckert, Karl (1820-1879). Der Koenig in Thule. Faust I, viii, 2759.

Festari C. V. (? - ?). Il re di Thule (The king of Thule). Translated from Goethe by G. Carducci. Faust I, viii, 2759. Milan: Ricordi.

Fink, Gottfried Wilhelm (1783-1846). Der Koenig in Thule, op. 18. Faust I, viii, 2759.

Fischer, Karl August (1885- ?). Gretchen vor der Mater dolorosa (Margaret before the Sorrowful Mother). Ach neige, du Schmerzen reiche (Incline, O Maiden, Thou sorrow-laden), op. 11, 1. Faust I, xviii, 3587. Berlin: Schlesinger.

Foergeois, F. (? - ?). Two Songs from Goethe's Faust: Es war einmal ein Koenig (The was a king in Thule). Faust I, viii, 2579. Es war 'ne Ratt im Kellernest (There was a rat in his cellar nest), op. 7. Faust I, v, 2126. Berlin: Challier & Co.

Francaix, Jean (1912-   ). Mephisto's Cantata for bass and string quartet.

Freundenberg, Wilhelm (1838-1928). Margaret's Prayer before the picture of the Sorrowful Mother. From Goethe's Faust for solo voice with orchestra. Faust I, xviii, 3587. Leipzig: Matthes.

Fritze, Wilhelm (1842-1881). The King of Thule, op. 17, 1. Faust I, viii, 2759. Margaret at the Spinning Wheel, op. 17, 2. Faust I, xviii, 3374. Prayer Before the Sorrowful Mother, op. 17, 3. Faust I, xviii, 3587.

Geilsdorff, Paul (1890- ?). Zum Sehen geboren (For seeing intended), song of Lynkeus. Faust II, iv, 11 288.

Glinka, Michail J. (1804-1857). Margaret at the Spinning Wheel. Faust I, xviii, 3374. Hamburg: F. Schuberth.

Gounod Charles (1818-1893). Margaret. Berlin: Fuerstner. Fausto, romanza di Siebel. Paris: Choudens, 1876. This is not from the opera.

Graben-Hoffmann, Gustav (1820-1900). Margaret's Spinning Song, op. 65. Faust I, xviii, 3374. Leipzig: Schuberth & Co.

Grimmer, Friedrich (1798-1850). The King of Thule, no. 5, from collection of 20 ballads and romances. Faust I, viii, 2759. Leipzig: Schuberth & Co.

Goenland, Peter (1761-1834). Angels' Easter Chorus, Christ ist erstan-
(S) den (Christ is arisen). Faust I, i, 737. The King of Thule.
     Faust I, viii, 2759. Leipzig: Breitkopf & Haertel.

G'schrey, Richard (1876- ?). Ach neige, du Schmerzen reiche (Incline,
     O Maiden, Thou sorrow-laden), op. 1. Faust I, xviii, 3587.

Haszlinger, Johann von (1822-1898). Margaret's Spinning Song, op. 5,
     6. Faust I, xv, 3374. Berlin: Haslinger.

Hauptmann, Moritz (1792-1868). Margaret Before the Image of the Sorrow-
(S) ful Mother, op. 3. Faust I, xviii, 3587. Leipzig: Peters.
     Piano acc. arranged for orchestra by Fr. v. Holstein. Leipzig:
     C. F. Peters, 1821.

Hetsch, Ludwig (1806-1872). Margaret's Spinning Song. Faust I, xv,
     3374. Bonn: Simrock.

Hiller, Ferdinand (1811-1885). The King of Thule. Faust I, viii, 2759.

Himmel, Friedrich H. (1765-1814). The King of Thule, set for solo male
     voice. Faust I, viii, 2759. Leipzig: Peters.

Hirschberg, Walter (1889- ?). Hoechste Herrscherin der Welt (Highest
     Mistress of the world), op. 34, 6. Faust II, V, vii, 11 997.

Hoesel, Kurt (1862-1929). Der Schaefer putzte sich (All for the dance
     the shepherd dressed). Dance and song from Faust I, ii, 949.

Jansen, Gustav (? - ?). Margaret's Spinning Song, for mezzo-soprano.
     Faust I, xv, 3374. Berlin: H. Mendel.

Jenner, Gustav (1865-1920). The King of Thule. Faust I, viii, 2759.

Jensen, Adolf (1837-1879). The King of Thule, op. 23, 6. Faust I,
     viii, 2759. Die Maulbronner Fuge von J. B. Scheffel, op. 40, 4.
     Dresden: Hoffarth.

Kaehler, Willibald (1866-1938). Was machst du mir (What dost thou
     here). Faust I, xix, 3682.

Kahn, Robert (1865- ?). Soldiers' Song. Burgen mit hohen Mauern und
     Zinnen (Castles with lofty ramparts and towers). Faust I, ii,
     884.

Kauffmann, Emil (1836-1909). Der Schaefer putzte sich (All for the
     dance the shepherd dressed). Dance and song from Faust I, ii,
     949.

Kienlen, Johann C. (1784-1830). Songs from Goethe's Faust for solo
(S) voice. 1. Burgen mit hohen Mauern und Zinnen (Castles with lofty ramparts and towers). Faust I, ii, 884. 2. Es war ein Koenig in Thule (There was a king in Thule). Faust I, viii, 2759.
3. Der Schaefer putzte sich zum Tanz (All for the dance the shepherd dressed). Faust I, ii, 949. 4. Verlassen hab' ich Feld und
Auen (Behind me, field and meadow sleeping). Faust I, iii, 1178.
5. Es war eine Ratt' im Keller-nest (There was a rat in the cellar nest). Faust I, v, 2126. 6. Meine Ruh' ist hin (My peace
is gone). Faust I, xv, 3374. 7. Was machst du mir vor Liebchens
Thuer (What dost thou here in day-break clear). Faust I, xix,
3682. Berlin: Schlesinger, 1817.

Kienzl, Wilhelm (1857-1941). Brander's Song in Auerbach's Cellar - Es
war eine Ratt (There was a rat). Faust I, v, 2126. Mephistopheles' Song in Auerbach's Cellar - Es war einmal ein Koenig (There
was a king once reigning), op. 25, 1 and 2. Faust I, v, 2211.
Angels' Easter Chorus - Christ ist erstanden (Christ is risen),
op. 76, 1. Faust I, i, 737.

Klein, Bernhard (1793-1832). Margaret's Prayer Before the Image of the
Sorrowful Mother. Faust I, xviii, 3587. The King of Thule. He
made two settings of this; one in A and one in G. Faust I, viii,
2759. Leipzig: Breitkopf & Haertel.

Klemperer, Otto (1885- ?). The King of Thule. Faust I, viii, 2759.

Kosmaly, Karl (1812-1893). Die Maerchen von Dr. Faust (The tale of Dr.
Faust), romance for bass. Berlin: Lischke.

Kraushaar, Otto (? - ?). Margaret's Spinning Song, op. 6, 1. Faust
I, xv, 3374. Cassel: Luckhardt.

Labarre, T. (? - ?). Mephistopheles. Ballad. Words by E. Hanappier.
Paris: Depot central de la Musique et de la Librairie, 1825?

Lang, Hans (1897- ?). Burgen mit hohen Mauern und Zinnen (Castles
with lofty ramparts and towers), op. 8, 1. Faust I, ii, 884.
Der Schaefer putzte sich (All for the dance the shepherd dressed),
dance and song, op. 8, 2. Faust I, ii, 949.

Lauer, A. B. von (? - ?). Brander's Song. Faust I, v, 2126. Mephisto's Song. Faust I, v, 2211. Uns ist ganz kannibalisch wohl
(As 't were five hundred hogs, we feel). Faust I, v, 2293. The
King of Thule. Faust I, viii, 2759. Margaret's Prayer Before
the Image of the Sorrowful Mother. Faust I, xviii, 3587.

Lecerf, Justus A. (1789-1868). Nine songs for Goethe's Faust. 2 vols.
(S)   Vol. I: 1. Ihr naht euch wieder (Again ye come). Faust I, ded-
ication, 1. 2. Burgen mit hohen Mauern (Castles with lofty ram-
parts). Faust I, ii, 884. 3. Der Schaefer putzte sich zum Tanz
(All for the dance the shepherd dressed). Faust I, ii, 949. 4.
Verlassen hab' ich Feld und Auer (Behind me, field and meadow
sleeping). Faust I, iii, 1178. 5. Es war 'ne Ratt' im Keller
nest (There was a rat in the cellar nest). Faust I, v, 2126. 6.
Es war einmal ein Koenig (There was a king once reigning). Faust
I, v, 2211. 7. The King of Thule. Faust I, viii, 2759. 8.
Margaret's Spinning Song. Faust I, xv, 3374. 9. Margaret's
Prayer Before the Image of the Sorrowful Mother. Faust I, xviii,
3587. Berlin: Schlesinger, 1835?

Lenz, Leopold (? - ?). Songs from Goethe's Tragedy Faust. 2 vols.
(S)   Vol. I: Margaret's Songs. 1. Two settings of the King of Thule,
in E and G. Faust I, viii, 2759. 2. Margaret's Spinning Song.
Faust I, xv, 3374. Margaret's Prayer Before the Image of the Sor-
rowful Mother. Faust I, xviii, 3587. Vol. II: 4. Brander's
Song. Faust I, v, 2126. 5. Mephisto's Song of the Flea. Faust
I, v, 2211. 6. Mephisto's Serenade. Faust I, xix, 3682. 7.
Peasants' Song. Faust I, ii, 949. 8. Soldiers' Song. Faust I,
ii, 884. Mainz: B. Schott's Soehne, c. 1871.

Liebling, Estelle (1894-   ). Faustiana; vocal fantasy for col. soprano based on the ballet music from Gounod's Faust. New York:
Galaxy, 1950.

Lindpaintner, Peter J. von (1791-1856). Six Songs from Goethe's Faust,
op. 81. 1. Brander's Song. Faust I, v, 2126. 2. Mephisto's
Song of the Flea. Faust I, v, 2211. 3. The King of Thule. Faust
I, viii, 2759. 4. Margaret's Spinning Song. Faust I, xv, 3374.
5. Mephisto's Serenade. Faust I, xix, 3682. 6. Margaret's Dun-
geon Song. Faust I, xxv, 4412. Soldiers' Song, op. 82, 2. Faust
I, ii, 884. Peasants' Dance Song, op. 82, 4. Faust I, ii, 949.
Margaret's Song Before the Image of the Sorrowful Mother, op. 138.
Faust I, xviii, 3587. Rostock: Hagemann & Tropp.

Liszt, Franz (1811-1886). The King of Thule for mezzo-soprano or tenor.
Faust I, viii, 2759. Berlin: Schlesinger.

Loewe, Carl (1796-1869). Margaret's Spinning Song, op. 9, III. Faust
I, xv, 3374. Du siehst mich, Koenigen, zurueck! (Thou sees me,
Queen, returned and free!), op. 9, VIII, 2. Faust II, III, 9273.
Lynkeus' Tower Song, op. 9, VIII, 3. Faust II, V, iv, 11 288.
Margaret's Song Before the Image of the Sorrowful Mother, op. 9,
IX, 1. Faust I, xviii, 3587. Maedchen, als du kamst ans Licht
(Maiden, when thou cam'st to light). Faust I, iii, 5178. Ariel's
Song. Faust II, I, 4613. The last two published, Leipzig:
Breitkopf & Haertel.

Lorenz, Carl A. (1837-1923). Margaret's Spinning Song, op. 6. Faust
I, xv, 3374. Berlin: Simmel.

Lortzing, Albert (1801-1851). Lynkeus' Tower Song. Faust II, V, iv,
ll 288.

Lothar, Mark (1902-   ). Mephisto's Song of the Flea, op. 39, 1.
Faust I, v, 2211. Mephisto's Serenade, op. 39, 2. Faust I, xix,
3682.

Lyra, Justus W. (1822-1882). Mephisto's Song of the Flea. Faust I, v,
2211.

Macfarren, George A. (1813-1887). Margaret's Spinning Song, op. 50.
Faust I, xv, 3374. Leipzig: Kistner.

Madeweis, Georg von (? - ?). Ihr guten Herrn (Good gentlemen). Faust
I, ii, 852. Leipzig: Kistner.

Marschner, Heinrich (1795-1861). The King of Thule, for baritone, op.
160, 1. Faust I, viii, 2759. Brander's Song, for bass, op. 47,
6. Faust I, v, 2126. Leipzig: Hofmeister.

Mayerhoff, Franz (1864-1938). Angels' Easter Chorus, op. 27, 5. Faust
I, i, 737. Lynkeus' Tower Song, op. 51, 7. Faust II, V, iv,
ll 288.

Mendelssohn, Arnold (1855-1933). Peasants' Dance Song. Faust I, ii,
949. Lynkeus' Tower Song. Faust II, V, v, ll 288.

Meyerbeer, Giacomo (1791-1864). Six Elégies et Romances. No. 6: la
Marguerite du Poete. Leipzig: Breitkopf & Haertel.

Meyer-Olbersleben, Ernst L. (1898- ?). Lynkeus' Tower Song. Faust II,
V, iv, ll 288.

Moszkowski, Moritz (1854-1925). Peasants' Dance Song, op. 44. Faust I,
ii, 949.

Muennich, Richard (1877- ?). Lynkeus' Tower Song. Faust II, V, iv,
ll 288. Manuscript.

Mussorgsky, Modest P. (1839-1881). Mephisto's Song of the Flea. Faust
I, v, 2211.

Nessler, Victor E. (1841-1890). Brander's Song, op. 54, 1. Faust I, v,
2126. Mephisto's Song of the Flea, op. 54, 2. Faust I, v, 2211.
Leipzig: Forberg.

Neuland, W. (? - ?). La Marguerite de Faust, ballade. Text by P.
Hedouin. Mainz: B. Schott's Soehne.

Nussbaumer, Fr. (? - ?). Margaret's Spinning Song. Faust I, xv, 3374. Munich: Falter.

Oberfeld, C. (? -   ). Vivent les grosses dames, fox trot from the
(C) film "Mephisto." Paris: Salabert, 1931.

Petzold, Eugen K. (1813-1889). Mephisto's Song of the Flea. Faust I,
    v, 2211. The King of Thule. Faust I, viii, 2759. Margaret's
    Spinning Song. Faust I, xv, 3374. Mephisto's Serenade. Faust
    I, ix, 3682. Composed, 1850. Manuscript.

Pfitzner, Hans (1869-1949). Margaret's Prayer Before the Image of the
    Sorrowful Mother. In Das dunkle Reich (The dark kingdom), with
    orchestra. Faust I, viii, 3587.

Prochazka, Rudolph, Frh. v. (1864-1936). The King of Thule, op. 22, 2.
    Faust I, viii, 2759.

Pueringer, August (c. 1870-1925). Mephisto's Serenade, op. 2, 4. Faust
    I, xix, 3682.

Reichardt, Johann F. (1752-1814). Goethe's Songs, Odes, Ballades and
    Romances. No. 8: The King of Thule. Faust I, viii, 2759. Leip-
    zig: Breitkopf & Haertel.

Rein, Walter (1893- ?). Lynkeus' Tower Song. Faust II, V, iv, 11 288.

Rochlitz, Johann v. (1769-1842). The King of Thule. Faust I, viii, 2759.

Schlottmann, Louis (1826-1905). Margaret's Prayer Before the Image of
    the Sorrowful Mother, op. 44, 9. Faust I, xviii, 3587. Berlin:
    Challier & Co.

Schneider, Johann G. W. (1789-1864). The King of Thule. Faust I, viii,
    2759. Brander's Song. Faust I, v, 2126. No. 7 & 12 in Mann's
    musikal. Almanach von 1805. Penig: Dienemann. Margaret's Spin-
    ning Song. Faust I, xv, 3374. Margaret's Prayer Before the Image
    of the Sorrowful Mother. Faust I, xviii, 3587. Berlin: Schles-
    inger.

Scholz, Bernhard (1835-1916). The King of Thule, op. 7, 5. Faust I,
    viii, 2759. Leipzig: Peters.

Schubert, Franz (1797-1828). Margaret's Prayer Before the Image of the
    Sorrowful Mother. Faust I, xviii, 3587. Angels' Easter Chorus.
    Faust I, i, 737. The King of Thule. Faust I, viii, 2759.
    Margaret's Spinning Song. Faust I, xv, 3374. Wie anders,
    Gretchen, war dir's (How otherwise was it, Margaret). Faust I,
    xx, 3776.

Schumann, Robert (1810-1856). The King of Thule, op. 67, 1. Faust I, viii, 2759. Arranged for solo voice by A. Horn. Lynkeus' Tower Song, op. 79, 28. Faust II, V, iv, 11 288. Leipzig: Breitkopf & Haertel. Song of the Smithy (Fein Roesslein ich beschlage dich), from Lenau's Faust, op. 90, 1. Leipzig: Kistner.

Schunke, Ludwig (1810-1834). Margaret's Spinning Song. Faust I, xv, 3374. Leipzig: Friese.

Seckendorff, Karl S., Frh. v. (1744-1785). The King of Thule. Faust I, viii, 2759. Dessau: 1782. This was the first musical setting of the ballad. Hoelle says he does not capture the ancient glow of the poem.

Seuberlich, B. (? - ?). The King of Thule. Faust I, viii, 2759. Leipzig: Kistner.

Siering, Moritz (? - ?). Zwei Lieder von Goethe (Two songs from Goethe). No. 1. Gretchen aus Faust. 2. Sehnsucht (Longing), op. 9. Gretchen vor dem Muttergottesbilde, und Verklaertes Gretchen, aus Goethes Faust (Margaret Before the Image of the Mother of God and Margaret transfixed), op. 11.

Siewert, Heinrich (? - ?). The King of Thule, op. 6, 3. Faust I, viii, 2759. Berlin: Challier & Co.

Simon, Hermann (? - ?). Vokale Kammermusik: Lieder zu Faust I for
(S) median male voice and four solo instruments (oboe, English horn, clarinet, viola, cello). Berlin: Lienau, c. 1939.

Sommer, Hans (1838-1922). Margaret's Prayer Before the Image of the Sorrowful Mother. Faust I, xviii, 3587.

Speidel, Wilhelm (1826-1899). Weh! Weh! Du hast sie Zerstoert (Woe! Woe! Thou hast it destroyed), op. 40. Faust I, iv, 1607.

Spohr, Louis (1784-1859). Margaret's Spinning Song, op. 25, 3. Faust I, xv, 3374. Vienna: Pietro Mechetti (now Cranz), 1815?

Stoepel, F. (? - ?). Margaret Before the Image of the Sorrowful Mother. Faust I, xviii, 3587. Erfurt: Suppus.

Streicher, Theodore (1874- ?). Scenes and Pictures from Goethe's
(P) Faust. Faust's Monologue. Edition for piano. Leipzig: Breitkopf & Haertel, 1911.

Taubert, Wilhelm (1811-1891). Weh! Weh! Du hast sie Zerstoert (Woe! Woe! Thou hast it destroyed), op. 26, 6. Faust I, iv, 1607. The King of Thule, op. 151, 6. Faust I, viii, 2759. Leipzig: Rieter-Biedermann.

Tomaschek, Johann W. (1774-1850). The King of Thule, op. 59, 2. Faust I, viii, 2759. Prague: Berra.

Truhn, Hieronymus (1811-1886). Mephisto's Serenade, op. 21, 3. Faust I, 3682. Peasants' Dance Song, op. 21, 4. Faust I, ii, 949. Maedchen, als du Kamst ans Licht (Maiden, when thou com'st to light), op. 21, 5. Faust II, I, iii, 5178. The King of Thule, op. 110, 1. Berlin: Paez.

Verdi, Giuseppe (1813-1901). Margaret's Prayer Before the Image of the Sorrowful Mother (Deh pietoso). Faust I, xviii, 3587. Margaret's Spinning Song (Perduta ho la pace). Faust I, xv, 3374.

Waghalter, Ignaz (1882- ?). Peasants' Dance Song, op. 10, 4. Faust I, ii, 949.

Wagner, Richard (1813-1883). Brander's Song. Faust I, v, 2126. Mephisto's Serenade. Faust I, xix, 3682. Church scene. Margaret's Prayer Before the Image of the Sorrowful Mother. Faust I, xviii, 3587. Zeitschrift fuer Musik, Vol. C, No. 2, Notenbeilage, 1933.

Weber, Franz (1805-1876). Margaret's Spinning Song, op. 7, 1. Faust I, xv, 3374.

Wetzel, Justus H. (1879- ?). Peasants' Dance Song, op. 8, 3. Faust I, ii, 949. Margaret's Prayer Before the Image of the Sorrowful Mother, op. 9, 1. Faust I, xviii, 3587.

Weinbrenner, August (? - ?). Margaret's Spinning Song, op. 3. Faust I, xv, 3374. Elberfeld: Betzhold.

Weitzmann, Carl (1808-1880). Margaret's Spinning Song. Faust I, xv, 3374. Berlin: Paez.

Weyse, Christoph E. (1774-1842). Ni Sange. No. 3: The King of Thule. Faust I, viii, 2759. Copenhagen: Lose & Olsen.

Wichmann, Hermann (1824-1905). Margaret's Spinning Song, op. 30, 3. Faust I, xv, 3374. Berlin: Trautwein.

Wiedebein, Gottlob (1779-1854). Margaret's Spinning Song. Faust I, xv, 3374.

Wilm, Nicolai von (1834-1911). The King of Thule. Faust I, viii, 2759.

Winterberger, Alexander (1834-1914). The King of Thule, op. 40, 1. Faust I, viii, 2759. Mephisto's Serenade, op. 40, 2. Faust I, xix, 3682. Leipzig: Kahnt.

Witting, Carl (1823-1907). The King of Thule, for bass, op. 22, 1. Dresden: Witting.

Wolf, Hugo (1860-1903). Margaret's Prayer Before the Image of the Sorrowful Mother. Faust I, xviii, 3587.

Wolf, Kurt, Frh. v. (also known as Wolfahrt)(1880- ?). Mephisto's Song of the Flea, op. 1, 1. Faust I, v, 2211. Peasants' Dance Song, op. 1, 2. Faust I, ii, 949. Soldiers' Song, op. 1, 3. Faust I, ii, 884. Hoechste Herrsherin der Welt (Highest Mistress of the World). Faust II, V, vii, 11 997.

Zelter, Carl F. (1758-1832). Margaret's Spinning Song. Faust I, xv, 3374. The King of Thule. Faust I, viii, 2759. Berlin: Schlesinger. According to Holle this setting reproduces the ancient glow of the poem.

Zenger, Max (1837-1911). Op. 31. Two Scenes from Goethe's Faust. I. Margaret at the Spinning Wheel. II. Under the Mater Dolorosa. For soprano and small orchestra. Leipzig: Kistner.

Zilcher, Hermann (1881-1948). Hoechste Herrscherin der Welt (Highest Mistress of the World), op. 32, 11. Faust II, V, vii, 11 987.

Music for Ensembles

Chemin-Petit, Hans (1902-   ). Kleine Suite fuer 9 Solo-Instrumente
(N)   nach der Musik zum Puppenspiel 'Dr. Johannes Faust'. Scored for oboe, clarinet, bassoon, string quintet and percussion. Contents: Ouverture, Melancholische Weise, Kasperles schnurriges Liedchen. Berlin: R. Lienau, c. 1940. Nachtlied, Erscheinung, Kasperles Tanz mit seiner Gretl.

Hirschbach, Hermann (1812-1888). String Quartet.

Mendelssohn, Felix (1809-1847). Octet in E Flat for 4 violins, 2 violas,
(NU) and 2 cellos, op. 2. According to Fanny Mendelssohn, the scherzo was inspired by the concluding lines of the Intermezzo of Faust, Part I, 4395-4398. Mendelssohn arranged this piece of full orchestra.

Roentgen, Julius (? -   ). Faust Sonata for violin and piano. Performed at the Goethe Bicentennial Celebration, Southern Illinois University, Carbondale, Illinois, 1949.

Sarasate, Pablo de (1844-1908). Faust Fantasia for violin (on Gounod's
(N)   melodies). In: Masterpieces for Violin and Piano, series IV. New York: Carl Fischer, c. 1911.

Wieniawski, Henri (1835-1880). Fantasy on Themes from Gounod's Faust, op. 20. London: Augener, Ltd., 1922. Begins with opening of overture in the piano. Typical violinistic fireworks. Ends with a short coda after the waltz episode.

Salon pieces and dances for piano
(2 hands unless otherwise designated)

d'Albert, Eugene (1864-1932). "Faust," diabolic waltz. Hamburg: Schuberth.

Andress, A. (? - ?). Marguerite. Adagio after the church scene of
(S) Goethe's Faust. New York: G. Schirmer, 1884.

Armster, H. (? - ?). Mephisto Galop, op. 20. Hamburg: Berens.

Canthal, A. (? - ?). Mephisto, polka diabolique, op. 121. Leipzig:
Schuberth.

Castellacci, Luigi (1797-1845). Valse de Faust. Paris: A. Petit,
(P) c. 1830.

Faust, Karl (? - ?). Mephisto Galop, Margaret (Gretchen) Polka, Famulus Quadrille. Frankfurt: Kresner.

Fitz-Gerald, John. (? - ?). The Mephistopheles Galop. London: Duff
(S) & Stewart, n.d.

Geisler, Paul (1856-1919). Episodes. Vol. II, No. 2: Mephisto's Song
in Auerbachs Cellar. No. 5: The King of Thule. Berlin: Bote &
Bock. Monologues. No. 6: Ja, kehre nur der holden Erdensonne
Entschlossen deinen Ruecken zu. No. 12: Pflueck ich ein Weib,
macht mir's mehr Skrupel nicht.

Gottschalk, Louis M. (1829-1869). Marguerite. Grande Valse brillante.
Boston: Oliver Ditson, n.d.

Graf, Wilhelm (? - ?). Mephisto Waltz, op. 51, concert transcription.
Prague: Wetzler.

Gregoir, Jacques M. J. (1817-1876). Faust (after Goethe). Musical poem
(B) for piano in two parts. Paris: Schott, 1847?

Harmston, J. (? - ?). Margaret at the Spinning Wheel (Gretchen am
(C) Spinnrade), op. 108. Boston: Oliver Ditson, 1917.

Hering, Carl (1766-1853). Wer ruft mir (Who calls me) and Er schlaeft
(He sleeps). Two fantasy pieces from Faust. Hannover: Nagel.

Horny, Eduard (? - ?). Margaret at the Spinning Wheel. Polka.
Prague: Hoffmann.

Lazare, M. (? - ?). Margaret at the Spinning Wheel. Caprice. Mainz:
B. Schott's Soehne.

Liszt, Franz (1811-1886). Gretchen, second movement of his Faust Symphony. Transcribed by the composer. Leipzig: J. Schuberth & Co., 1876. Mephisto Polka. Berlin: Fuerstner. Der naechtliche Zug, Mephisto Waltz, no. 1. Two Episodes from Lenau's Faust. Mephisto Waltzes nos. 2, 3 and 4. Leipzig: Schuberth.

Loeffler, Richard (? - ?). Margaret at the Spinning Wheel, op. 114, 4. Vienna: Haslinger.

Mihalovich, Edmon de (1842-1929). Faust Overture. Composed for piano, four hands.

Neuer musikalischer Merkur, 1808. Jahrgang I, Heft I. Dresden: Hil-
(S)   schersche Musik Handlung, 1808? Contains: Tanz von Faust und Caspar aus Doctor Faust, Jaeger-Tanz aus Doctor Faust, and Laternen Tanz aus Doctor Faust by an unidentified composer.

Pedrell, Felipe (? - ?). Faust rhapsody for piano, on motives from Gounod's Faust, op. 22. Madrid: Sociedad Editorial de Musica, n.d.

Rosenthal, Ernst (? - ?). Margaret at the Spinning Wheel. Compositions for piano, no. 2. Braunschweig: Bauer.

Rost, Ernst (? - ?). Mephistopheles. Polka francaise, danse carac-
(S)   teristique. Dresden: A. W. Rost, 1896.

Schubert, C. (? - ?). Faust aux Enfers (Faust in Hell), quadrille. Mayence: Schott.

Schulz, C. (1845-1913). Tanzphantasieen zum Trauerspiel Faust (Dance fantasy for the tragedy Faust) by Klingemann. Leipzig: Hofmeister.

Winterberger, Alexander (1834-1914). Drei Skizzen zu Faust von Goethe
(S)   (Three Sketches for Goethe's Faust), op. 37. No. 1: Mephistopheles. No. 2: Am Dom (In the Cathedral). No. 3: Faust and Margaret. Leipzig: Forberg, 1875.